Fred Matheny's Complete Book of Road Bike Training

Fred Matheny's Complete Book of Road Bike Training

Your Year-Round Guide to Greater Speed, Strength, Power and Endurance

BY FRED MATHENY

Photos by Fred Matheny, Deb Matheny, Ed Pavelka, Nico Toutenhoofd
Cover design by Mike Shaw

RBR Publishing Company • **Chapel Hill, North Carolina** • **USA**

Fred Matheny's Complete Book of Road Bike Training
Copyright © 2002 RBR Publishing Company

ISBN: 0-9714619-1-0

First edition.

Printed in the USA.

RBR Publishing Company / www.RoadBikeRider.com
3141 Forest Knolls Drive
Chapel Hill, NC 27516-5727, USA

Fax: 208/248-3968
E-mail: RBRpublishing@roadbikerider.com

To purchase additional copies of this book or other RBR publications, please visit our website at www.RoadBikeRider.com.

Reviews Continued from Back Cover

"In the early 1980s, Fred Matheny's *Beginning Bicycle Racing* was the first book to really put it all together for aspiring American racers. This new volume leaves no stone unturned. It could easily be the book that beginning European racers will soon be scrambling to translate."

Don "Captain Dondo" Cuerdon
Cycling writer, category racer

"Whether you're hoping to complete your first century or preparing to race, and whether you're 16 or 60, this great book has the information you need to reach your potential. It's chock full of secrets, tips, professional advice and programs, all explained in the easily understood style Fred's famous for."

Jim Langley
Cycling writer, fitness rider

"Fred Matheny knows his stuff and 'completely' shares this wisdom with us in his newest book. I highly recommend it."

Joe Friel
Coach, author of *The Cyclist's Training Bible*
www.ultrafit.com

"What Hemingway was for the bullfight, Fred Matheny is for road bike training. Practical, yet extremely thorough and descriptive, this information has applications for fitness enthusiasts and elite cyclists. This book is a great tool that will take you to the next level."

Ed Burke, Ph.D.
Physiologist, author, Olympic team manager

"I know of no other journalist with Fred's knowledge of training and his ability to turn that knowledge into a practical, powerful game plan for becoming a better rider. I can't wait to start using this book!"

Scott Martin
Cycling writer, category racer

"Fred Matheny's background as a teacher, coach and cyclist makes this the perfect learning tool for all levels of road cyclists."

Lon Haldeman
Race Across America winner, cycling camp director
www.pactour.com

"Fred has done a supreme job of taking the mystery out of road training and making it approachable for everyone. This book has everything you need to succeed."

Alex Stieda
Coach, Tour de France yellow jersey holder

RoadBikeRider.com
Weekly Newsletter & Website

You're invited to visit the website and subscribe to the *RoadBikeRider.com Newsletter,* an e-mail publication distributed every Thursday by Fred Matheny and Ed Pavelka. New subscribers receive a complimentary copy of the eBook, *29 Pro Cycling Secrets for Roadies.*

RBR Publishing Company specializes in expert "how to" road-cycling advice to help you ride with more skill, performance and enjoyment. If you like what you read in this book, you'll love what you find on our website and in our newsletter.

To
Deb and Ross

Contents

PART 2: OFF-SEASON TRAINING

PART 3: SPRING TRAINING

About the Author

Fred Matheny has written about cycling for nearly 3 decades, including 11 books and hundreds of articles. He served as *Bicycling* magazine's training & fitness editor for 5 years. In researching his writing, he has interviewed (and ridden with) many of the world's top racers, coaches and exercise physiologists. He has coached at numerous cycling camps and authors the "Ask Coach Fred" column in the *RoadBikeRider.com Newsletter*.

Fred began cycling in the early 1970s after an athletic career that included football and track in high school and football at Baldwin-Wallace College in Ohio, where he was named all-league and his team's outstanding offensive lineman. After he moved to Colorado, cycling helped him lose 50 pounds he had gained to play college ball. He enjoyed riding so much that it became his passion.

Fred rode his first race in 1976. A category 2 competitor since 1978, his top placings include a cat 3 win in the Mount Evans Hillclimb; a world record of 5 days, 11 hours, 21 minutes in the 1996 Team Race Across America; first place in the Colorado Masters Time Trial Championships; and third place in the Masters National Time Trial Championships.

Fred and his wife of 34 years, Debbie, live in Montrose, Colorado, where both have had long teaching careers. In addition to his work in cycling journalism, Fred taught high school senior English for 27 years. Their son Ross also is in the teaching profession.

With his business partner, Ed Pavelka, Fred operates RBR Publishing Company, which includes the www.RoadBikeRider.com website, the weekly *RoadBikeRider.com Newsletter* and a book publishing division.

Acknowledgments

Many people have been instrumental in the development of this book.

Deb, my wife, has given me her support, encouragement and help during 25 years of writing about cycling. She critiques my copy, puts up with my absences when I'm off at cycling events and hikes my legs off when I get home.

Ed Pavelka has edited my books starting with *Beginning Bicycle Racing* in 1980. There's no higher praise for an editor than this: Ed has never made a change in my manuscripts that didn't make them better.

Alan Ardizone is the owner of Cascade Bicycles in my hometown of Montrose, Colorado. His mechanical expertise, ace wheelbuilding and insights into the cycling industry make his shop everything a good bike shop should be.

Finally, thanks to all the cyclists I have ridden with during my many years in the sport. Every one of you, from Tour de France winners to novices, has helped me write this book.

Introduction

This book brings together and reshapes all of the key information from 4 eBooks I've written for RBR Publishing Company. Included are *Basic Training for Roadies*, *Off-Season Training for Roadies*, *Spring Training for Roadies* and *Supercharge Your Training for Roadies*.

Do you get the notion that we're a road-oriented company? Road riding was my first love and it remains my favorite type of cycling. Ed Pavelka and I founded RBR in 2001 to provide roadies with a dedicated source of "how to" information for riding better and getting more fun and fitness from the sport. The support we've received has been gratifying.

This book is a payback of sorts. It's simply the best collection of road riding and training information that I could assemble.

The 4 parts, being an amalgam of the eBooks, naturally touch on similar key topics. For example, you'll find a discussion of all-important lactate threshold training in several places. In each part it's treated differently, oriented to the time of year and specific training goals. You'll benefit from this perspective as you develop your own training plan with the recommendations provided. (By the way, you'll see a good deal of information about lactate threshold training credited to Lance Armstrong's coach, Chris Carmichael, who says LT workouts are the key to Lance's astounding success.)

Because of this approach, each part of the book provides all of the essential information necessary, standing alone so you can enter at the best place for your needs. You don't have to start at page 1, for instance, if it's March and you're on the doorstep of the new season. In this case, start with *Part 3: Spring Training*. Virtually everything you should know for the spring period is in that section. Then read the rest of the book, particularly *Part 1: Foundation Information*, to fill in the overall picture and get additional perspectives on key training topics.

Fred Matheny
fredmatheny@roadbikerider.com

FOUNDATION INFORMATION

CHAPTER 1

Training vs. 'Just Riding'

Some years ago while in Erie, Pennsylvania, to speak at a cycling event, I went for a ride. The locals were joking about how their terminology changed as they'd gotten more serious about cycling. Where they had previously "ridden" now they "trained."

But I know several fast, strong and accomplished cyclists who won't let the word "training" pass their lips. They feel the word connotes a level of seriousness that's unhealthy at the least and, at worst, could dim their enjoyment of the sport. They simply "go for a ride."

Of course, there's nothing wrong with riding in an unstructured way, cruising along with the breeze in your face, going fast when the spirit moves you, slowly when the spirit lags. Riding like you feel can generate fine fitness.

That said, there are still some great reasons to allow the "T" word into your vocabulary.

REASONS TO TRAIN

- **The challenge of improvement**. All of us like challenges, especially when we can see improvement that's commensurate with the effort we put in. That's why training on the bike (as opposed to "just riding") is so exciting. When you make the decision to go from occasional rides to a regular schedule, you'll experience big fitness gains. Add one more step—a modest increase in intensity once or twice a week—and you'll bump up your performance another notch. In this book, I'll show you exactly how to reap these training benefits—without getting obsessive about training.

- **The ability to ride like an athlete**. Increased fitness means you don't have to merely sit on the bike and plod along. The greater your strength, power and endurance, the more you can ride with the verve and style of an athlete. Get out of the saddle and jam over small hills. Sprint for county line signs. Outrun a snarling canine attacker and laugh in his doggy face. Take on long, tough hills that used to reduce you to a gasping wreck—and top the summit with a smile. Build your fitness and you'll feel like Kobe Bryant on 2 wheels.

- **The fun of going fast**. Bicycles, scientists tell us, represent the perfect marriage of a machine with the human body. We bipeds on bikes can go faster and cover the miles with less effort than with any other method of human locomotion. Think of the bike not as a device for transportation but rather as a machine for creating fun—zooming around corners, flattening hills, dropping your buddies. When you're fit, you can use this remarkable invention to its fullest.

- **The dynamics of group rides**. When I got into cycling, I rode alone. In the early '70s, no one else in my small Colorado town had discovered the sport. But when experienced rider Don Christman showed up, he invited me to ride from Gunnison to Montrose, a rollicking, 65-mile roller coaster of a road. On the flats heading west he introduced me to drafting. It was a revelation. Soon I sought out groups to ride with and began road racing. As I wrote at the time, "Part of the thrill of cycling is how bikes handle around other bikes—the vacuum, suction, lightening sensation of a big pack, the psychedelic patterns of alloy and jerseys, the sense of shared enterprise and momentary alliances, the way the pack develops a mind and will of its own, independent of, and yet connected to, each rider's perceptions and personality." It takes a minimum level of fitness to ride in a group and have all this fun. I'll show you how.

- **The fitness to go the distance.** Among the most popular cycling events these days are weekend charity rides and weeklong cross-state rides. Many riders dream of doing a transcontinental—riding across the United States. It takes training to be able to pedal between 50 and 100-plus miles day after day. But it's achievable on a surprisingly limited time commitment. If you long for the open road, keep reading.

- **The cultivation of riding skills.** When you build fitness, bike-handling ability comes as part of the package. Remember that old saying about practice making perfect? It's true when it comes to riding a bike well. Gaining fitness requires you to get on the road—and that's where you'll also accumulate the experience necessary to feel connected to the bike, like your were born to it.

- **And don't forget those buffed legs!** Vanity may not be the purest of motives for getting fit, but so what? Cycling strips the excess fat off your legs and torso. It tones your quads until they look like they'll rip through the skin. But best of all is what happens inside where you can't see it—better cardiovascular fitness, an improved cholesterol profile, more stamina for daily activities, and the post-ride calm of a Zen master. Now that's something to be vain about!

CHAPTER 2

Benefits for Body and Mind

That's a pretty attractive list of benefits in chapter 1. But there's more. A regular riding program creates even greater positive physiological changes. Exactly what happens when regular exercise becomes a habit? And what effect does this have as we grow older?

YOUR IMPROVING BODY

Here's what you can expect as your fitness increases:

- **Resting heart rate decreases**. Your heart is a pump composed of muscle. When it's stressed and then allowed enough time to recover, the heart muscle gets stronger to meet the demands placed on it. It doesn't have to beat as often during normal daily activities. Because of this, it's not uncommon for a beginning rider to experience a resting heart rate decrease of around 15 beats per minute (bpm). The average sedentary person has a resting rate of about 75-80 bpm while fit cyclists' hearts purr along at 50-60. Pro cyclists may have resting rates under 40. Five-time Tour de France winner Miguel Indurain reportedly thumped along at 28 bpm!

- **Stroke volume increases**. While resting heart rates decrease in fit athletes, their maximum heart rates don't increase. If that's so, why do they go faster? Doesn't the heart have to beat more rapidly in order to pump more blood and oxygen to the working muscles? No. Although the elite cyclist's heart beats fewer times per minute than an average couch potato's ticker, his heart also pumps more blood per beat compared to his sedentary brethren. Think of it this way: The slacker's heart puts out a squirt of blood with each beat while a Tour de France rider's heart blasts out a tidal wave. As a result, the pro's heart can beat less frequently.

- **VO_2 max rises**. VO_2 max is a measure of how much oxygen your body's working muscles can use. It's a gauge of your oxygen delivery system. Elite male riders can process 70-85 milliliters of oxygen per kilogram of body weight. Some figures in the low 90s have been reported. Elite women endurance athletes average about 10 ml/kg lower. In contrast, sedentary people usually languish in the 30s. Athletes in non-aerobic sports (baseball for instance) average in the low 40s. Although how high you can drive your VO_2 max is genetically determined (see chapter 4), regular training will boost your score about 25 percent.

- **Blood pressure drops**. Troubled by hypertension? Regular training on the bike is one of the best ways to lower your blood pressure without medication. Exercise can reduce blood pressure about 15 percent—equivalent to the results of most medications but without the side effects. (Of course, don't stop taking medication without your doctor's permission.)

- **You can ride longer near your max heart rate**. Ever wonder how hard Lance Armstrong was working when he won all 3 time trials in the '99 Tour de France? Was he working as hard as you do in your local 10-mile TT? Probably harder. The average sedentary person can work for only about 30 minutes at an intensity of around 70-75 percent of maximum heart rate. A fit cyclist can time trial for an hour at 85-90 percent of max. But the redoubtable Mr. Armstrong, due both to great genetics and a highly developed pain tolerance, can rage down the road for an hour at more than 93 percent of his max heart rate. Ouch!

- **You can generate more power at a given heart rate**. It's one thing to tolerate a high percentage of max heart rate for a long period. Plenty of weekend racers can crank till they croak and suffer with the best of the European pros. Why do cash riders go faster for the same degree of suffering? They generate more power at a given intensity—say 90 percent of max heart rate—than sub-elite riders. Don't despair, though. In this book, I'll show you how to put out more power-per-grimace.

- **Body fat melts.** The average American man totes at least 20 percent body fat while U.S. females carry about 25-27 percent. In contrast, fit recreational male cyclists typically are 12-15 percent fat. Elite male riders consistently range from 10 percent down to 3 percent. Female riders tend to average about 5 percentage points more than their male counterparts, although extremely fit women can reach male levels.

- **Cholesterol profile improves.** Study after study shows that regular exercise lowers cholesterol without medication and without a change in diet.

- **Mood brightens**. If all of these positive physical benefits of training don't make you happy, consider this: Fitness invariably yields a significantly improved mood. Classic studies by William Morgan from the 1970s show that athletes' scores on psychological tests demonstrate the so-called "iceberg profile:" high in vigor and enthusiasm, low in anxiety, apathy and depression.

> **CAUTION!** Here's a case of too much of a good thing. When athletes *overtrain*, the desirable psychological benefits of exercise vanish and are replaced by the "reverse iceberg profile:" low values for vigor and enthusiasm, skyrocketing scores for anxiety and fatigue. More is not always better. In chapters 8 and 36, I'll show you how to avoid overtraining so you can keep smiling all the way through your ride—and the rest of the day.

AGE-RELATED CHANGES

What happens to your body as you age? Lots—and it isn't good. As the human body approaches middle age, it begins an inexorable decline. Medical science hasn't figured out a way to halt this slide, genetic advances notwithstanding. Here's the bad news (don't worry—the good news is coming up shortly):

- **Endurance** peaks in the late 20s, can be sustained for about 10 years, and then declines about 1 percent per year. Another way to put it: A century ride gets longer as you get older.

- **Power** peaks in the late 20s along with endurance, but power declines even faster. This means your sprint is compromised. (Whoever heard of a 40-year-old world-class sprinter?) In addition, your lessened ability to hammer over short hills makes even small bumps grow in proportion to your age.

- **Strength** hangs on longer, to the late 40s, then deteriorates slowly. By age 70, strength has often declined by 50 percent compared to your hale and hearty 20s.

- **Recovery time** lengthens because aging slows metabolism. Muscles, in turn, are slower to refuel and repair. Masters cyclists often cite the need for more recovery time as the first sign that they aren't spring chickens anymore.

- **Body fat** increases as muscles wither (a process called *sarcopenia*). It's not uncommon for a male to weigh the same at age 60 as he did at 25—but have 20 percent more body fat.

What can you do about this catalog of woes? The answer is simple—keep exercising! Consider these benefits:

- While sedentary people experience a decline in VO_2 max of at least 1 percent a year, training can slow this frightening slide by more than 50 percent—to an almost imperceptible 5 percent per decade.

- Regular training helps you retain muscle volume, thus slowing the accumulation of fat.

- Muscular strength can be retained and even increased with a simple weight training program. If you retain strength, you'll preserve much of your power and sprinting ability, too.

- Regular training slows the inevitable lengthening of recovery time. Bodies that are forced to get ready for consecutive days of training adapt even in advancing years (albeit more slowly than for youngsters). Recovery may take longer, but not as long as for your sedentary peers.

I'd like to tell you that regular training, both on the bike and in the weight room, is a fountain of youth, that cycling is a panacea and if you ride you'll never grow old. I wish I could be a prophet of immortality achieved by exercise. As we've seen, it doesn't work that way. Aging and decline are inevitable. But—and this is the most important qualifier you're likely to find—riding your bike is the best way to combat the aging process so you can live a healthy and active life right up to your last pedal stroke.

CHAPTER 3

The Ways We Improve

So far I've talked a lot about improvement. Most people assume that if they exercise, they'll get fitter. Few people, however, know much about the principles that lead to greater fitness. In fact, the body's ability to adapt to various demands placed on it is one of the wonders of physiology. Here's how your body does the trick.

PRINCIPLES OF TRAINING

- **Stress leads to adaptation**. All training is based on the body's stress adaptation system. In a process known as the "general adaptation syndrome," the body responds to stress by becoming stronger. When a stress (like training) is applied, the body becomes better able to withstand that stress. If the training isn't hard enough, improvement doesn't take place or, if it does, it occurs at an extremely slow rate. On the other hand, stress the body too much with insufficient time for recovery and the adaptation mechanisms are overwhelmed. Next comes chronic fatigue.

- **Stress is cumulative**. Remember to factor in all the stressful events in your life when you calculate your ability to recover. It isn't just the day's training that applies stress to your system. Long hours on the job, family responsibilities, marital problems, financial woes—all these stressors combine with the rigors of training. They all add up. Can you fall into chronic fatigue and stalled improvement on only 6 or 7 hours of riding each week? You bet. If you're constantly stressed by the demands of everyday living, additional stress in the form of training might be more than you can handle.

Because of this:

- **Training should be specific.** Adaptation correlates to the stress that's applied. If you train by riding long, slow miles, your body will get better at riding long and slow. If you change your training by reducing mileage and doing sprints, you'll get faster but your endurance will decrease. That's why goals are so important. If you don't know what you want to accomplish in your training, you can't take advantage of the body's blind adaptation to specific training.

- **Training should be individualized.** We're all unique in our response to training. An endless fascination is watching how the body responds to the combination of workout intensity, workout duration and rest.

- **Training should be regular**. Steady doses of training are better than periodic bursts. Studies show that aerobic exercise 3 times a week allows you to keep the fitness you have, while 4 workouts per week mean you improve. Five sessions per week are thought to be optimum, allowing plenty of miles to stress the body for improvement along with 2 recovery days.

- **Training should be predictable**. The body doesn't like surprises. If you're accustomed to a leisurely 25 miles each day on flat roads and you get suckered into a fast 75-miler in the hills, you'll end up sore, injured, demoralized—and probably dropped. A regular training program leads to optimum improvement when it's founded on steady and moderate increases in effort plus plentiful rest.

- **Training should be periodized.** The same training schedule day after week after month will destroy continued improvement and your desire to ride. Different months require different approaches to training. Periods of complete recovery in late fall, crosstraining in winter, building a base in early spring—these are ways that smart riders introduce variety into their program. It's what this book is about.

CHAPTER 4

The Limits to Improvement

When I started riding, I was fascinated by my improvement. I charted my declining times up a local hill or on a 5-mile time trial course and projected them through to the following race season. I had a naïve faith in infinite progress and was convinced that if I continued my rate of improvement, I'd be a Cat 1, a 50-minute time trialist, and a national champion in less than 2 years. It didn't work that way. I soon learned that improvement isn't a continually ascending curve.

WHY IMPROVEMENT ISN'T FOREVER

The curve of improvement flattens markedly as we approach the upper levels of our genetic potential. Improvement often becomes uneven. It proceeds in fits and starts—a noticeable jump over several weeks, then months of stagnation or even deterioration.

Genetic upper limits are tipped off by performance plateaus, chronic fatigue and other clear physiological signals. As we sense our improvement slowing, we often react by training more. There's less time for recovery. The result is overtraining. Improvement stops.

> **EXAMPLE!** West of my Colorado town there's a rolling 3-mile course where I have timed myself through the years as a way of gauging my progress. One year in July, I rode my fastest time ever. Four days later, I knocked off another 4 seconds. The Mount Evans Hillclimb was coming up, so I continued to do intervals twice a week and added 2 additional hard 6-mile climbs up to Black Canyon National Park just outside of town.
>
> Soon I was cooked but wouldn't admit it. My intervals became slower and my times up Black Canyon increased. A week before Mount Evans I timed myself on the 3-mile course. It was incredibly painful, far more than on the previous record rides. When I crossed the line and punched the watch, I was sure I had shattered my old record. I had put in massive amounts of hard work in the previous month. Why wouldn't I blow away the record?
>
> Then I looked at the time—27 seconds slower. Overtraining had blown *me* away. Needless to say, on Mount Evans, the mountain won.

Workouts have to be altered in both intensity and duration as you approach your genetic ceiling. The training that elicited big jumps in performance when you started riding doesn't work as your fitness increases. Just riding around casually is a big shock to the sedentary system, so reformed sofa spuds get better in leaps and bounds. But as you become a regular rider—and then a regular trainer—it takes more intensity, more structure and more rest to improve.

If 7 carefully planned hours of training each week make you a 60-minute finisher in a 40K time trial, doubling your training time may produce additional improvement measured in seconds rather than minutes. Or it may stress you so much, given less than adequate time to recover, that you'll get slower instead of faster. It's a physiological version of the law of diminishing returns.

THE GENETIC CEILING

I've mentioned a genetic ceiling to performance. The hard fact is that some people have more inherited talent for endurance exercise than others. That shouldn't be surprising. There isn't any magic.

There aren't many 7-footers walking around but they tend to make the best NBA centers. If you're 5-10, all the post moves in the world won't get you to the big show. You can't see cycling talent like you can hoops potential—unlike height and a tall vertical jump, a predilection for endurance sports takes place in the cardiovascular system and the muscle cells. Great cyclists, especially great climbers, tend to cut rather scrawny, unimpressive figures.

The heritability of endurance talent was highlighted by the recent Heritage Study. Sports scientists gave several hundred people identical training programs—12 weeks of interval sessions on exercise bikes. The subjects' VO_2 max was measured before and after the training. The scientists reasoned that if there were no genetic component to endurance improvement, the same training would produce the same rate of improvement in all the subjects. Conversely, if different people had varying ability to improve, it's logical that some subjects' VO_2 max would skyrocket while others wouldn't budge.

The results showed that while some subjects experienced VO_2 max increases of a whopping 40 percent, others didn't improve at all. Imagine weeks of intense interval training—and no improvement. These people may as well have spent the time on the couch.

DUCKING UNDER THE CEILING

Wait! Before you sell your bike and retire poolside, note these important points:

Only a small number of people scored at either end of the Heritage Study range. As you'd expect, subjects' scores produced a bell-shaped curve. Most people fell in the middle third, exhibiting a healthy ability to improve about 25 percent. Even if VO_2 max increased modestly or not at all, the health benefits of riding remained. So-called "low responders" may not have the inherited gifts to become elite racers, but they become healthier through exercise.

Remember, VO_2 max isn't everything. Although it's a good marker of endurance potential, the sheer ability to process oxygen is only a start.

EXAMPLE! Let's go back to our basketball players. All 7-footers have the height to play basketball at a high (pardon the pun) level but not necessarily the coordination, the work ethic or the strength. In the same way, a high VO_2 max doesn't mean that an athlete can produce high rates of power at a given level of oxygen consumption. It doesn't mean that he understands how to train to take advantage of his talent. And it certainly doesn't follow that he's a master tactician.

So here's the take-home lesson: Training trumps genes. Sure, it's helpful to have picked your parents properly if you want to be a great endurance athlete. Having a really tough grandmother is a bonus. But regardless of how blessed your family tree, regular training will improve your health, make you a better rider (regardless of your VO_2 max) and let you experience the joys of the open road. Those are things that can't be passed down by natural selection.

CHAPTER 5

Learn the Lingo

Every human activity has its own jargon, a unique set of words (or a unique way of using familiar words). Learning the lingo is the key to understanding the activity and getting accepted by its practitioners. Training on the bike may not be as jargon-ridden as medicine, yachting, pipefitting or musical counterpoint—but it comes close.

For instance, take the word *jam*. Once when I was in a small group that contained a novice rider, the leader yelled that we were going to jam to the next stop sign. Hearing only the word—and not knowing its cycling application—the rookie started looking around for the snack stop and got left behind. To help you avoid similar embarrassing situations (and so you know terms necessary to understand subsequent chapters), here's a list of absolutely vital definitions. For words not covered here, check the Glossary at the end of the book.

P.S. Don't ignore these definitions or you may get in a jam!

TRAINING TERMS TO KNOW

- **Circuit training**: Usually this term refers to a weight training technique in which you move rapidly from one resistance exercise to another with very short rest breaks or none at all. New research shows that your lactate threshold (and therefore your ability to maintain a higher cruising speed on the bike) is increased by alternating a resistance training exercise like bench presses or squats with a hard effort on the indoor trainer. (See chapter 49.) As a result, circuit training that combines weights with aerobic activity is becoming popular for off-season workouts.

- **Crosstraining**: Using different sports for mental refreshment and physical conditioning, especially during cycling's off-season. Examples are running, swimming, Nordic skiing, skating, rowing, weight training, and court sports like basketball. Some crosstraining activities even simulate the pedaling motion. A good example is snowshoeing, one of my favorites. The motion of lifting the 'shoe out of the snow and pulling it forward for the next step strengthens the muscles that pull the pedal around the back of the stroke and move it to the top, ready to push down again. Some forms of certain activities are more helpful to cyclists than others. For instance, running on the flats doesn't seem to improve cycling specifically whereas running uphill works the quads in a similar way to pedaling.

- **Fartlek**: A Swedish word meaning "speed play," it's a training technique based on unstructured changes in pace and intensity. It can be used in place of timed or measured interval training. Of course, structured training has a place in any cyclist's plan, but fartlek training is less demanding psychologically (although just as demanding physically). A cyclist employing speed play would warm up and then do whatever faster riding seemed appropriate. Jam each short hill, time trial to the silo a mile down the road, or sprint for 200 yards every time you see a bluebird or white mailbox. It's a fun, free-flowing way to add intensity to training.

- **Intervals**: A structured method of training that alternates brief, hard efforts with short periods of easier riding for partial recovery. Alternating hard efforts with rest allows you to do more work than you could if you did just one long, hard repeat. Intervals also make it easy to vary workout intensity. Several variables can be manipulated: length of the work phase, recovery time, heart rate (or wattage output) and number of efforts. It's important that recovery is incomplete. Usually heart rate is allowed to drop only to about 120 bpm before another hard effort is begun.

- **Jam**: A period of hard, fast riding. Jams are completely unstructured. You simply go faster for as long as you feel like it (or as long as other riders make you). The terrain can dictate the length of a jam, too—harder to the top of a hill, faster on the flats when you have a tailwind or you're trying to beat a thunderstorm home. Group rides often feature jams when the pack decides to chase down a rider or when riders are jockeying for position to contest the city limit sign sprint.

- **Jump**: A quick, hard acceleration. The ability to jump is vital to cycling skills. A good jump initiates the longer effort of a sprint. Most coaches suggest that riders work on their jump at least once a week with several quick, out-of-the-saddle accelerations in a moderate gear.

- **Lactate threshold (LT)**: This is the exertion level beyond which you can no longer produce energy aerobically. Additional intense work means your body can't deal with the resulting buildup of lactate (lactic acid). You experience muscle fatigue, pain and shallow, rapid breathing. LT is vital to training because the more power you can generate without going over your lactate threshold and becoming anaerobic, the faster you can ride at a given heart rate. LT workouts are the key component in Lance Armstrong's training program, but they're not just for elite racers.

- **LSD**: Long, steady distance is a training technique that requires an even aerobic pace for at least 2 hours. Many cyclists do long rides too fast and can't sustain the pace for the distance. Others do them too slowly and fail to achieve an optimum increase in endurance. Most coaches suggest that long rides be done at heart rates from 70 to about 85 percent of max, a pace that feels "moderate" or "brisk."

- **Power**: The combination of speed and strength. Measured in watts using an on-bike computer either indoors or out.

- **Repetition** (*rep* for short): Each hard effort in an interval workout. Also, one complete movement in a weight-training exercise. Varying the number of reps is one way to manipulate the difficulty of intervals or resistance training.

- **Set**: In intervals or weight training, a specific number of repetitions. Riders (or weight trainers) divide their reps into sets so they can recover and do more total work. For instance, a common weight training prescription is "3 sets of 10." This means you'd do 10 repeats of an exercise, rest briefly, then repeat the process 2 more times for a total of 3 sets. On the bike, you might do 3 climbs of 2 minutes each with 2 minutes of easy spinning between each climb. That's 1 set. Then you might do the 3 climbs again. That's the second set.

- **Snap**: The ability to accelerate quickly. Snap is different from a jump because snap refers to a quick acceleration any time, not a formal out-of-the-saddle explosion. A rider with snap can simply remain seated and accelerate quickly with 10 or 15 pedal strokes to close a small gap after a corner or power over a short hill.

- **Soft pedal**: To rotate the pedals without actually applying power. This skill is crucial in a paceline if you're in danger of running up on the wheel in front. You shouldn't grab the brakes to slow because the resulting jerk of your bike might take down another rider. And if you abruptly stop pedaling, your bike will move "backward" in the paceline, endangering the rider behind you. The trick is simply to keep the pedals going around while putting less (or no) pressure on them. You'll drift back to a safe distance from the wheel you're following without spreading a ripple of concern among your companions. Then smoothly begin applying power again.

- **Speed**: The ability to accelerate quickly and maintain a very fast cadence for brief periods. Most non-racers don't work on speed but it's important for everyone who wants to ride athletically. Going fast for short periods makes your fast-twitch muscle fibers (the ones with little endurance but great capacity for speed) fire rapidly and often. Without occasionally being asked to do some quick pedaling, fast-twitch fibers get little stimulation. Occasional bursts of speed are like weight training on the bike.

- **Speedwork**: A general term for high-velocity training such as sprints, time trials and motorpacing. Use this training to improve your acceleration and top-end speed. Speedwork is similar to interval training but with this important difference: Each "on" effort is shorter and more intense, and you must allow complete recovery between efforts. Speedwork is tough. One session per week is plenty. If you race, particularly in criteriums, speedwork is the key to coping with the many sprints out of turns. For all riders, speedwork gives you the ability to do things like accelerate away from chasing dogs, get through a traffic light before it turns, or win the group sprint. You'll also develop the ability to stay in full control of the bike when pedaling with maximum speed and power.

- **Spin**: To pedal with a quick cadence. There are 2 ways to make a bike go, say, 22 mph. You can pedal a big gear at a relatively low cadence or you can pedal a smaller gear at a faster cadence. Learning to spin is crucial because a fast cadence means the effort each leg has to produce is divided into smaller units. You have to pedal more frequently but you don't have to push as hard each time. You can save your leg muscles for later in the ride. *Spinning* also is used to describe an easy ride done at a brisk cadence with low effort. And it's the term for stationary training in a health club, using one-speed, fixed-gear "spinning" bikes.

- **Suppleness**: A quality of well-conditioned leg muscles that allows a rider to pedal at high cadence with smoothness and power. Also known by the French term, *souplesse*. It's developed by hours of high-cadence riding. Many cyclists also develop suppleness by riding a fixed gear, like on a track bike. Because you can't coast, you're forced to develop a round, smooth stroke.

- **Tempo**: Fast riding at a brisk cadence. Tempo is done at a heart rate of about 75-85 percent of max. This isn't as hard as a time trial so it can be maintained for long periods. Tempo rides often are done in the early season to build the base needed for intervals and other strenuous training later in the year.

- **Time trial** (TT): A race against the clock in which individual riders start at set intervals and cannot give or receive a draft. For this reason it's often called the "race of truth." Time trials are great for training, too. Working at 85-90 percent of max heart rate for extended periods (15 to 60 or more minutes) increases your lactate threshold and thus the speed you can maintain for a given level of effort.

- **Watt**: A measurement of the power you're producing. It tells how much energy you apply to the pedals over time. A power output of 100 watts will illuminate a 100-watt light bulb. The average recreational racer can generate 200-250 watts for about 30 minutes. Lance Armstrong is reputed to pump out more than 450 watts for that amount of time.

CHAPTER 6

The Periodized Training Year

Sally and Jane have different approaches to training. Sally rides year round, aiming to keep a high level of fitness at all times. She wants to hang with the fast group during the first training ride in March but she also wants to rock in evening club races in July. Jane, on the other hand, carefully plans her training to include specific periods of rest, weight training, base mileage and intervals. Because she crosstrains in the winter and does weight work instead of pedaling, she often can't keep up on those March rides. But because she has patiently built endurance and strength in the early season, she can introduce hard intervals by spring. As a result, by midsummer she is much faster than Sally.

Jane has learned the importance of periodization—planning specific workouts at pre-determined times of the year in order to peak for important events. It's a crucial technique for recreational and fitness riders, too. It helps avoid boredom, it automatically includes variety in the yearly training plan, and it ensures that you'll be riding your best in the big rides you pinpoint.

Of course, some riders don't like structured plans that tell them what to do each day all year. They'd rather decide how to ride—an easy spin, hard intervals or a long endurance session—based on how they feel during the warm-up. That works, but it may mean they won't reach their full potential.

Here's an important point: Structured plans don't have to be set in stone. If they're designed well, there's plenty of room for flexibility.

CRAFTING YOUR PLAN

This book is all about training. I'll be very detailed in the coming pages about what to do at various times of the year. But first, you need to answer 2 questions:

1. What you want out of cycling? Do you want to improve your fitness? Set a PR in a local time trial or century? Keep up with the Sunday group rides? Get on the podium at masters nationals? These are all worthy goals, but some of them require more time and energy than others. You alone know how much psychological capital you can afford to invest in the stress of training. And you are the best judge of your total training load—how much will make you better, how much more will break you down.

2. How much time do you have to train? Your goals should be related to how much time you are willing to spend to reach them. If you have a family, a job and home chores, you'll have little energy for an extensive training schedule. Set goals that fit in the parameters of the rest of your life.

Got your answers? Great! Now:

- **Set goals**. If you don't know where you're going, any road will do. But cyclists who have specific goals can set up a plan to meet them. Choose a couple of events—races, centuries, tours—where you want to be at your strongest and mark them on the calendar.

- **Train for success**. Set short-term goals in small, attainable increments so you can reach them. If you rode a 2-mile training time trial in 6 minutes, set your goal for next week at 5:45. Don't set it for 5 minutes. You probably won't reach it, and then what? You've been training for failure. Success and failure in cycling are relative terms. You can decide what they mean for you. So when you set goals, define them in such a way that you'll frequently achieve small but significant successes. Success breeds more and bigger success, but failure often breeds more failure and frustration until finally you're fed up with the sport.

- **Create a plan**. When you go on a trip, you take a map. When you attend a meeting, you get an agenda. When you repair a flat, you follow ordered steps. In the same way, when you train you need a plan. After you've decided which events are important, set up your training so you peak for them. Why do hard intervals in March if you want to break your PR in a September century? You have a limited amount of energy. Wise training choices enable you to use it when it counts the most.

At the end of this chapter, I'll show you how to design a simple but effective individual yearly plan. But first, keep these principles in mind:

- **Build slowly**. If your longest ride ever is 35 miles, don't tackle a 75-miler this weekend. Your body is much happier—and less likely to get injured—if distance increases are incremental and small. The time-honored rule is to increase mileage no more than 10 percent from week to week.

- **Include variety**. If you go on a trip and a bridge is washed out, you look at your map and choose from other roads. If your plan calls for a scheduled hard ride on Tuesday and you feel washed out, choose from a variety of easier workouts. Put varied types of rides and other training into your schedule. And don't be reluctant to alter your plan when conditions warrant. You'll find that goals are easier to reach if you alter your training frequently. You probably get plenty of sameness in your job and daily routine. Why continue the pattern on your bike? Cycling is supposed to be recreation. So re-create.

- **Vary the pace**. The better the rider, the greater the gap between his speed on recovery days and the speed he goes when he's racing or interval training. Pros can average more than 30 miles per hour for a hundred miles. But on their recovery days, they just creep along, taking a walk on the bike. Nearly anyone can keep up. Pros know that fast rides provide the impetus for improvement and slow rides allow the body to recover and get stronger. The big mistake? Going the same speed day after day. If you always ride at a moderate pace, your body has no way of knowing what going fast is all about.

- **Vary the volume**. Just as you vary the pace, you should also ride different distances during the week. You won't feel comfortable going 40 miles if every training ride is 90 minutes long. But if you gradually increase the time of one weekly ride, soon your body will adapt and 40 or 50 miles will be easy.

- **Do intervals**. Interval training has a bad rap among cyclists. It's hard, they argue, and it's so structured that it takes all the fun out of riding. The hard part can't be denied, but that's what makes it effective. A large body of research shows that the intensity of interval training is the most potent producer of fitness. It's also the most time-efficient way to get better. Intervals don't have to be by-the-clock drudgery. Instead, simply go faster when the spirit moves you—sprint over short hills, go hard to the next stop sign, try to catch the rider up ahead. Such random efforts are known by the Swedish term, *fartlek*. They're a great way to increase your intensity.

- **Take rest days**. Training is built around a paradox: You don't get better when you're training hard, you get better when you're resting. That's when your body rebuilds from physical stress. So take at least one day each week completely off the bike. Two may be better. Do some yard work, upper-body resistance training, bike maintenance—or prop up your feet and sip a cold lemonade.

- **Keep it fun**. Training should never be drudgery. Unless you're a pro, you're riding a bike for recreation and to improve your fitness. Explore different routes. Go mountain biking on dirt trails. Ride alone if you always go with a group, and vice-versa. Try to break your personal record for the local killer climb. Join in the local club's weekly training race. The world of cycling is huge so there's no reason to get stale.

PERIODIZATION IN PRACTICE

Here's an overview of how structured, periodized training works. In the rest of this book, we'll look at the particulars of each segment.

- **October:** *Active Rest Period*

Active rest is the best way to recover and refresh from a season of cycling. Take days off, do other aerobic sports, go fishing, play tennis or work in the yard. Keep active but don't worry about a formal training plan. Here's a sample weekly schedule:

Monday	Light weight training
Tuesday	30-60 minutes of easy aerobic activity
Wednesday	30-60 minutes of easy aerobic activity
Thursday	Light weight training
Friday	Rest day
Saturday	Easy ride or rest
Sunday	2-hour group ride or other aerobic activity

- **November and December:** *Preparation Period*

During these 2 months, think general fitness. Lift weights with the goal of increasing your upper-body and core (low back, abdominal) strength. Use relatively light weights and do 10-15 reps. Begin resistance work for your legs with weights that allow 15-25 reps.

Improve your aerobic fitness, but don't worry about riding your bike if the weather in your area is harsh and roads are dangerous with ice and snow. A mountain bike with knobby tires is safer in such conditions. Early darkness is another obstacle. There's no need to force rides by installing lights and venturing into the cold darkness. If that's your only choice for riding after work at this time of year, do your pedaling on an indoor trainer instead. Use weekends for getting on the road, weather permitting.

Better yet, crosstrain with other aerobic sports you enjoy. Uphill running, Nordic skiing, snow-shoeing and skating are great aerobic activities that complement cycling. Here's a sample weekly schedule:

Monday	Rest day
Tuesday	Weight training
Wednesday	60-90 minutes of aerobic activity
Thursday	60-minute ride outside or on trainer
Friday	Weight training
Saturday	60-minute ride outside or on trainer
Sunday	Group ride if possible, or other aerobic activity

- **January, February and March:** *Preseason Buildup Period*

Continue to lift weights with added emphasis on the legs. I outline a program in chapter 23.

As the weather improves, gradually increase your time on the bike. Remember the 10 percent rule—increase mileage only 10 percent each week. You have 3 months to build up, so don't rush it.

Go on weekend group rides when the weather cooperates. You'll learn pack-riding skills or refresh them if you're an experienced rider. Here's a sample weekly schedule:

Monday	Rest day
Tuesday	60-minute ride followed by light weight training
Wednesday	90-minute ride with speedwork
Thursday	Weight training
Friday	90-minute ride with speedwork
Saturday	Easy aerobic ride or other aerobic activity
Sunday	Group ride for endurance, progressing to more spirited outings toward the end of this period

- **April through September:** *Cycling Season*

Scale back your weight training to a maintenance program. Once or twice a week do 1 or 2 sets using light weights. You want to keep the strength you built during the winter but avoid using too much energy that should go to riding.

Now is the time to build up to specific events, capitalizing on the base fitness you established during the winter and early spring. Here's a sample weekly schedule:

Monday	Rest day
Tuesday	60-90 minutes with speedwork
Wednesday	Longer endurance ride
Thursday	60-90 minutes with intervals
Friday	Maintenance weight training
Saturday	Easy 60-minute ride
Sunday	Group ride, race, century, etc.

CHAPTER 7

All About Intensity

I made a serious mistake when I started cycling. I enjoyed it so much—climbing passes in Colorado, swooping around corners, hammering into the wind—that I soon rode so much and so hard that I got tired and stopped improving. In that era before heart monitors, there was no objective way to measure how hard I was going. I relied on "listening to my body" and my body gave me bad information. It was misled by my head, which was having so much fun that it forgot to feel exhausted. My body eventually remembered.

It's crucial to know how hard you're working. Train too easily and you won't stress your body enough to improve. Train too hard without adequate recovery and your performance will deteriorate. You'll be too tired to mow the lawn. Friends and family will remark on your contentious personality.

FOUR MEASUREMENTS OF INTENSITY

1. Speed. Runners have it easy because there's a strong correlation between speed and effort while running in the controlled conditions of a track. A 75-second lap on Tuesday probably takes the same effort as running that speed on Thursday. Things aren't so simple on a bike. External factors have a large effect because you're riding on roads exposed to the elements. It's easy to go 20 mph with a strong tailwind but much harder—maybe impossible—to ride back into the gale at that pace. Speed on a bike, measured with a cyclecomputer, rarely correlates well with how hard your body is working.

2. Heart rate. Heart monitors have revolutionized training in the last 15 years. They're a window into the body, revealing how hard the cardiovascular system is working. But as the sole indicator of intensity, heart rate isn't perfect. That's a little-known fact. Most riders assume that any time they're riding at a heart rate of, say, 140 bpm, they're generating the same number of watts and their physical systems are working at the same rate. However, heart rate can vary widely for a given amount of power output because of factors such as hydration status, mental state and muscle fatigue. If you ride for an hour at a steady effort, your heart rate will rise gradually even though you maintain the same pace. This phenomenon, called *cardiac drift*, is caused by overheating and dehydration. You have to know how to interpret the number on the monitor.

> **EXAMPLE!** Day after day of hard effort on a tour or in a stage race often makes heart rate drop as the event goes on, even though you're putting out the same effort. When Ed Pavelka, Skip Hamilton, Pete Penseyres and I set the senior world record for Team Race Across America, we knew from training exactly what heart rates were necessary to ride our 30-minute shifts as fast as possible.
>
> But as the second morning dawned, our heart rates were down as much as 25 beats compared to the first day. Try as we might, we couldn't get them higher. We were going just as fast because we averaged nearly the same number of miles (530) each day. Our hearts were pumping slower but pumping more blood per beat.

Max Testa, M.D., a pro team physician, reports that the same phenomenon is common in stage races lasting more than a few days. And Lance Armstrong's coach, Chris Carmichael, says that riders time trial at a lower heart rate at the end of the Tour de France compared to the prologue TT that starts the 3-week event. It's no wonder that when cyclists rely on heart rate alone to determine intensity, they often accuse themselves of being incredible slackers.

3. Wattage. The best way to determine how much power you're putting out is to measure it directly with strain gauges mounted in the crankarms or rear hub. Recently available is a device from Polar that measures wattage by calculating chain tension. Power is measured in watts. Health club exercise bikes have wattage readouts, but it has proven more difficult to develop affordable, lightweight, weather-sealed systems for outdoor use. (See chapter 42.)

4. Rating of perceived exertion (RPE). The old-fashioned method of gauging intensity—how you feel—still works for experienced riders. It has gotten more sophisticated with the introduction of various ratings of perceived exertion such as the Borg Scale. Here's a simple system: A rating of **1** means you're completely motionless while **10** means you're riding as hard as you can. An easy spin along the bike path is **5**. Light effort is **6**. At **7**, you begin to breathe steadily and rhythmically. At **8**, your breathing intensifies but you're not panting. When you begin gasping and are unable to carry on a conversation, you've reached **9**. With a little practice, you'll be able to stay in a given RPE zone as you ride. The key transitions are from 7 to 8 (when you become aware of your breathing and conversation becomes difficult) and 8 to 9 (when breathing goes from steady and measured to panting and gasping, when talking ceases and your quads burn).

PICK YOUR POISON

Heart monitors can be pricey, and watts-measuring devices can drain a good portion of junior's college fund. Fortunately, it isn't necessary to go into debt to know how hard you're riding. Simply use RPE. Think about it when you're on the bike and you'll acquire a keenly tuned sense of your effort level.

Of course, the best way to measure intensity is to use all 4 methods: speed, heart rate, wattage, RPE. By checking the first 3 while at the same time being aware of perceived exertion, you'll have a precise measure of your absolute intensity—and how your body is reacting to it.

EXAMPLE! Suppose you're doing repeats up a hill that takes about 5 minutes to climb. When you feel good, your heart rate hits 160 in the last minute, your wattage averages around 250, and your RPE is 9.

On another day, the climb feels as hard as usual, maybe harder, but your heart rate won't go above 150 and your average wattage sinks to 200. This combination indicates that you haven't recovered from past training. You're tired. You should rest, eat well and re-hydrate before attempting another intense workout. Your numbers will confirm when you're ready.

In this example, if you had relied only on how you felt, you would have guessed that all was well—you were climbing as hard as you usually do. But had you keyed off the depressed heart rate and the lower wattage readout, they would have led you astray by telling you to go harder.

HOW TO GO HARD

Most riders find it difficult to go hard in training. It takes enormous willpower to make yourself hurt. But there's no escaping the fact that you have to do it if you're going to improve. Experienced riders know that there are 2 sure-fire ways to make it easier to go hard.

1. Ride hills. Climbing is a basic cycling skill. Unless you live on pancake-flat terrain, you have to go uphill occasionally or even frequently. Do a cross-state tour like Colorado's Ride the Rockies and you'll be climbing several thousand vertical feet each day. Don't avoid hills, seek them. Once or twice a week, pick a hilly route. Climbing builds strength, technique, and teaches you to apportion your effort to the top. And it's work with a built-in reward—you get to fly down the other side. In this way, climbing provides a natural form of interval training. Hard effort going up, rest going down. If the only climb in your area is a highway overpass, ride it twice from each direction. No overpasses? Grind into the wind in a big gear to get a similar training effect as hills provide.

2. Ride in a group. Go out with riders who have similar goals. Learn to ride safely and predictably in a paceline. There's something special about the speed and the feeling of being pulled along in a group of riders. It can't be duplicated when you're grinding away by yourself. Hard effort doesn't feel as difficult and the miles fly by. The feeling of shared effort, of a group enterprise, is addictive.

CHAPTER 8

Overtraining and Recovery

Hard training doesn't always lead to better performances. Combine it with inadequate recovery and you'll almost certainly get worse instead of better. How can you avoid this depressing phenomenon, known as *overtraining*? How can you recover better?

STRESS IS CUMULATIVE

Pro cyclists rarely overtrain. They ride enormous mileage (on the order of 400 to 600 miles a week) and they slug it out in long stage races. But pros have plenty of time for rest and recuperation. All they do is ride, eat and relax. On the other hand, recreational riders usually log only 5 to 10 hours a week. This is deceiving, though, because their workweeks stretch to 40-plus hours and most have additional responsibilities at home. In fact, the average recreational cyclist probably has a lower miles-to-rest ratio than a pro.

Never forget that stress is cumulative. If the boss is ragging on you about that overdue report and your personal relationships are coming unglued, you'll have little energy left even for modest training. You'll also have less ability to recover from the training you do manage to fit in.

SYMPTOMS

Overtraining symptoms aren't always clear cut. But if you experience several of the following, beware.

- **Lowered performance**. When your time or speed worsens even though you're training hard, suspect overtraining. Here's the rule: If you're getting worse despite hard training, you're probably getting worse because of hard training. This is one of the most difficult things to learn—and believe.

- **Apathy**. If you have to pry yourself out of bed for the Sunday morning ride, you may be suffering from chronic fatigue. When you've lost your normal enthusiasm for cycling, it's a clear signal that you aren't fully recovered and your body is crying for rest. It's not a sign of personal weakness.

- **Desire to quit**. This is a classic symptom that you've pushed too hard. Organized events should make you eager to ride hard or compete. If you're lethargic, tired and feel like taking the shortcut home or not riding at all, you've left your competitive fire out on your training roads.

- **Increased irritability**. Family members provide the best early warning of overtraining. They're the first to notice when your normally sunny personality turns grumpy.

- **Disrupted sleep**. Overly tired cyclists often fall asleep easily in the evening. In fact, they usually feel drowsy in the afternoon. But they often awake at 3 or 4 a.m. unable to relax. This pattern is a sure tip-off that you've overdone it.

EXAMPLE! It was my second season of bike racing. Along with my wife and infant son, I moved to Boulder to take an 8-week class at the University of Colorado. Boulder was rapidly becoming the center of the U.S. cycling world, home to the Red Zinger Bike Race (later to become the Coors Classic), the germinal American stage race. I was coming from a small town with no other cyclists, so Boulder was a revelation—riders training everywhere and frequent races.

I was a newly minted cat 2 and got caught up in the enthusiasm. Up at 5:30 a.m. to meet a teammate, we did intervals twice a week, a long ride in the mountains on a third day, and raced on the weekends. I also tried to lose weight. I had been a football lineman in college, but cycling had peeled off 40 pounds automatically. Now I wanted to lose another 10, so I severely restricted my calories. I wasn't eating enough to fuel such demanding workouts, and "running on empty" meant that not only did I feel miserable all the time, I couldn't sustain the training volume or intensity.

Soon my performance began to drop drastically. I had gone through the lower categories quickly and placed well in the district time trial, but I was having trouble staying with the cat 1-2 pack despite all the interval training. My motivation took a similar nosedive. When I began the early-morning interval routine, I didn't need to set my alarm. I was so excited about the dawn hammerfest that I woke automatically. That didn't last. Before long I was nearly comatose when the alarm went off. Rousing a hibernating woodchuck would have been easier. Worse, I found my mind wandering during class and I had to fight a monumental battle with myself to head for the library to study in the afternoon instead of taking a nap.

I fell asleep at 9 p.m. but woke in the middle of the night and stared at the ceiling for hours before sinking into oblivion again. And I was beyond grumpy. My wife noticed that a lot sooner than I did. I needed a whole off-season of easier activity to recover. And ever since, it has taken much less of a training load to bring on the symptoms again.

Intensity is a drug. As we have seen, hard training makes you better—until you exceed your capacity to recover. Then hard training makes you worse. So think of intervals, racing and tough group rides as powerful medicine, medicine that can, in the right dosage, make you improve. But prescribed incorrectly, it can make you ill indeed. This isn't just a metaphor. If you suffer through a bout of overtraining and chronic fatigue, *illness* will seem exactly the right description.

PREVENTION

First, learn to ride slowly. Most cyclists feel guilty when they aren't hammering, but a fairly large percentage of each week's training should be spent at heart rates around 65-75 percent of maximum (RPE of 6 and 7).

Why ride slowly if you're training to get faster? Easy rides promote recovery because they stimulate blood flow to the muscles without stressing them. They're psychologically beneficial, too, because they provide the fun of cycling without the stress of training. And some authorities argue that riding at low intensity helps capillary development and thus increases endurance. If you have trouble restraining yourself and easy rides have a way of becoming fast and hard, try these tricks:

- **Wear a heart monitor**. Set the upper limit alarm at 75 percent of your max heart rate. When it beeps, back off.

- **Ride with slower people**. Easy days are great opportunities to ride with friends who couldn't normally keep up with you.

- **Don't "train."** Just ride to the coffee shop or do errands on your bike.

- **Ride a slow bike**. You associate your fast road bike with speed and intensity, so use your town bike or beater to give you an easy-ride attitude.

- **Ride on bike paths or dirt roads**. Take a leisurely "walk on the bike" on routes that naturally inhibit speed.

- **Avoid hills**. Stay in terrain that doesn't force you to work at higher heart rates.

- **Ride indoors**. It's easy to control your intensity while riding on rollers or a trainer. Simply limit your gears. Watch TV or read a book.

- **Schedule down time**. It's appropriate to designate every fourth week a rest week, cutting volume and intensity about 30 percent. It's far better to plan a rest week than be forced into one by fatigue. Rest before you're tired, not when you're cooked.

Studies show that significant gains in fitness come not *during* the hard efforts of training, but while resting and recovering *after* training. That's when your muscles repair themselves and grow stronger. To ensure sufficient recovery:

- **Evaluate your total stress load**. When non-cycling demands are unusually high, cut back on scheduled training. If you're building a new house or starting a new and challenging job, training may have to go to the back burner and be reduced to a simmer. That's okay.

- **Eat and drink enough**. Be sure you're well hydrated and eating enough carbohydrate to replace the muscle fuel that training consumes. Consider a post-ride carbo replacement drink. Many cases of overtraining have roots in insufficient calories and poor hydration.

- **Monitor your body**. Learn the overtraining symptoms above and be keenly aware of how you feel. If you're experiencing symptoms, reduce training *now*. Don't make the mistake of thinking you can ride through fatigue and come out stronger. It won't happen. You'll only sink deeper.

YOU OVERTRAINED. NOW WHAT?

Rest! It's a sad truth, but rest is the best remedy. Nap instead of training. Eat high-carbohydrate meals. Pump the fluids. When you're feeling better in several days, resume normal training but avoid the excessively hard work and insufficient recovery that got you in trouble.

Are you really recovered? It's often difficult to be sure. Sean Kelly, the great Irish pro, said he knew he had lively legs when he could power over small hills without standing. A general rule: If you feel eager to ride, you're rested. If warming up is a chore and you still feel tired and flat 30 minutes into the ride, you need more rest, not training. Turn around, go home and put your legs up.

CHAPTER 9

Building the Base

Most cyclists realize the importance of a good endurance base. We know the litany: steady miles (1) develop the ability to process huge amounts of oxygen, (2) prepare the cardiovascular system for high-speed training, and (3) reduce body fat so climbing is improved. Endurance is important for long one-day rides, centuries, cross-state treks and tours.

In chapter 13, I discuss how to prepare specifically for these events. But before you can ride long distances with style and comfort, you must learn to pedal efficiently.

THE IMPORTANCE OF BETTER PEDALING

Here's an eye-opening fact: When you ride steadily for an hour, you make about 5,400 pedal strokes. A century ride may mean 40,000 turns of the crank. Any flaw in your pedaling style gets magnified by the sheer number of times you perform the motion. Poor technique leads to premature fatigue and overuse injuries. It's obvious that honing your pedal stroke is the first step to building endurance and well worth some effort.

> **EXAMPLE!** A few years ago, I was riding in Boulder, Colorado, a road bike mecca where it isn't unusual to see hundreds of other cyclists during a morning spin. Sporting the latest trade team jerseys and shorts, they look, to the casual eye, like pros.
>
> Then I noticed a lone rider coming at me. Something about him screamed "Pro!" even though he wore a nondescript jersey. It wasn't the clothes, it was the pedal stroke that set him apart: rock-solid shoulders, relaxed arms and a silky spin that seemed effortless even though he was going uphill into a brisk wind off the mountains.
>
> It was 7-time Tour de France rider and Giro d'Italia stage winner Ron Kiefel, out for a leg-loosening spin. No way for this retired pro to hide—the elegance and efficiency of his pedal stroke gave him away.

I know what you're thinking: Why should you care about looking elegant? Why devote any effort to honing a silky spin when a choppier style probably gets you down the road nearly as well?

- **A smooth stroke is more efficient on long rides**. Although the difference between the pedal strokes of Ron Kiefel and those of an average rider may be miniscule for each revolution, over thousands of repetitions it results in significant energy savings. A small improvement in form pays off in less fatigue and faster average speed.

- **A smooth stroke reduces injuries**. Pushing down hard on the pedal in a lurching, square stroke increases the chance of damage to the tendons around your ankles and knees. When you smooth out your stroke, you distribute the workload among all the leg's structures, lessening the chance of straining any given part.

- **A smooth stroke allows you to pedal faster**. And fast pedaling, according to coach Chris Carmichael is the key to developing power. At 100 rpm, the leg muscles have to push down with much less force on each stroke compared with going the same speed at 50 rpm. A faster pedal stroke lets you use suppleness and agility rather than brute strength to power your bike.

HOW TO IMPROVE YOUR STROKE

- **Practice pedaling during each ride.** Just 10 minutes of specific pedaling practice as part of your warm-up can bring quick improvement. Spin for a few minutes, then choose a relatively big gear and a slow cadence of around 50 rpm. By pedaling slowly so you can think about the motion. Then pedal fast to make it automatic. You'll soon smooth your stroke at normal cadences. The idea is to feel the pedaling motion all the way around. Pull the pedal through the bottom of the stroke like you're scraping mud off your shoe. To get the pedal over the dead spot at the top of the stroke, envision pulling your knee toward the handlebar.

  Then, on a gradual downhill or tailwind section, shift to a lower gear and increase cadence to the point where you start bouncing on the saddle. Slow down slightly until your hips become steady. Hold that rpm for at least one minute. Focus on pedaling smoothly and applying force throughout the 360-degree pedal circle.

- **Add one-leg training**. Start on an indoor trainer because it's safer. Unclip one foot and rest it on a stool beside the bike or hook it over the trainer back by the rear axle. Pedal a moderate gear with the other leg, trying to stay smooth. As you fatigue—it won't take long—your stroke will get ragged. As you try to pull the pedal over the top, you'll feel a "clunk" in the drivetrain when your leg muscles stop firing. Alternate legs every couple of minutes. At first, your stroke will quickly deteriorate as you tire. But progress will be fast. Soon you'll feel your stroke get smoother and more powerful.

  You can do this drill outside, too. Find a slight uphill on a safe road with little traffic. Unclip one foot, hold it out to the side, and pedal as you did on the trainer. Soon you'll be able to roll along one-legged to the amazement of your friends and bystanders. In fact, you may have to explain to someone what you're doing. Once a friend stopped his car to ask if I'd hurt my knee and needed a lift home.

- **Consider a fixed-gear bike**. Track bikes have no freewheel. When the rear wheel turns, so do the crankarms—you can't coast. Thus, you're forced to make smooth, round pedal circles. Old-time road racers spent a month or more each winter riding a fixed gear on the road to re-program their muscles and nervous systems with the proper pedaling motion. Current roadies such as Lance Armstrong are doing the same.

  A good bike shop will be able to help you set up an old road frame with a fixed gear. Practice in an empty parking lot until you're comfortable with being unable to coast and can get into and out of your pedals safely. Two rides a week on the fixed gear will produce improvement you can feel.

- **Ride rollers**. Rollers are like a treadmill for bikes. The rear wheel sits on 2 low cylinders while the front wheel rests on one. All 3 cylinders spin as you pedal, so the bike's wheels turn just like in regular riding. Because nothing holds the bike in place, any ragged pedaling can cause it to bob and veer. You must turn the crank smoothly and evenly to stay in control. This makes rollers a great way to find and fix pedaling flaws that you might never notice outdoors. When you can ride rollers without bouncing or wavering—and even ride no-hands—your stroke is sound.

- **Get dirty**. Studies done at the Olympic Training Center in Colorado Springs show that mountain bike riders have the most supple stroke in cycling. Surprised? This is because our dirt brethren have to apply even pressure all the way around the pedal circle or the rear wheel will break free on loosely surfaced climbs. If you have a mountain bike, seek rubbly uphill trails and practice riding them smoothly. Or, try this tip from Ron Kiefel: ride non-technical singletrack climbs on your road bike. If you can pedal uphill through loose dirt on a smooth road tire while maintaining traction, you know you've got a stroke as smooth as a pro's.

PUTTING IN THE MILES

Okay—your pedal stroke is as silky as Kiefel's. Now it's time to work on endurance. Most riders think that developing endurance is simple—just ride more—but it's slightly more complicated than that.

- **Ride long once each week.** Most recreational riders and weekend racers find that one long ride every 7-10 days is sufficient to keep their endurance up. How long is "long?" It's usually about 40 percent of weekly mileage. So if you average about 100 miles per week, your long weekend ride should be about 40 miles. Don't boost mileage too quickly. Increases of 10 percent from one week to the next are usually well tolerated and effective.

- **Keep your speed comfortable.** Do long rides well within your aerobic zone. If you're using a heart monitor, keep intensity between 65 and 80 percent of your max heart rate—a comfortable level of effort. At the start of the ride the correct pace should feel easy. But after several hours, it will begin to feel difficult. It's fine to go a bit harder on climbs or headwind sections, but stay below your lactate threshold. You should feel like you're cruising. Your breathing should never become labored. Finish the ride mellowly tired but never exhausted.

- **Be a chowhound**. The keys to a successful long ride are food and fluids. As ultramarathon cyclist and coach John Hughes says, "No matter how fit you are, endurance is limited by what you eat and drink during a ride." Start with plenty of sports drink, energy bars and other food. Finish with empty bottles and jersey pockets. A good rule of thumb: Drink at least one large bottle of sports drink and eat at least one energy bar or equivalent (5 or 6 fig bars, for example) every hour. On rides lasting more than 2 hours, use a backpack-style hydration system for additional fluid capacity, or plan stops at convenience stores to refuel. Don't bonk!

- **Work at recovery**. Immediately after your ride, consume between 50 and 100 grams of carbohydrate with a little protein. The exact amount depends on your body weight. You'll do well by eating a large bowl of cereal with a banana and skim milk, or a bagel with jam and a piece of fruit. Studies say that the sooner you start the refueling process, the faster the body makes glycogen (muscle fuel) and transports it into the working muscles. Many riders like to use commercial recovery drinks. They're quicker to prepare than food and may be easier to digest when you're tired.

BEYOND ENDURANCE

Endurance is only part of the cycling equation. You need speed and power, too. I discuss how to develop these skills in chapters 11 and 12. However, speed and power will come easier if you mix them into your early-season endurance rides.

> **EXAMPLE!** Pete Penseyres trained for his first Race Across America victory in 1984 with plenty of long, steady miles. He commuted 35 miles to work in the morning and took a longer route home so he totaled about 100 miles a day. On the weekend, he did a 24-hour ride.
>
> But in preparing for his second win in 1986, he changed his training, substituting faster riding for some of the long slogs. He did training races and time trials to put more speed in his legs. The result was an average speed record for solo RAAM that has yet to be broken. Penseyres averaged 15.4 mph for more than 3,000 miles, including time spent off the bike (not much!).

You probably do only a fraction of the training distance that ultramarathon riders log. But even a modest diet of slow and steady endurance work can sap your snap. So, while concentrating on building an endurance base, also work on speed of various kinds during one ride each week. Here are 3 types of speed, plus a sample workout to develop each. Always warm up for at least 20 minutes before making hard efforts.

- **Sprint speed**. On a flat road and in a moderate gear, stand up and sprint—not all-out but at about 90 percent of your maximum for 10-15 seconds. Spin easily for 5 minutes to recover. Repeat 3-5 times.

- **Climbing speed**. Find a moderately steep hill that takes 2-4 minutes to climb. Climb it 3 times. On the first ascent, stay seated and use a relatively small gear so your cadence is 80-90 rpm and your heart rate rises to about 90 percent of max. On the second ascent, use a larger gear and stand all the way at a cadence of around 75. Again, aim for a finishing heart rate of 90 percent of max. On the final climb, every 30 seconds alternate standing in a large gear with sitting in a low cadence while spinning a smaller gear. If you don't have hills in your area, do these repeats using a big gear into the wind.

- **Time trial speed**. Find a 2- or 3-mile stretch of lightly traveled road, preferably with a wide shoulder and no stop signs or lights. Ride at a steady pace at 80-90 percent of your maximum heart rate. Use a moderately large gear and a cadence of about 90 rpm. Recover by riding slowly back to the start. Repeat 2-4 times.

CHAPTER 10

Raising Lactate Threshold

If you read articles about training (or hear other cyclists talk about their training programs) you can't avoid the term *lactate threshold*. It's so common it has become a buzzword, as in "What's your LT?" or "I went over my LT on that hill and blew up." Lactate threshold is essential to effective training, so let's see what it's all about.

LT DEFINED

Lactate threshold is the exertion level beyond which you can no longer produce energy aerobically. Additional intense work means your body can't deal with the resulting buildup of lactate (lactic acid). Excess lactate is marked by muscle fatigue, pain and shallow, rapid breathing. The lactate threshold was formerly called the anaerobic threshold (AT) and you might still encounter this term, but it's now dated. In scientific papers, lactate threshold is sometimes referred to as OBLA (onset of blood lactate accumulation).

HOW LT IS MEASURED

LT can be measured in the lab with a relatively simple but invasive procedure. On a stationary bike, the cyclist rides at steadily increasing resistance while the lab technician takes a blood sample from his fingertips every minute. Lactate circulates in the blood, and LT is defined as a specific amount—usually 4 millimoles.

LT also can be measured, although not quite as accurately, on the bike—and you won't have to suffer getting your fingertips perforated. Basically, LT is the maximum intensity a rider can sustain for a 30- to 60-minute time trial. This intensity can be measured in watts or heart rate. Ground speed, the simplest method, can be deceiving because it takes more power to ride at, say, 25 mph into a headwind than with a tailwind.

To determine your lactate threshold, wear your heart monitor, warm up thoroughly, then ride a time trial of at least 10 miles on a flat course. Your average heart rate for the distance is your LT. (It's ideal to have a heart monitor that calculates average heart rate.) To double check, do this test again at least one week later. Be well rested for each test.

> **CAUTION!** Lactate threshold testing and LT training are extremely strenuous. Please get your doctor's approval, especially if you are over 35, have any type of cardiovascular problem, or are not used to this type of exertion. Play it safe so you can train with confidence.

WHY LT IS IMPORTANT

The more power you can generate without going over your lactate threshold and becoming anaerobic, the faster you can go at a given heart rate.

That's fine for racers, but why is LT important for recreational riders? The ability to produce more power at a comfortable heart rate means you'll go faster with the same effort. Your time for centuries will improve. When your companions on the weekend group ride are gasping on a climb, you'll still be in your comfort zone.

> **EXAMPLE!** Suppose Mick generates 300 watts at LT while Rod puts out 250. On a race's early hills, Mick pushes the pace at an effort equal to 280 watts. He's still under his LT, riding hard but in control. To keep up, Rod has to go over his LT and into oxygen debt. On the last and deciding climb, guess which rider still has something left?

THE ARMSTRONG SECRET

LT's significance for all riders has risen lately because it's been identified as the key component in Lance Armstrong's training program. In May, 1999, shortly before Lance's first Tour de France victory, his coach, Chris Carmichael, revealed the secret of the rider's overwhelming fitness. I heard it firsthand at the Boulder Center for Sports Medicine's Science of Cycling Seminar.

First, a little background. Most training programs are complicated because cycling requires a vast range of seemingly conflicting abilities—the endurance to ride 150 miles, the power to win 53x12-gear sprints, and the aerobic capacity to time trial at better than 30 mph. Training these diverse skills is like asking a champion marathoner to also win the 100-meter sprint or an NFL quarterback to play nose tackle, too.

However, Carmichael's training philosophy is extremely simple. He has distilled the sport to one skill—the ability to produce great power at lactate threshold. The coach says that Armstrong's power at LT has grown steadily during his career from about 340 watts in 1993 to more than 400 in 2001. (For comparison, the average age-group bike racer generates about 220 watts.)

"The issue," Carmichael stated at the conference, "isn't merely to produce power. Anyone can produce 400 watts. But most riders can't produce 400 watts for very long without going anaerobic and slowing abruptly. So, power isn't the issue. It's the ability to produce significant power while remaining under your LT and in control. All of Lance's training revolves around increasing his power at LT.

"The secret," Carmichael concluded, "is to do most of your hard training a little below, at, or slightly above your lactate threshold."

LT-BOOSTING WORKOUTS

Here are typical workouts to boost lactate threshold. Remember to warm up for at least 15 minutes. Wear a heart monitor to regulate your effort.

- **LT tempo**. Ride for 30 minutes at a heart rate about 10 beats below your LT heart rate.

- **Two tens**. Ride for 10 minutes at an average heart rate about 5 beats below LT. Spin gently for 15 minutes, then repeat the 10-minute hard effort.

- **Hill repeats**. Find a hill that takes 3-5 minutes to climb. Go up at your LT heart rate. Coast to the bottom, spin gently for 5 minutes on the flats, then repeat the climb 2-5 times, depending on your fitness level.

- **Grinders**. Find a long climb that takes 10-30 minutes. Ride it steadily at just below your LT. Choose a gear that allows you to maintain a relatively high cadence of 80-90 rpm.

- **Time trials**. Many bike clubs have a time trial series. They're usually around 10 miles on a weekday evening. Check at your local bike shop for details. Riding these events is great LT training—and you'll have the benefit of competition to give the hard effort another purpose.

LT TRAINING TIPS

- Do only 2 LT workouts per week, separated by at least 2 recovery days. We mortals don't have as much time to train and recover as pros like Lance Armstrong.

- After 3 weeks of LT training, ride easily for an additional week to let your body recover and consolidate the gains you've made from hard training.

- Don't do LT training all year. After 8 weeks of lactate threshold work (2 cycles of 3 weeks of LT training twice a week, then one week easy), spend one month riding steadily at about 30 beats below LT to build your endurance.

- Remember! Get your physician's permission before you do LT work or any strenuous training.

CHAPTER 11

Building Power

When do you get dropped? If you're like most riders, you don't lose contact with the group (or your buddy) when the pace is moderate. Even if things get a little frisky you can hang. Nope, most riders get dropped when it suddenly gets really hard—on a steep hill, when someone attacks, or when the road briefly turns into the wind. To stick with the group in these conditions you need power—the ability to put the hammer down for 30 seconds to 3 minutes—and then recover when the pace slows.

Strong at 60: Tucker, left, leg presses half a ton.

Power like this isn't easy to develop. It takes time. Start by establishing a solid strength base in the off-season with resistance training. I'll cover this in the book's part 2. Then after a weight program, you need to devote 8 weeks to specific power-building on the bike.

Strength in the weight room is a necessary precursor to power on the bike. I'll define strength here as low-repetition movements—how much you can lift in a given exercise from 1 to 15 times. Power, on the other hand, is work over time. It's characterized by the multiple repetitions of the pedal stroke while going fast up a hill, for instance.

At first glance, low-rep grunt-and-groan strength has little to do with riding. But the emerging model for building crank-busting power on the bike starts in the weight room. The trick, as we'll see, is to build strength first, then convert it to cycling-specific power.

EXAMPLE! Colorado masters rider Scott Tucker holds the U.S. time trial record for the 55-59 age group, a blistering 51:56 for 40 km (24.7 miles).

Although he weighs only about 160 pounds and is now over 60, his goal in the weight room each winter is to build to 1,000 pounds in the leg press for at least one rep.

Not bad for a slender senior citizen! That's an amazing amount of strength that Tucker successfully converts to national-class time trial power.

PEDALING FOR POWER

When it's spring and you've survived winter in the weight room, your power in the leg press or other leg exercises will be high. Now you're ready for the on-bike portion of power building. Here are the guidelines:

- Develop a solid fitness base before you attempt power workouts—at least 1,000 miles of varied riding in the previous 3 months in addition to the weight room work.

- Do 2 power workouts per week, such as the ones below. I describe springtime power building in more detail in part 3 and include power workouts in daily training schedules at the end of that section.

- Each week, do one longer ride at a moderate pace to keep your endurance up. The rest of the week, ride very easily at about 65 percent of max heart rate to recover. Don't cheat and go harder. You need rest if you want to improve.

- Always warm up for 20 minutes before you attempt a power workout. Start by spinning easily, then progressively increase gearing and cadence until you're sweating and your heart rate is about 80 percent of max.

- Wear a heart monitor for at least some power workouts to gauge your effort. Always wear it for recovery rides to guarantee you're going easy enough.

- Don't do power workouts if you now have or have had knee problems!

WORKOUTS

Here are 5 types of training rides that are guaranteed to develop your power.

- **Drag races**. On a flat road, roll along slowly in the saddle in your biggest gear. Hold the handlebar in the drops. Remain seated. Accelerate as hard as possible for 15-20 seconds. Practice good pedaling form. Don't thrash all over the bike. Spin very easily for 5 minutes between each effort. Do 3 reps the first time and build to 5.

- **Accelerations**. Roll along at 15 mph on a flat road in your biggest gear. Hold the bar in the drops, rise from the saddle and accelerate as hard as possible for 20 seconds or until you are turning the gear at 100 rpm. Maintain good pedaling form. Spin easily for 5 minutes between accelerations. Do 3 reps the first time and build to 5.

- **Sprinter's hills**. Find a steep hill that takes 20-30 seconds to climb when you're going fast. Even a highway overpass works if traffic isn't a problem. Roll into the hill, then sprint hard to the top while out of the saddle. Maintain good pedaling form. Choose the correct gear. It's right if you spin a bit too fast at the bottom of the hill but can barely maintain a cadence of 75 rpm at the top. Do 3 reps the first time and build to 5.

- **Three minutes of pain**. Find a moderate hill that takes about 3 minutes to climb. Wear a heart monitor for this workout. Climb the hill nearly as fast as possible. Attain a heart rate of about 90 percent of max at the top. Alternate sitting on one ascent and standing on the next. Do 3 reps the first time and build to 5.

- **Monster sprints**. Find a gradual climb about half a mile long. Use a large gear and roll along at a moderate pace of 15-17 mph. Sprint for 30 seconds. Don't go all out at first, but gradually increase the effort until you're going 100 percent—but retaining good form—in the last 5 seconds. Do 3 reps the first time and build to 5.

With this on-bike work following a winter weight-training program, you *will* substantially increase your power. Let your riding buddies beware!

CHAPTER 12

Developing Speed

A rider once told me about the greatest display of speed she ever produced. No, it wasn't in a race. She was riding along minding her business when a huge Doberman, jaws dripping saliva and teeth glinting in the sun, rocketed out of a suburban yard and took dead aim on her calf. Speed isn't just for racers! Our heroine jumped out of the saddle, accelerated for all she was worth and vanished down the road, leaving Fang frustrated and panting.

How did she develop such a doggone good burst of speed? She's no natural sprinter and she doesn't do hard intervals, but she'd been taking advantage of opportunities to get faster. Here are the secrets for more speed with less work.

RULES FOR GETTING FASTER

- **Don't force it.** Speed training doesn't require a gut-busting effort with eyeballs bulging and knuckles white from gripping the handlebar. You can go nearly as fast if you learn to float along in a brisk but relaxed way. Don't think "Pedal harder!" Think "Pedal faster!"

- **Speed doesn't have to mean sprint.** I look at how to sprint below. But speed doesn't necessarily require an explosive burst for 10 seconds. Aim for relaxed speed that is sustainable for a minute, speed you can repeat several times on a ride without feeling stressed.

- **Train for speed by yourself (most of the time).** Your idea of speed may not be the same as someone else's. Your friends may be faster or slower than you. The only thing that matters is your improvement. So with few exceptions, train for speed alone—at your speed.

- **Use a group to develop speed (sometimes).** When you feel comfortable with going faster from your solo training, venture out in a spirited group. Riders will attack, sprint for roadside signs and bump up the pace on hills. Trying to stick with the group is a fast way to develop a turn of speed. The competition revs your engine in a way that solo riding can't.

SPRINTING FORM

Use these tips to reach high speed quickly.

- **Choose your gear.** Start the sprint in a gear that you can turn comfortably at about 80 rpm—a bit lower than your normal cadence. Your initial jump will get you above 100 rpm. Then, while still standing, shift to a higher gear, pedal it up to a fast rpm and shift again. It's easier to shift while standing if you ease off pedal pressure slightly just as you make the gear change. Practice will quickly give you the feel for this technique. Thanks to indexed brake/shift levers, you can start your sprint in a gear low enough for rapid acceleration, then shift to a higher gear to reach max velocity while still standing.

- **Trust your thrust.** To jump effectively, hold the handlebar in the drops. Rise from the saddle as you thrust strongly with your dominant leg. (Which is your dominant leg? It's probably the one that's forward when you descend with your crankarms horizontal.) At the same time, pull up on the handlebar with the arm that's on the same side as the leg that's pushing down. The downward thrust makes the bike tip toward that side. Pulling up counters the force that would otherwise topple you over. After the first explosive downstroke, continue to pedal powerfully while rocking the bike just enough to counteract your leg thrusts. Don't throw the bike excessively from side to side. That wastes energy and scrubs off speed. It's a danger to other riders, too.

> **EXAMPLE!** I attended Greg LeMond's training camp that he ran with his friend, Canadian rider Steve Bauer. Famous as a road sprinter, Bauer often dueled with American Davis Phinney in Colorado's legendary Coors Classics in the 1980s. Bauer personified power. A former hockey player, he was built like a powerlifter from the waist down.
>
> At the camp Bauer gave us a demonstration of his sprinting prowess. We stood by the side of the road while he rolled along slowly in a big gear until next to us. Then he jumped hard. The bike creaked like it was cracking. Within 20 yards he was a blur. We could hear his tires humming on the pavement.

- **Watch your line.** Sprinting with your head down or your eyes locked and blurry is a recipe for disaster. The best sprinters are like running backs in football. They see the whole field all at once so they can anticipate and make split-second decisions.

- **Stay grounded**. Powerful riders often have trouble keeping the bike's rear wheel on the pavement when they sprint. It hops slightly on each pedal stroke, losing traction, wasting speed and risking control. Avoid the "hops" by keeping your hips back to weight the rear wheel. When you stand, concentrate on raising your hips above the saddle, not moving them forward toward the handlebar. Your shoulders should stay behind an imaginary vertical line through the front hub.

SOLO SPEED-PLAY DRILLS

Want to develop snap and speed on your everyday rides like our Doberman defier? Try these solo drills. Always warm up first with at least 15-20 minutes of steadily increasing effort.

- **Chase the bluebird.** Pick a cue that appears fairly frequently on your route: bluebirds, adopt-a-highway signs, white mailboxes, silos. Whenever you spot one of these cues, sprint for 20-30 seconds. Don't go quite all out. Sprint, sit, settle in, spin.

- **Pickups.** On an obstacle-free stretch of road, pick up the pace gradually until you're pedaling briskly at about 80 percent of your max heart rate. The pace should feel quick but comfortable. Concentrate on a smooth spin and a relaxed, flowing pedal style. Continue for about one minute then gradually back off to an easy pace. Repeat 3 times during the ride with at least 5 minutes of easy spinning between each effort.

- **Rollercoaster**. Find a course with 3 or 4 short hills spread over several miles. Or look for a short loop with 1 or 2 hills. It should take no more than 20 seconds to sprint over each hill.

Roll gently between the hills, then attack each rise out of the saddle. Your gear choice should let you spin about 110 rpm at the bottom and at least 90 rpm at the top. Again, don't go all out. You want to ride briskly but not exhaustively.

TIPS FOR COMPETITIVE SPRINTS

Okay, you've been sprinting on your solo rides and you know you're faster. But how can you snag bragging rights in a group sprint against several friends?

Position is everything. You'll rarely win if you lead out a sprint, especially into a headwind. Position yourself 1 or 2 riders back, take advantage of their draft, and wait until the last minute to jump and come around. The exception is a slightly downhill sprint or one with a tailwind. Sometimes you can jump early by surprise and hold your gap to the line.

Cheat! Feign fatigue and sit on the back, or time your pulls so your last turn comes about a mile from the line. Then you can hide in the paceline until it's time to fire your afterburners.

CHAPTER 13

Increasing Endurance

Increasing your endurance seems easy—simply ride more miles. It isn't that easy in practice, however, for several of reasons. First, you need an important goal to stay motivated. You need more time, too. And you need to know how to increase mileage safely and effectively. It's common to do too much too soon and fall prey to overtraining, overuse injuries or plain old boredom.

Let's look at perhaps the best way to increase endurance. It's worked for countless riders over the years. It begins with this simple declaration:

"I'm going to do the _____ century ride."

Fill in the blank with a 100-miler near you. There's sure to be one. More than a thousand organized centuries are held in North America each year. By choosing one that's at least 2 months away, you can make tremendous strides in your endurance before the big day. This chapter will show you how.

The benefits will extend far beyond the event you're training for. When you're able to ride a century with strength and energy to spare, you'll have the fitness and confidence to ride any distance shorter than 3 figures, too.

It's important not to underestimate the challenge. One hundred miles is a long way on a bike, no doubt about it. It'll likely take 6 or more hours—a daunting prospect if you're a first-timer. But it's also important not to overestimate the challenge. Building up to a century isn't the overwhelming task that you may fear. In fact, if you can spin along comfortably for 60 to 90 minutes right now, you can get century-fit in only 8 weeks of training.

YOUR CENTURY TRAINING PLAN

This 8-week training schedule will get you through a century with a smile on your face.

I'm assuming that you can ride about 30 miles when you start the program. I'm also assuming that your training time is limited. Isn't everyone's? The plan starts with only about 4 hours a week on the bike and gradually builds to 9 hours.

A century can be done on such a modest time commitment because it's a one-day ride, not a multiday tour requiring consecutive long days in the saddle. As a result, each century training week includes only one *long* ride. It accustoms you to the endurance demands of the event.

I've also included a weekly *fast* ride. Studies show that short-but-brisk training sessions provide as much benefit as dawdling through long rides, good news for time-challenged cyclists. Adding intensity to one workout each week develops the power to combat headwinds and hills, and you'll be able to join a fast paceline if you choose.

In addition to each week's brisk ride (for fitness) and long ride (for endurance), add 3 *easy* spins of about an hour each, for recovery. Separate the endurance ride and the speed ride by at least 2 days. Take 1 or 2 days completely *off* the bike. You can do light exercise such as walking or upper-body weight training if you like.

Get your doctor's permission before you start any training program. This is essential if you've been sedentary, are over 35, or have had any medical problems. Once you're cleared to begin, always start rides with 15 minutes of easy spinning before doing harder efforts. For a more formal and thorough warm-up, follow the schedule I lay out in chapter 41.

WEEK 1: Endurance day Speed day	1 hr. and 30 min. at moderate effort (about 75% of max heart rate) 1:00 including 3 miles at a brisk pace (about 80%)
WEEK 2: Endurance day Speed day	1:45 at moderate effort (75%) 1:00 including 5 miles at a brisk pace (80%)
WEEK 3: Endurance day Speed day	2:00 at moderate effort (75%) 1:10 with a long climb (15-20 min.) or against headwind for 20 min.
WEEK 4: Endurance day Speed day	2:30 at moderate effort (75%) 1:10 including 5 miles at a fast pace (85%)
WEEK 5: Endurance day Speed day	3:00 at moderate effort (75%) 1:15 including 4 short climbs (20-45 sec.) just below max heart rate
WEEK 6: Endurance day Speed day	3:30 at moderate effort (75%) 1:15 with a long climb (15-20 min.) or against headwind for 20 min.
WEEK 7: Endurance day Speed day	4:00 at moderate effort (75%) 1:30 including 8 miles at a fast pace (85%)

WEEK 8: You're almost ready! Here's how to train and taper during the final week so you can ride your best:

Sunday	Endurance. 4:30 at moderate effort (75% of max heart rate)
Monday	Rest day
Tuesday	Speed. 1:30 with 5 short climbs (20-45 sec.) at a hard pace (85%)
Wednesday	Spin. 1:00 at an easy pace (65%)
Thursday	Rest day
Friday	Spin. 1:00 at an easy pace (65%)
Saturday	Ride a great century!

During the long rides, get in the habit of nibbling and sipping throughout. The key to endurance is your stomach, not your legs. Even the best-trained riders pack only enough fuel (glycogen) in their muscles for a couple of hours of strenuous cycling. Fluid stores evaporate even faster. Eating and drinking before, during and after the ride is crucial. Remember that fluid replacement is essential during training, too. Routinely drink at least 8 big glasses of water each day. Your urine should be pale yellow and you should need the restroom every couple of hours. Failure to drink enough will result in chronic dehydration and reduced performance.

CENTURY PREPARATION

Training isn't just for accumulating mileage. Long rides help you sort out all the logistics and comfort issues that accompany a day in the saddle. Use your endurance training to test your equipment and food. Do your shorts chafe? What kind of energy bars and sports drinks go down easily? Training is also the time to get comfortable in a paceline. If you're apprehensive about group riding, opt to ride the century on your own or with a friend.

Resist the urge to cram extra training into the week of the event. You're much better off riding fewer miles and starting the century rested rather rolling out with heavy legs. Cut your mileage by at least half in the 6 days before the ride.

Find out about the course. Is it hilly? Are headwinds probable? Severe conditions can add more than an hour to your finishing time. Pack emergency food and make sure your gearing is low enough for the terrain. Check to see how many rest stops are provided, where are they and what's on the menu. If they have only water, you run the risk of *hyponatremia*, a potentially serious sodium deficiency. Although this condition is rare in events of 100 miles or less, sports drinks that contain sodium are better than water alone. They also supply carbohydrate calories in a form that provides quick energy.

If you can't stomach the food or drinks being offered, carry your own. Or make arrangements with non-riding friends to supply you along the way. They must not drive on the course because vehicles pose a hazard to riders, but they can use adjacent roads to meet you at rest stops or in towns.

THE BIG DAY

Great! You've done your training and your scouting and you're ready to go. Here's your strategy for a successful century.

- **Eat aggressively the night before.** This will top off your muscles with glycogen. Emphasize carbohydrates like pasta, vegetables, whole grains and fruit. Don't skip dessert.

> **EXAMPLE!** When pro cyclist Henk Vogels was asked what was on his dinner menu before Colorado's grueling 138-mile Saturn Cycling Classic, he replied: "Three or four plates of pasta, ice cream, and go to bed bloated." You get the idea, but be careful about hitting the hay with a full stomach because you might not sleep well. Schedule dinner to finish at least two hours before bedtime. Also, stop hydrating at about the same time or your sleep could be interrupted by multiple trips to the bathroom.

- **Lay out all your equipment.** You don't want to be fumbling around the next morning. Pump tires, prepare food and fluids, put out rain gear in case of inclement weather and pin on your number if the event provides one. Then set 2 alarm clocks so you don't worry about oversleeping.

- **Eat an ample breakfast.** Thanks to cycling's smooth pedaling motion, you can eat about an hour before the start of this or any other noncompetitive long ride without risk of stomach upset (unless there are immediate hills). And you'll need a full tank because a century ride incinerates about 4,000 calories. Breakfast should total about 60 grams of carbohydrate if you're an average-size woman, 80-100 grams if you're a man. For example, cereal, skim milk, a banana and a bagel with jam equals about 90 grams of carbo. Add some protein and fat, such as scrambled eggs or an omelet, to stick with you miles into the ride.

- **Drink 16 ounces of a sports drink** during the hour before the start. Hit the restroom just before you depart so a full bladder doesn't hinder your early miles.

- **Don't begin too fast**. In the excitement of a big event that you've prepared so well for, it's hard to control the adrenaline surge. A good rule: Ride the first 30 miles at an easy pace, and the next 40 moderately. Then hold that pace—or pick it up—to the finish.

- **Take advantage of pacelines.** But only if you're comfortable in them. Pacelines in large century fields can be disorganized and dangerous. They may be too fast for your fitness level. Riding with several friends is often a better choice.

- **Drink before you feel thirsty**. Your sensation of thirst lags behind your need for fluid. Remember to grab your bottle every 15 minutes and take a couple of big swallows (4-6 ounces). Set your watch's countdown timer to beep as a reminder.

- **Eat 20 grams of carbohydrate each half hour**. That's the equivalent of half an energy bar, several fig bars or half a banana. Constant nibbling will ensure that you don't bonk.

- **Don't dwell at rest stops**. Long breaks mean stiff legs when you get rolling again. Fill your bottles and grab enough food to last to the next stop. Then eat and drink once you're back on the road. On the other hand, if the century offers a festive lunch stop with tempting food, stay and enjoy it if you aren't riding for a fast time.

- **Fuel the finish.** The last 25 miles is the crux of any century ride. Switch from energy bars and other solid food to energy gels or sports drinks. They digest faster so they'll kick in before the finish. Be sure to wash gel down with plenty of fluid. Consider a caffeinated beverage late in the ride. If you use caffeine regularly you won't get much of a boost. But it can give infrequent users a physical and mental lift.

AFTER THE RIDE

You finished—and had fun. Congratulations! Now there are only 3 things left to do.

1. **Rehydrate**. No matter how much you drink during a long ride, you'll finish dehydrated. Drink until your urine is pale yellow and plentiful, and your weight is back to normal.

2. **Refuel**. Eat and drink carbohydrate as soon as you're off the bike. Replenishment of muscle fuel becomes progressively less efficient as time passes, so snack while you stand around and talk to friends. Down about the same amount of carbo as before the ride.

3. **Recap**. If you're like most riders, you'll be eager to ride another century—and ride it better. Jot down training and tactical errors while lessons are still fresh, then work on fixing them.

MULTI-DAY RIDES

While centuries and other long one-day rides are fun, multiday tours are even more challenging and satisfying. You can take off on a tour by yourself with your bike loaded with camping gear. Or you can join an organized tour that hauls your stuff so you can ride unencumbered. Some tours offer motel accommodations in destination towns. On others, riders set up a tent city on local athletic fields. Some rides are charity events, others are commercial ventures. Many are cross-state treks.

Several years ago, I rode the PAC Tour Northern Transcontinental from Seattle to the Virginia shore. Along with 45 other cyclists, I covered the 3,400 miles in 24 consecutive days of riding, averaging 140 miles per day. It's recommended that anyone contemplating such a rapid transcontinental be able to ride back-to-back 150-milers and cover 200 miles in 14 hours.

By comparison, it's relatively easy to develop the endurance necessary for a week of the 50- to 80-mile rides that most tours require. The key is to follow the 8-week program on page 40 but do an endurance ride *each* weekend day. This conditions you to the demands of riding long on consecutive days. Here's what the weekends look like. "Moderate effort" is about 75 percent of max heart rate.

WEEK 1:	
Saturday	1 hr. and 30 min. at moderate effort
Sunday	1:45 at moderate effort
WEEK 2:	
Saturday	1:45 at moderate effort
Sunday	2:00 at moderate effort
WEEK 3:	
Saturday	2:00 at moderate effort
Sunday	2:15 including 2-3 hills of 5 min. each
WEEK 4:	
Saturday	2:30 at moderate effort
Sunday	2:45 including 3-5 hills of 5 min. each
WEEK 5:	
Saturday	3:00 at moderate effort
Sunday	3:15 including 4-6 hills of 5 min. each
WEEK 6:	
Saturday	3:30 at moderate effort
Sunday	3:45 including 4-6 hills of 5 min. each
WEEK 7:	
Saturday	4:00 at moderate effort
Sunday	4:30 at moderate effort

Week 8: Begin the tour!

CHAPTER 14

Limited-Time Training

"If only I had more time to train, I'd be in super shape." Ever overhear that comment on the club ride? I bet you have. You may have even said it yourself. It ranks way ahead of other cycling "if onlys"—wishes for more power, a faster sprint or a lighter bike. Give me 20 hours a week on the bike, we fantasize, and Lance would be in trouble.

Sorry. More mileage, by itself, is unlikely to make us better riders. And that's good consolation for riders fighting a time crunch.

Let's examine why a modest amount of training time allows you to unlock nearly all of your genetic potential. Then I'll show you how to reach a very high level of fitness by training only 7 hours per week.

MORE MILEAGE DOESN'T GUARANTEE MORE FITNESS

When some people start riding, 10 miles is a real demand. But soon they can ride longer, and their average speed improves markedly. However, as we saw in chapter 4, after some months they reach a depressing plateau. Average speed stagnates and it's harder to tack an additional 15 miles on weekend rides. Even when they increase training mileage substantially, performance refuses to budge—and it may even deteriorate if they wind up overtraining,

Each of us has inherited limits to our abilities. Simply adding mileage won't shatter that genetic ceiling. In fact, riding too much can slow us down rather than make us faster when we exceed our capacity to recover.

EXAMPLE! Runners are more susceptible to injury than cyclists because of the high-impact nature of their sport. As a result, runners get harsh reminders from their bodies that they're overdoing it.

Sports scientists agree that the injury rate for many runners jumps sharply at about 30 miles per week. Stay below this number and most runners can perform almost as well as they would at 50 or 70 miles a week—and have a far lower incidence of injury.

Because cycling is a compliant, non-impact sport, we don't get such a dramatic warning that we've reached our mileage limit. But current thinking places it at about 110 to 150 miles per week for people who work for a living. That's 6 to 9 hours of riding.

As Olympic road cycling champion Connie Carpenter-Phinney has noted, "If you work full time, 10 hours of riding each week is a lot."

There's one more fallacy of wishing for unlimited time to ride: You'd probably get bored with cycling. Isn't gonna happen—you love to ride, right? But if all you did was ride—no weight training, no hiking, no leisurely Saturday mornings puttering around the house—you'd eventually come to dislike the bike.

DECIDING HOW MUCH TO TRAIN

Pro cyclists often ride 20-30 hours a week. Riders training for ultramarathon events may log even more. Recreational racers (category 3, 4, 5 and masters) usually put in about 10 weekly hours, although some get by on 5 or 7 quality hours if their events are short. Most people with careers, families and other time constraints find that 7 hours a week is plenty of riding to meet their goals. Fast centuries require occasional training rides of 4 or 5 hours, but other weekly jaunts can be shorter.

All of this said, trying to ride a set number of hours each week—and getting frustrated if you don't meet that goal—is exactly the wrong approach.

You're an experiment of one. That's what running philosopher and physician George Sheehan used to say and he was right. We're all individuals. The training program that makes Lance Armstrong fit enough to win the Tour de France would make most of us too tired to get a leg over the bike. The secret? Ride when you can, and have fun when you do. You shouldn't punch a time clock when you get on your bike.

TOP FITNESS IN 7 HOURS A WEEK

You can get in excellent cycling shape on an average of only 60 enjoyable minutes of riding each day. This will leave plenty of time to mow the lawn, buy the groceries, say hi to the spouse and maybe even hold down a job.

Even though this program allots 7 hours, avoid simply riding an hour each day. That can't give you endurance or recovery. Instead, ride longer some days and take other days completely off the bike. Your personal schedule will determine the exact mix, but most people ride more on weekends when they're off work. They schedule non-cycling days for weekdays.

Here's a weekly schedule that works for many riders:

Monday	Rest day with 15 minutes of resistance training
Tuesday	Ride 1 hour with 3-8 sprints or other short, hard efforts
Wednesday	Ride 1 hour at a steady, moderate pace
Thursday	Ride 1 hour including 20 minutes of hard effort (time trialing, jamming short hills, ascending a long climb, pushing into a headwind, and so on)
Friday	Rest day with 15 minutes of resistance training
Saturday	Ride 1 hour at an easy pace
Sunday	Ride 3 hours at a varied pace (group rides or hilly courses are good choices)

Remember, intensity is one key to this program. If you could ride 200 to 400 miles per week, sheer volume would guarantee a high level of fitness. But you can't. Instead, make up for missing miles by including intense efforts at or above your lactate threshold (see chapter 10). Mix short, hard efforts like sprints with longer, steady efforts on hills or into the wind. Spirited group rides raise intensity, too.

The key is varying the intensity during the week. If you always go at a medium pace, your fitness will be mediocre. So, when you go hard, go *really* hard. When you go easy, go at a pace that Colorado cycling coach Skip Hamilton calls "guilt-producingly slow." You must learn to go slowly.

A second key is sufficient rest. Intense workouts boost your speed and power, but this increased fitness comes at a price. Put the hammer down too often and soon you'll be tired, irritable and slow—all the hallmarks of overtraining. This is why I recommend staying off the bike at least 2 days each week. Lift a little, take a relaxing walk, prop up your feet and read a good book. When the time comes to train hard or to beat up your friends on weekend rides, you'll be rested and ready.

Don't forget to squeeze in some resistance training. Cycling is great in many ways, but it doesn't do much for the upper body. Maintaining muscle volume is crucial as we age. So, cheat on the 7-hours-a-week maximum and find 15 minutes 2 days each week for some basic upper-body exercises. Pushups, pull-ups, crunches for the abs and a low-back exercise (such as back extensions) are all you need. Knock off a couple of sets of each to complement your saddle time. A good time to do this simple-but-effective resistance program is right after easy rides when you're warm.

Are you so busy that finding even 7 weekly hours looks like mission impossible? The trick is to examine your daily schedule and look for small segments of free time. For example:

- Can you get up early and **ride before work**? With modern lighting systems, pre-dawn rides are safe. It's cooler, less windy and the traffic is often lighter.

- How about a **lunch-hour workout**? With a little planning, you can change, get in a brisk 60-minute ride, clean up and be back at the desk in 70 to 75 minutes. Eat half your lunch at your midmorning break and the rest during the afternoon.

- **Late evening** is a good time for many people to exercise. Dinner is over, you've had some family time and a great workout is a lot better for you than slouching on the couch in front of the cardiac tube. Again, modern lighting systems make after-dark rides a snap.

- **Ride indoors**. If you don't like riding in the dark or nasty weather, consider pedaling on a trainer. An hour passes quickly if you vary your workouts, use a big fan for cooling, drink plenty of fluids and watch race videos as you pedal. Chapter 26 is devoted to tips, tricks and techniques for making indoor cycling productive and as enjoyable as possible.

- **Commute**. A 5- to 10-mile ride to work with a longer loop home provides an automatic 1 or 2 hours of cycling each day. Why sit in a car and stress about finding time to ride when you could use your bike for daily transportation?

Finally, ride smart. Is there a negative to this 7-hours-a-week program? Of course. In lengthy events such as centuries or week-long tours, you won't have the endurance of riders blessed with more training time. The solution is to realize your limitations and ride accordingly. Sit in a paceline, back off a bit on climbs, eat and drink often. You'll do fine.

CHAPTER 15

Tapering and Peaking

Have you ever had an injury or illness disrupt your cycling just when you were reaching top fitness? "Rats!" you say as you settle in for a period of convalescence, sure that your hard-won fitness will vanish. But then a funny thing happens. After a week or 2 spent chomping at the bit to ride again, you're finally recovered. You hop on the bike expecting to be feeble—and you're flying! Far from destroying your fitness, the downtime seemed to enhance it.

Pro racers encounter this phenomenon frequently. A late-spring injury seems poised to destroy a rider's season. But when he comes back, he finds a whole new level of fitness.

> **EXAMPLE!** In 1999, Oscar Freire was just another young Spanish racer, buried in the peloton and trying to make a name for himself. Worse, his early season was compromised by injury. He was able to race only 11 times. However, as he began to build after the enforced rest, often training alone, he felt stronger and stronger. In October, he astounded everyone by winning the world road championship.

Racers and recreational riders alike can experience the wonders of tapering in order to reach a peak performance. Sports science has shown us that most riders in regular training programs are hovering on the edge of overtraining. If they attempt to go directly to an event that demands a top performance, they'll be unable to produce it. Lingering fatigue will sabotage their efforts. But if they schedule some rest and recuperation (or even if it's forced upon them), their bodies will rebound and they'll be ready for a breakthrough performance. Another example is Greg LeMond, who missed part of the 1983 season with a broken wrist, then came back strong to win the world road championship.

Want to harness the power of tapering for your next big event without having to get injured first? Here's how.

SIX PRINCIPLES OF TAPERING

1. **Decide how long to taper.** For most events, you'll need a longer taper than you think to reach peak form. Just taking a day off during the week and spinning gently the day before won't accomplish much. Plan on a week-long taper for best results. Remember that athletes differ in their time requirements. Some extremely well-trained (and therefore chronically tired) riders could benefit from a 2-week taper. Newcomers to training may want to ride right up to a century or fast club ride. In the latter case, the rider may not have had time to get sufficiently tired to benefit from a pronounced taper. Also, the shorter and more intense the event, the shorter the tapering period. If your goal is a PR in the local 10-mile time trial, you only need about 3 days of lessened intensity and volume.

2. **Reduce riding time.** The key to tapering is to ride less. Sounds obvious, but it's amazing how many cyclists can't force themselves to write down fewer miles in their training diaries. For most events, reducing mileage about 50-65 percent during the tapering period works well. You heard me right—cut your mileage (or time on the bike) by at least half. I know that sounds horrifying to dedicated trainers, but it's necessary.

3. **Don't reduce riding days.** If you normally ride 5 days a week, continue doing so. But reduce the mileage each day. You want your muscles to "remember" how to ride, so give your body its usual lesson. Just keep it short.

4. **Maintain intensity.** Even though you're riding fewer miles during the taper, you'll still ride fast at times. If you normally do short intervals on Tuesday and longer repeats or climbing on Thursday, continue the schedule. The difference? Reduce the number and length of the hard efforts. For example, if you've been doing 8 sprints on Tuesday, cut down to 4 but keep the intensity high. Accustomed to climbing 5 hills hard on your Thursday ride? Do only 2 but with your usual vigor.

> **RESEARCH!** A classic study on peaking and tapering was done in Canada in the late 1980s. Runners who averaged 50 miles per week in normal training cut their mileage drastically to only 6 miles—a reduction of almost 90 percent. However, nearly all of this reduced mileage consisted of fast 500-meter intervals. In spite of (or perhaps because of) the reduced mileage combined with speedwork, their performances improved 22 percent compared to 2 other groups of runners who had done no training or 18 miles of jogging, respectively, during the taper period.

5. **Make slow rides very slow.** What about the other rides during the taper? Make them slow and easy. Don't feel any pressure on the pedals. Ride the flats or, if you can't avoid hills, use your lowest gear. If you wear a heart monitor, keep exertion below 75 percent of max.

6. **Plan peaks in your season schedule.** Many authorities argue that athletes can peak successfully only 2 or 3 times a year. They suggest planning your objectives so you don't waste a peak. Make sure you're feeling great for the events you care most about.

Interestingly, some coaches are now recommending more frequent tapers—as often as one week out of every month. The idea is to lessen the workload regularly so training (as well as racing) can be high quality. Experiment to see what works well for you.

PEAKING FOR RACING

To see how all of this works, here's the schedule I used to peak successfully for the Masters National Time Trial Championship in 2000. I'd been training regularly and had raced both the Colorado time trial and road championships about a month before. The week before nationals, I suspended normal training and reduced on-bike time by about 50 percent. I rode easily but included some fast 2-minute efforts, starting with 4 repeats. I reduced them by one each day. So, my week before the race looked like this:

- 7 days to go: 2-hour easy ride.
- 6 days to go: 1:00 ride with 4 x 2 minutes at time trial pace.
- 5 days to go: 1:25 ride with 3 x 2 minutes at time trial pace.
- 4 days to go: 2:00 ride with 2 x 2 minutes at time trial pace.
- 3 days to go: 1:45 easy ride.
- 2 days to go: Flew to the race. No ride.

- 1 day to go: Rode the course in 1:20 on my time trial bike at a moderate effort, checking the corners and working out what gearing to use on the short hills.

How did it work? I was pleased to clock 57:33 for the 40 km (24.7 miles) on a rolling course with several tight corners. It was good for third place in the 55-59 age group. Winning a national championship medal was nice, and so was feeling good after the finish and not being completely drained on subsequent days.

CHAPTER 16

Nutrition

Proper nutrition is the most contentious issue in cycling. Whether you use Shimano or Campagnolo components, favor steel or titanium frames, wear your sunglasses over your helmet straps or under them—all of these quarrels fade to insignificance compared to tiffs about the percentage of carbohydrate in your diet. Cyclists can be rational about equipment, training and tactics, but calm reason deserts them in a flash when diet is mentioned.

Pros are no guides to nutritional strategies that work well. Some are incredibly precise in their daily diet. Lance Armstrong says in his book, *It's Not About the Bike*, that he weighs food portions so he can control the exact number of calories he consumes each day. On the other hand, I once saw a racer fuel himself for competition with a huge bowl of cornflakes topped with bananas, mounds of white sugar and chocolate milk.

Nutritional experts are no less conflicted. Some books extol the virtues of low-carbohydrate regimens while others suggest the "Three-B Diet"—bagels, bananas and bread—and abhor fat to the extent of suggesting that true believers wash off the last vestiges from low-fat cottage cheese.

Given this lack of consensus, what's a rider to do? I believe the answer, as in so many things in life, is found in moderation. Here are my 5 simple rules for resolving the nutrition controversy.

FIVE RULES TO EAT BY

1. **Avoid fanaticism**. Any dietary regimen that requires iron will is doomed to failure. Athletic training requires enthusiasm, time budgeting and a certain inescapable amount of will power. Don't add to these requirements with a set of arbitrary dietary rules. In fact, a fanatical approach to one diet can offend friends and alienate family. It also can convince you that if you don't get a perfect blend of fat, carbohydrate and protein, you won't perform well. Dietary adaptability is crucial for racers who travel to events, but it's also important for us recreational riders who leave work on Friday evening to drive to a century ride, fueling up along the way wherever it's convenient. If you're convinced that you only ride well on penne pasta and vegetables lightly stir-fried in olive oil, what will you do when faced with one choice of road food—burgers and fries? No, such foods aren't good for you when consumed regularly. But it pays to be omnivorous when choices are limited.

2. **Eat a varied, moderate diet**. A wide selection of food, eaten in moderation, ensures that you get the optimum mix of nutrients without overdoing the calories. Many nutritionists agree that there are no "bad" foods. An occasional bowl of ice cream won't destroy your fitness. There's no steely-eyed dedication needed here. Simply stop and think before you eat something, and make smart choices.

3. **Go easy on fat**. An enormous number of calories can be eliminated from your diet if you cut down on unhealthful fat. For instance, a plain lettuce salad has about 20 calories. Add a dollop of dressing and it increases that innocent bowl of lettuce to 120 calories. Most of the additional calories are the kind of fat that clogs arteries. Try a squeeze from a lemon wedge instead. Likewise, some muffins contain nearly 400 calories, more than half of which come from fat. How about 2 slices of whole wheat bread instead, spread with low-sugar jam? Of course, some fat in the diet is necessary. Sports nutritionists prefer it from fish and nuts.

4. **Emphasize carbohydrate**. I won't go into the continuing controversy over so-called "40-30-30" diets that restrict carbohydrate intake in favor of more protein. I'll simply point out that studies dating back almost 50 years have shown carbohydrate to be the body's preferred fuel for endurance activity. Carbohydrate is simply the best source of glycogen (muscle fuel), and without glycogen you'll ride nowhere fast. That said there's no need to go overboard and eat carbo to the exclusion of other nutrients. A classic study looked at the percentages of carbohydrate, protein and fat in professional racers' diets during the Tour de France. The researchers found that when given a choice of food, racers naturally selected a ratio of about 60-65 percent carbo, 20 percent protein, and around 15 percent fat. This is a good guide to daily nutrition for recreational riders, too.

5. **Eat enough**. Many riders are obsessed with body weight. They think that if they could just drop that "last 10 pounds," their performance, especially on hills, would improve markedly. I'll talk about responsible weight loss in a moment. But remember that riding a bike takes a lot of energy. So do the demands of the rest of your life. And energy comes from calories. Of course, if you eat too much—especially if your food choices are high in fat—you'll gain weight. But if you eat too little, you won't have enough fuel for daily training. You'll feel miserable. Your performance, especially on hills, deteriorates rapidly when your tank is empty.

FIVE ON-BIKE NUTRITIONAL STRATEGIES

> **EXAMPLE!** It happened on a long ride in Colorado—the dreaded bonk. I'd neglected to carry enough food to fuel an endurance-building spin in sparsely populated ranch country. An hour after my last energy bar, I succumbed. One minute I felt great. The next minute I was "pedaling squares," seeing black spots and hallucinating bagels. The cows beside the road didn't know it, but they were in dire danger. Cheeseburgers on the hoof, anyone?

Once you've suffered the bonk, you won't forget it. This word is cycling slang for weakness and sudden fatigue resulting from failure to eat enough during extended hours in the saddle. Not just recreational riders fall victim. Bonked pro racers have been known to lose significant time to the leaders on a single climb. In the 2002 Giro d'Italia, a depleted Cadel Evans dropped 17 minutes in the final 5 miles to a mountaintop stage finish. So what's the solution? Eat and drink enough, of course. But you also have to eat and drink smart. It's not just the amount of food and fluids you put down. Timing is crucial, too. Let's look at 5 nutritional strategies to help you feel great on the bike—and so you can stop casting carnivorous glances at ol' Bess.

1. **Eat before the ride**. If you do much running, you know how hard it is on a full stomach. The jarring associated with each foot strike makes it supremely uncomfortable. Not so with cycling. The smooth pedaling motion means you can eat shortly before and during rides unless you're going flat-out. In fact, it's good to start with a full tank if the ride stretches over 90 minutes because cycling at a brisk pace consumes around 40 calories per mile. About one hour before you get on the bike, eat 55-65 grams of carbohydrate if you're an average-size woman, 80-100 if you're a man. How much is that? Most energy bars contain about 40 grams of carbo and a banana packs about 30. Or try a bagel with jam and a handful of raisins or a fruit bar.

2. **Prehydrate**. You need food before the ride but you also need to be sufficiently hydrated. Most people are chronically dehydrated because they drink coffee, a mild diuretic, and they don't drink enough water during the day. If this sounds like you, you may be starting rides dehydrated—and it only gets worse from there. So, drink copiously all day. Keep a water bottle on your desk at work and sip and refill all day long. Research shows that it's difficult to hydrate fully with water alone, so an hour before you ride, drink about 16 ounces of a sports drink. Urinate just before the start to avoid unwanted pit stops.

> **TIP!** How do you know if you're drinking a sufficient amount daily? Two rules: If you aren't getting up at least once in the night to urinate, you aren't drinking enough. Also, your urine should be pale yellow (not dark) as well as plentiful.

3. **Eat and drink during the ride**. Eating and drinking on the fly isn't easy. We associate food and fluids with sitting down at a table with white napkins and soft music, not with flying down the road astride a bike. That doesn't qualify as fine dining. But getting enough calories and fluids while riding is surprisingly easy. It just takes a little planning and awareness. Get in the habit of drinking frequently, before you feel thirsty. Your body's sensation of thirst lags behind its need for liquid. When you realize you're thirsty it's already too late. Make it a habit to reach for your bottle every 15 minutes and slug down 4-6 ounces (a couple of big swallows). If you can't remember, set the countdown timer on your wristwatch to beep every 15 minutes. That's a signal to eat, too. About every 30 minutes, down 20 grams of carbohydrate, the equivalent of half an energy bar. Several fig bars, half a banana, or a piece of bagel also work well.

4. **Hydrate after the ride**. No matter how much fluid you ingest while on the bike, in summer weather you'll finish a long ride with a deficit. There's a simple way to be sure you rehydrate sufficiently: Weigh yourself before and after each ride, then compare the figures. If you've lost weight, it is, unfortunately, water you've sweated out, not fat you've burned. Drink 20 ounces of fluid for each pound of bodyweight you're down. Keep drinking until your weight is back to normal.

5. **Use the glycogen window**. One last step—and it might be the most important. Studies show that your muscles replace their fuel (glycogen) much faster and more efficiently if you eat carbohydrate immediately after a ride. The longer you wait, the less eager your muscles cells become to refill with glycogen. The goal is to eat about 60 grams of carbohydrate if you're an average-size woman, or 80-100 grams if you're an average male, as soon as possible after you get off the bike. Your muscles will re-fuel best if you down this chow within 15 minutes. The refueling process becomes progressively less efficient during the 2 hours post-ride. Notice that the amount of carbohydrate is the same that's recommended before a ride. Some recent research indicates that if you mix 4 parts carbohydrate with one part protein, your glycogen stores will top off more quickly and more fully. In fact, several post-ride recovery drinks are based on these findings. It should be noted, however, that the results of at least one of these studies has been challenged. Doubters argue that the protein/carbo mix produced greater glycogen levels only because the subjects getting that mix received more total calories than the subjects who got only carbohydrate (no protein) after exercise. So, the jury is still out. But in a practical sense, it's hard to eat only carbohydrate. Most riders prefer post-ride meals like a bowl of cereal or a turkey sandwich. As long as there's ample carbohydrate in the food, it's probably best to heed your body's cravings.

If you follow these 5 strategies, you'll feel great while riding and then recover faster. Just think of cycling as a license to eat heartily! Refuel properly and you'll be able to ride faster and stronger for longer, thus getting a better workout and building superior fitness.

FOODS WITH ABOUT 50 GRAMS OF CARBO PER SERVING

- Bagel
- Two slices of bread and 8 oz. low-fat milk
- English muffin, 1 tbs. jam, 8 oz. low-fat milk
- Popcorn (4 cups) and 8 oz. fruit juice
- Cold cereal (1 cup), 8 oz. low-fat milk, piece of fruit
- Pasta (1 cup) and marinara sauce (1 cup)
- Pancakes (3 large) and syrup (2 tbs.)
- Pretzels (1 oz.) and 8 oz. fruit juice
- Rice (0.5 cup) and beans (0.5 cup) and corn tortilla
- Thick pizza (1 slice) and 12 oz. soda
- Rice (1 cup) and broccoli (1 cup)

RESPONSIBLE WEIGHT LOSS

Light body weight and climbing success are related. Studies show that losing 10 pounds can improve your time on a 5-mile climb by about 2 minutes. The most famous example is Lance Armstrong's conversion from a 175-pound classics specialist to a 158-pound Tour de France winner and dominating climber. But Lance lost weight due to the chemotherapy he underwent for testicular cancer—not the weight loss strategy of choice. There's a better way, and you can do it. Just follow the 3 steps below and you'll fly up those hills. Well, at least you'll climb faster than you do now. Only one drawback: You'll have to buy smaller cycling shorts.

Before you begin, make sure you really need to lose weight. Unless you are certain that you're heavier than you should be, get a body fat analysis from a physician or sports medicine clinic. Using one of several methods—skinfold calipers, underwater weighing, electrical impedance—they'll pinpoint the percent of your bodyweight that's fat.

Elite male riders carry 4-10 percent fat; elite women about 5 percentage points more. In contrast, sedentary American males are around 20 percent fat and American women are 25 percent or higher. If your body fat percentage is already at low levels, don't undertake a weight loss program. You may be heavier than other riders, but if it's muscle it's unhealthy to cut weight.

Successful weight loss is a long-term project. Crash diets have one thing in common: They don't work. Sure, you can lose weight quickly, but keeping it off is another matter. Weight loss of about a pound a week is the most likely to permanently reshape your body.

Although human metabolisms are quite variable, losing weight is essentially as simple as burning more calories than you consume. A pound of body fat is equivalent to 3,500 calories. If you decrease dietary calories and increase caloric immolation through exercise, and the deficit equals 3,500 calories a week, you'll lose one pound every 7 days. At this rate, you can safely drop 20 pounds in just under 5 months.

STEP 1: Cut calories painlessly. You only need to cut about 500 calories a day. That's about the number of calories in 2 energy bars, 3 cups of whole milk or 4 teaspoons of butter. Think about each food choice so you eliminate unnecessary calories, especially those from excessive fat. Here are some ways. You'll quickly find others.

- Eliminate fatty processed snacks and substitute fruit
- Use skim or one-percent milk rather than whole milk
- Substitute low-fat yogurt for butter, margarine and salad dressing
- Order meats and fish grilled rather than fried
- Eat 1 cookie instead of 2 (or 10)
- Eat half a bagel with jam rather than a high-fat muffin
- Cut down on alcohol. Beer, wine and mixed drinks can add significantly to your daily caloric total. Quench your thirst with water.

STEP 2: Increase your metabolic rate. Cycling burns calories while you're pedaling, and it also elevates your metabolic rate for a period after a ride. Studies show that intense exercise increases and prolongs this effect. So, include 2 or 3 rides each week that drive your heart rate past 85 percent of maximum. You can get the same effect in the off-season on the indoor trainer or with crosstraining activities such as running, snowshoeing or cross-country skiing.

TIP! Commuting is great way to keep your metabolism smoldering. Two-a-day rides seem to burn more calories in 24 hours than a single ride of equal duration.

Longtime roadie Ed Pavelka has noticed this effect. When he moved to North Carolina to take a new job, he lost lots of riding time in the transition. Weekend-only rides through the winter left him 23 pounds overweight as the new season approached. He started commuting to work, riding between 15 and 42 miles each way. Without any dietary changes, the fat weight came off in 2 months.

Ed discovered another trick while this was going on. To feel fuller and not actually eat more because of the commuting, he started drinking more water at the office. Often he'd put down 4 liters a day. This also helped him combat the risk of dehydration from 2 rides a day in the Carolina humidity.

Weight training is important, too. Only muscle mass burns calories. Fat just sits there inertly, going along for the ride. Gain muscle volume and you'll have more calorie-consuming potential.

STEP 3: Increase your miles. It's hard to boost mileage because it requires a time investment. It's even harder in winter. It gets dark early and in most parts of the country it's cold. But if you can increase your total weekly cycling (or crosstraining activity) by an hour or 2, you'll consume an additional 500 to 1,500 calories, depending on intensity.

Above all, be consistent. Schedule workouts like any other obligation. You can find the time if you are willing to treat exercise as a necessary part of your day.

CHAPTER 17

Wisdom of the Cycling Coaches

I've been in the cycling game for 3 decades. The bad news: I'm racing in the Paleolithic age group. But my, ahem, maturity means that I've had the chance to meet and work with many of the top coaches in the sport. What I've found is that they all have elaborate training philosophies, making it difficult—and usually misleading—to condense their ideas. But whenever I've been around these maestros of cycling technique and training, I've come away with 1 or 2 gems that I can use right away. I'll share 5 with you to close this section of the book.

CYRILLE GUIMARD: *Rest Before an Event*

Credentials: Until the mid 1980s, European pro cyclists trained by accumulating lots of slow miles in the winter. Then they raced into shape in spring events. France's Guimard revolutionized training methods by insisting on a carefully periodized plan. His riders worked on specific abilities at set times of the year. His approach helped Greg LeMond win 3 Tours de France and 2 world championships. I learned about Guimard's methods from LeMond.

Quote: "When you have a big event on Sunday, take Friday off the bike, not Saturday. Many riders like to rest the day before the event, but it works better if you schedule down time two days before. The day before, ride about an hour at a good endurance heart rate and throw in four or five sprints to get your body warmed up."

What you can do: It's tempting to train right up to your target event, but that usually means you'll be tired when you wheel up to the start line. Hard training often masks fatigue until it's too late. Resting 2 days before an event reveals your fatigue in time to rest the day before, too, in case you need additional recovery.

CHRIS CARMICHAEL: *The Primary Training Objective*

Credentials: A former pro rider and U.S. Olympic Cycling Team coach for the 1992 and '96 Games. He coaches Lance Armstrong and other top pros, as well as recreational riders, through his Carmichael Training Systems (CTS) coaching service.

Quote: "The most important goal in training is to raise a rider's power at lactate threshold. This is the maximum intensity possible for 30-60 minutes. The issue isn't the ability to produce power. Anyone can generate 450 watts, at least for a few seconds. The trick is to produce significant power while still staying below your lactate threshold."

What you can do: Carmichael suggests building power starting early in the season by improving strength with weights. Next, convert that strength to cycling-specific power on the bike in 3 ways:

1. Hard efforts on hills in a big gear using low pedal cadence of around 50 rpm

2. Intervals, done by starting in a big gear at walking speed and accelerating as hard as possible for 15 seconds while remaining seated

3. Tempo rides of 10-30 minutes at an intensity slightly below your time-trial pace.

EDDIE BORYSEWICZ: *Marry the Bike*

Credentials: Eddie B, a rider and coach in cold-war Poland, revolutionized American cycling in the late 1970s when he came to the U.S. with Eastern-bloc training methods. He led a pack of talented Americans—including Connie Carpenter, Davis Phinney, Alexi Grewal, Ron Kiefel, Mark Gorski and Steve Hegg—to 9 medals in the '84 Olympics and then to success in major European races.

Quote: "From early March it is the summer program. Now you must ride each and every day, seven days a week. Now you deal with the bike full time. No car rides around town. All your local transportation must be by bike. You live with the bike, you are married to the bike. I am sorry for you if you think this is not necessary. Believe me, this is what it takes to be a top rider."

What you can do: You probably don't want to marry the bike, but you can intensify the relationship. A good way to squeeze more cycling into your busy life is by commuting to work. Commuting guarantees a daily dose of riding. In the summer when there's more daylight, take a longer route home and train just as you normally would.

MAX TESTA, M.D.: *Overtraining*

Credentials: Physician for 7-Eleven, the first American team to succeed in Europe. Now Testa works with Eric Heiden's sports medicine clinic in California.

Quote: "I used to prescribe lots of intense workouts for my riders, but maybe they were a little overtrained. They sometimes lost power when they did hard workouts instead of becoming more fit. Sometimes they had bad psychology for races. So now, I watch carefully for signs of overtraining like decreased power, irritability and dumb crashes that indicate a poor attention span. When these symptoms appear, I prescribe rest."

What you can do: It's easy to get caught up in the thrill of improvement and keep pushing even when you're tired. One hard workout or race leads to another, and pretty soon you're too tired to play ball with your kid, much less improve your cycling performance. So, schedule rest days once or twice each week. Especially as we get older, we need more rest and recovery between hard workouts.

TOM EHRHARD: *Beat the Bonk*

Credentials: U.S. Military Cycling coach, one of the most innovative thinkers in the sport. Ehrhard was one of the first cycling coaches to employ periodization in his training plans.

Quote: "If you bonk during a training ride or race, that's a big medical problem. Most riders bonk and they think they can just eat and drink that evening and they'll be fine the next day. That's wrong. It takes two weeks of rest and easy riding to recover from a major bonk. It's a medical emergency."

What you can do: Don't bonk! Always carry enough food and fluids to last the length of your ride. If you're riding in areas without convenience stores or other places to fuel up, carry extra food and drink in case you get lost or are delayed. It's much easier to avoid the bonk than to recover from it.

PART 2

OFF-SEASON TRAINING

Introduction

" The off-season is the most important training period of the year. It's when you make your biggest gains. Lance wins the Tour de France in November, December and January."
Chris Carmichael, Armstrong's coach

"Winter training is the time when a rider can make a difference in his preparation for next season. It's the only time of year when a pro can work on fitness for three consecutive months without the stress of racing and traveling."
Max Testa, M.D., former pro team physician

Cycling is traditionally a summer sport. Feeling the breeze on your bare legs and the sun's warmth on your back is as much a part of riding a bike as lubing your chain. There's something deeply wrong, many casual cyclists would argue, about riding in the cold with snowflakes sticking to your sunglasses.

Traditionalists may contend that you need a break from training. Do something besides ride in winter, they counsel. Run, ski, play basketball. Wean yourself from the bike, and from serious exercise, to build enthusiasm that will carry you through the 3 seasons of cycling. In this view, only serious racers should train all year round—and only because they are getting paid to.

It's certainly true that year-round training has been a key reason for the higher performance of pro riders. As recently as 15 years ago, European pros got off the bike in September and started training again in January, often having gained 10 or 15 pounds. They put in a desultory 2,000 miles and used early-season races to "ride into shape." Eager neo-pros who went off the front were sternly chastised for their irrational exuberance. They soon learned to slow down and play the game.

That relaxed approach to winter has changed dramatically. German pro Eric Zabel, many times a stage winner in the Tour de France, is famous for riding a minimum of 6,000 miles between seasons and coming out strong in spring classics. Time off the bike has shrunk from 3 months to 3 weeks—and those precious 3 weeks aren't consecutive but are spread through November and December.

No one has focused on the off-season like 3-time (and counting) Tour de France champion Lance Armstrong. But what about us recreational riders and amateur racers? Why should we train—on the bike and maybe in the weight room, too—in winter? We're not pros. No one is paying us to ride. Our goals are much more modest than winning the Tour. Most of us want to complete a century ride, hang with the lead group in the local Sunday morning hammerfest, maybe get on the podium in age-graded racing.

Of course, you can take the winter off and still have fun riding next summer. You can even achieve modest cycling goals. But it's a lot more effective—and better for your health—if you stay in shape and even increase your fitness in the winter. And believe it or not, off-season training can be just as much fun as riding during the traditional cycling months.

Here are my 10 good reasons to train through the calendar:

1. Expand your cycling season. I bet you like to ride—you wouldn't have purchased this book if cycling didn't rate high on your list of preferred activities. So why stop doing one of your favorite things for several months just because it gets cold, wet or dark early? With the right techniques, clothing, lighting and other equipment, cycling can be a year-round activity at latitudes only polar bears could love.

2. Preserve last season's fitness gains. If you finished the season flying—or at least feeling good—it's depressing to think about all that hard-won fitness disappearing during the winter. The "use it or lose it" syndrome is at work here. Exercise physiologists call it "detraining," and some studies show that it occurs with frightening rapidity. Several aspects of fitness—power output in short efforts, for instance—can tail off in just a few weeks of not training.

> **RESEARCH!** In a study of 16 cyclists done at Florida State University, their VO_2 max remained high despite much less time devoted to exercise during the winter. Only anaerobic power (short sprints and explosive efforts up steep hills) declined significantly.
>
> But these riders weren't completely sedentary all winter. They did other aerobic sports such as running, and some were in the weight room. Also, thanks to Florida's climate, many of them rode, albeit at a lower intensity and volume than during the season.
>
> The bottom line: It doesn't take much activity in the off-season to keep fitness from vanishing. But maintaining fitness—or increasing it—requires a bit more investment in time and effort.

3. Improve your riding skills. Winter is a great time to practice the bike-handling techniques necessary to feel comfortable in testy conditions. Riding an old bike on snow or through the mud of a cyclocross course teaches you how to relax when the rear wheel skids. Get a few friends together for snow criteriums in a frosty field, and I guarantee that come spring, the wettest, slipperiest roads will seem tame in comparison.

4. Avoid SADness. Does winter make you depressed, sap your energy and give you an advanced case of cabin fever? Seasonal affective disorder (SAD) is a common affliction of people in northern latitudes. It's related to lack of natural light, so getting outside to exercise is one of the best ways to beat it. What a deal—stay fit and lift your mood all at once!

5. Avoid weight gain. In the above-cited study, the cyclists averaged 11.6 percent body fat at the end of winter—about 2 percentage points higher than would normally be expected in riders of their age and category. That's not extreme. Moderate weight gain (3 to 5 pounds) can actually be good because it provides reserve energy for demanding spring training. Greater amounts of winter lard are best avoided, however. The time it takes to ride it off with long and relatively slow early-season miles could be better spent honing speed and power. Carmichael states this limit: "It isn't advisable to gain more than 10 pounds over the winter."

EXAMPLE! We need look no further than Jan Ullrich to see the danger of too much winter weight gain. The German is making a career out of finishing second in the Tour de France, even though he's called the most talented rider in the peloton.

Ullrich traditionally packs on 20 pounds during the same period that Lance Armstrong is doing his effective winter program. In the early season, Ullrich shows up bloated and struggling to ride off his excess weight so he can be competitive again, especially on climbs.

By Tour time in July, Ullrich is back to racing weight, but Lance has been there for months. That's one difference between winning and losing.

6. Boost your confidence. Belgium has the most depressing winter weather imaginable—an endless round of cold rain, sleet and wet snow. Yet Belgian riders train through the worst that northern Europe has to offer. In the spring classics (usually in the same abominable conditions), they regularly beat up on riders who spent the winter putting in their miles in balmy Mediterranean climes. Indeed, there's a name for these masochists, *flahutes*, meaning hard riders who revel in wretched weather. It also makes them great bike handlers in slick conditions, a skill that comes in handy on the slimy cobbles of springtime race courses.

EXAMPLE! Andy Hampsten, who often trained in sleet and snow in Colorado, won the 1988 Giro d'Italia on the climb over the Gavia Pass in a snowstorm. It was so slippery and cold that most of the field abandoned or rode merely to survive the stage. But because Andy was toughened by riding Colorado's passes in January or sliding through snowy trails on his mountain bike, he knew exactly how to handle the conditions.

It works for us non-pros, too. My RBR colleague, Ed Pavelka, has ridden through 20 winters in Vermont and Pennsylvania. He still remembers one 8-hour ride on a dark-gray February day when the temperature hovered at 35 degrees and a slushy snow fell throughout. Ed will tell you, "I felt like a Belgian that day." He got some fitness from that ride, but more important he got confidence. Even now, a dozen years later, he'll think about that experience when the going gets tough. Because he did that ride, he feels he can do any ride.

7. Enjoy riding more next spring. If you get out of shape over the winter, spring is going to be tough. You'll struggle to lose weight and struggle again to keep up with your friends. It can be dispiriting. But if you maintain and even improve your fitness, you'll be the one handing out the hurt.

8. Beat aging! Never let yourself get out of shape and you'll forestall most of aging's deterioration. Studies show that each year it becomes harder to regain your previous level of fitness after a period of inactivity. But if you maintain your fitness, age-related deterioration can be minimized to nearly undetectable levels. While sedentary people fall victim to a decline in VO_2 max (their ability to consume oxygen for energy) on the order of one percent each year after about age 35, year-round training with an occasional dose of appropriate intensity can limit this loss to less than half a percent per year.

9. Add variety. What if you live in a climate where winter cycling is ideal? Maybe you're in Arizona, Florida or another place so hot in summer that the off-season is actually the most comfortable time to ride. The risk here is falling victim to overtraining and stalled enthusiasm. Being able to ride all year is a double-edged sword. It helps you maintain fitness, but it can get boring and predictable, too. In this book, we'll see how to vary training with the seasons. This will help you remedy your weaknesses so you'll be fast and strong when it counts.

10. Realize your hope. Even racers who've had an abysmal year will be full of hope again by Thanksgiving. The off-season's 3 or 4 months of uninterrupted training can revive dreams and restore confidence. All cyclists, whether they compete or not, get an annual midwinter feeling that anything is possible next summer.

Unfortunately, all too often these dreams are followed by another season without that long-sought century PR, 10-mile time trial record, or sprint victory against weekend training buddies. Why? Because we tend to do the same ineffective training each winter. My brother Mike calls it "the futility cycle." To misquote Alexander Pope:

Hope springs eternal in the human breast.
A cyclist never is, but always to be, fast.

But from now on, winters will be different. With the information I'm about to give you, you'll learn how to train right during cycling's off-season—and come out flying in the spring. When daylight saving time is gone, the temperature is plummeting and snow is in the forecast, it's the perfect time to train—correctly—for cycling. Let's do it!

HOW TO USE THIS SECTION

Off-season training is, in some very important ways, much more complicated than training during warmer months. You have to deal with cold weather, for one thing. More sports are involved (because you'll be crosstraining), and this means learning new skills. Weight training introduces a whole new discipline to master. And as Chris Carmichael noted, the very importance of off-season training adds to the complexity. You need to do it right because it serves as the base for your whole season.

So, it's not enough merely to skim through this section and get started. You need a sequential plan of attack. The disparate elements must merge into a program that builds on your unique strengths and meets your personal goals. With this in mind, the material is organized so that you can read about topics in the order you'll want to employ the information.

Before you begin off-season training, read about rest, goal setting and self-testing. Next come the tools for training—dressing for cold weather, resistance training, crosstraining, reaching ideal weight and indoor cycling.

I include a separate chapter on how to build power by combining weights, high-cadence pedaling and intervals. And because bike-handling skills are such an important part of becoming a better rider, I devote a chapter to drills and activities to help you keep the rubber side down.

What about a training schedule? What should you do each day? In chapter 28, I tell how to set up 18-week off-season training programs for 3 different cycling interests:

- **Fitness**
- **Recreation**
- **Competition**

Because everyone has different goals and time available for training, the guidelines in chapter 28 are general by necessity. They will help you set up your personal program divided into 6-week blocks. I include a sample week's schedule for each block. You'll be ready to write an ideal schedule for yourself after reading chapters 18 through 27.

You don't have to start your off-season program on a particular date. Normally, you'll get underway sometime between early November and late December, depending on when the weather curtails outside cycling in your region. But the program I present makes sense any time of year if your goal is superior cycling fitness or you have just started riding and want to get in shape. It's an effective fitness program no matter when it's used.

CHAPTER 18

Rest, Recovery, Remediation

The most important way to prepare for a successful cycling season is, paradoxically, to rest thoroughly and well to start the off-season. All good winter programs begin with a complete recovery from the rigors of the summer.

According to former Motorola team physician Max Testa, M.D., "Pros start the winter with a two- to three-week vacation where they keep active, play a sport like tennis, and go mountain biking three or four times a week." Testa's advice is just as good for recreational racers as well as riders who do centuries or just hammer hard while having fun.

If you didn't have a "last season" because you're just beginning to shed a sedentary lifestyle and starting to ride, you can still jump into the training outlined below. But if you rode substantial miles last summer and want next season to be your best ever, include the 3 R's—*rest, recovery, remediation*—in your November and December training plan.

REST

I've been using the word *rest* in its normal sense—relaxation that ranges from mild activity to slouching on the couch. But rest is different from *recovery*. As a result, I'll be more precise and define rest as no training and no physical exercise at all, except for the activities of daily life.

Rest is the most neglected part of training. We have been schooled to equate improvement with hard work. In our success-oriented society, we automatically assume that the harder we work, the more success we'll achieve—and the faster it will come our way. That's not what happens. Sure, it's important to keep your nose to the grindstone. There's no substitute for hours in the saddle, a precise dose of intense riding and enough technique practice to keep you and your bike upright. But hard work by itself is useless. On a week-by-week basis during the season, you improve only when your body has enough down time between one session of hard riding and the next. We improve while we're resting, not while we're out hammering ourselves into exhaustion.

For the same reason, at the end of the cycling season you should give your body a deep rest. This will heal any lingering physical problems (like saddle sores) and refresh you mentally so you're eager to get back on the bike.

TIP! How many weeks of rest do you need? It depends on how hard your previous season was and how fatigued you feel as winter approaches.

Chris Carmichael recommends that "recreational riders take two breaks of two weeks each. One break should come right at the end of the riding season, and the other over the Christmas holidays. Don't take all four weeks at once—you'll lose too much fitness."

Too many riders fall prey to the "flying in February, fried in July" syndrome. They are so eager to reach great fitness that they train hard all winter. They're out in the cold and gloom of January doing intervals. Or worse, they spend 3 months in their basement, suffering on an indoor trainer while watching old cycling videos and counting how many drops of sweat per minute cascade down their nose and onto the top tube. No wonder they're mentally and physically fatigued just when the real cycling season begins.

But don't misunderstand—there's nothing wrong with indoor training. As we'll see in chapter 26, 48 and 49, carefully planned sessions on rollers or a resistance trainer can help you maintain and even improve your fitness. The trick, in your mid-winter enthusiasm, is to avoid overdoing it. Listen to famed exercise scientist Tudor Bompa, Ph.D.: "The key isn't hard work, it's intelligent work."

RECOVERY

Okay, you're rested. But when you start off-season training, you must make time for recovery after exercise whether on the bike, crosstraining or in the weight room. By recovery I mean "active recovery"—easy exercise that aids recuperation. The best recovery activities are aerobic. This may be walking or riding easily to do errands around town. Unlike complete rest, mild exercise stimulates blood flow to tired muscles and improves how quickly they're ready for the next hard workout.

> **TIP!** Tudor Bompa suggests this after a hard training session: "Take 30 minutes for regeneration. Drink a carbo replacement beverage, lie down with your legs elevated, relax mentally and do five minutes of self-massage."

REMEDIATION

Remediation means fixing things. Devote some off-season time to physical maintenance.

Now that you aren't training as much and have extra hours, see your doctor for an annual exam, get your eyes checked and visit your dentist. You don't want to train for months only to miss an important event because a vague ache in your mouth has become a raging toothache. In Max Testa's view, "Winter is the time to resolve physical problems inherited from the previous season, and to prevent damage to overall health."

Get all cycling-related problems fixed, too. Here's a list of common ailments that cyclists often brush off during the season:

Saddle sores. Cyclists usually continue to ride after they sprout small midsummer saddle sores. They tough it out—and a tiny pimple becomes a full-fledged boil. These lesions often calm down when riding tapers in the fall, but they may lie dormant and erupt again as off-season training begins.

Use the late-autumn break to eliminate these troublesome infections. Your doctor may prescribe antibiotics for moderate cases. Sometimes the boil has to be lanced, a procedure that should be avoided because it hurts like heck and it means you can't ride for 2 or 3 weeks.

Use any downtime to figure out what caused the problem. Is your riding position correct? Has your saddle broken down, putting pressure on one area and causing irritation and infections? Do you have a leg-length inequality? Are your shorts old with a thin, worn liner that's abrading your crotch?

> **RESOURCE!** For detailed expert advice about saddle-related problems, bike fit, riding position, tendinitis and many other cycling injuries, see *Andy Pruitt's Medical Guide for Cyclists*. This RBR Publishing Company paperback is available in the online bookstore at www.RoadBikeRider.com. Pruitt was chief medical officers of the 1996 U.S. Olympic Cycling Team and headed the U.S. Cycling Federation's sports medicine program for many years.

Tendinitis. Knees are where tendon inflammation most commonly strikes cyclists. This irritating pain packs a double whammy: Once you're afflicted, it's hard to ride and it's difficult to do lower-body weight training, too.

The upper body is also at risk. Some riders suffer from tendinitis of the elbow (an affliction similar to "tennis elbow") from leaning on the handlebar for hours at a time. This problem is easily ignored during summer, but it makes weight lifting difficult in winter. As a result, sufferers don't do the strength training that might alleviate the problem—and the tendinitis gets worse as they start building mileage in the spring.

If you're struggling with tendinitis anywhere in your body, see a physical therapist, who will have various treatments to resolve the problem. Remember that it may take quite a while to relieve the pain and limited motion. The earlier you address tendinitis, the faster you'll be back training at full strength.

Suspicious skin spots. Cyclists spend months with substantial amounts of skin exposed to direct summer sunlight. No matter how much sunscreen you slather on, dangerous UV rays scald you every time you ride. When you have your exam, ask the doc to check your skin, especially areas exposed while riding—the back of your neck, ears, arms and legs. Don't ignore any unusual bumps, spots, moles or scaly places you notice. They could be cancerous.

BIKE AND EQUIPMENT MAINTENANCE

Great! Your body is all checked out for next season. Feels good to know that, doesn't it? Now let's turn attention to your bike. You can inspect and service your own equipment or pay a good bike shop mechanic to do it for you.

Inspect everything—frame, handlebar, stem, seatpost, derailleurs, brakes, cables, tires, rims—everything. Replace any part that's suspect. Be especially vigilant with weight-bearing equipment: crankset, pedals, stem, handlebar, saddle, seatpost, wheels.

There are 2 times when you don't want an equipment failure—in the season and in the off-season. Having an important summer event ended by a malfunction is one thing. Being stranded far from home on a frigid winter day is potentially dangerous as well as frustrating.

EXAMPLE! One recent winter I noticed a creak coming from my bike near the seat. I checked the saddle rails and even greased them where they contacted the seatpost clamp. But the vague squeak kept chirping in the background like a cricket in the basement. Soon I forgot about it.

Then one Sunday morning I was chatting casually in the paceline when my saddle suddenly tilted back. The nose pointed at the sky and nearly slid me onto the rear wheel. The top of the seatpost had sheared off.

Moral: Never ignore unusual sounds from your bike. Check the location carefully in strong light, looking for telltale cracks that might indicate material failure.

Service or replace the bearings—headset, bottom bracket and hubs. Purchase items that will wear out and need replacement—chains, cables, brake pads, tires, tubes, handlebar tape, cassette, maybe chainrings. Get your clothing in order. Buy your shorts, jerseys, shoes, socks, gloves and other summer items during off-season sales. Also, get the winter riding garb you'll need, depending on your climate. (See chapter 21.) Stockpile miscellaneous items when you see a good price. These are things like chain lube, chamois lube, sunscreen, lip balm, sunglasses, bottles and so on.

SHOULD YOU HIRE A COACH?

This is one of the most important decisions heading into the off-season if you're serious about maximum improvement. This book is dedicated to helping you make great strides without any extra guidance. However, Chris Carmichael argues, "Getting a coach is critical, and the program with your coach should start in the off-season."

Sure, Chris is in the coaching business as president of Carmichael Training Systems. You'd expect him to offer this advice. But although self-coaching has been the norm in cycling even among pros, we're realizing that having a coach is better. In other sports, coaches are accepted without question. Now more cyclists are beginning to see the light.

Why hire a coach when you can set up your own training program?

- If you're a beginning rider, a coach can teach you the correct way to train from day one.

- If you're an experienced rider whose progress has stalled, you can benefit from a coach's objective opinion. A coach can set up a new program to help you rise to the next level.

- Maybe you've taken on a big cycling challenge—a cross-state tour, the quest for a century PR or a season of racing—and you want to give yourself the best possible chance of succeeding. A coach who has worked with other riders having similar goals can customize a program based on your unique abilities.

EXAMPLE! Even experienced riders may find that a coach helps them improve. I learned this in 1996 when training for Team Race Across America.

I had raced for 20 years and written 4 books on training. Certainly I could set up the team's program. But I talked cycling coach Tom Ehrhard into developing a periodized training plan, and his insights helped us approach preparation in a new light. We went on to set a senior (50+) world record for the event, riding 2,905 miles from Los Angeles to Savannah in 5 days, 11 hours, 21 minutes.

Too often, experienced riders do the same training year after year. They need a fresh approach, an objective outsider to come in and shake things up. Tom Ehrhard filled that role for us.

After all, if you keep doing what you're doing, you'll keep getting what you're getting!

HOW TO FIND A COACH

The governing body of American bike racing, USA Cycling, certifies coaches. Most work with non-racers and competitors alike. Visit the website at www.usacycling.org. In addition, your community may have highly qualified and experienced cycling coaches who have never taken the time to get certified but whose knowledge is outstanding. Check at bike clubs and shops for recommendations.

A number of excellent coaches offer their services over the Internet and by phone. Coaches with programs I can vouch for include:

- **Arnie Baker, M.D.**, *www.arniebakercycling.com*

- **Chris Carmichael**, *www.trainright.com*

- **Joe Friel**, *www.ultrafit.com*

- **John Howard**, *www.johnhowardschool.com*

- **John Hughes**, *JHnFriends@aol.com*

CHAPTER 19

Dreams, Goals, Limiters

Many hard-driving, successful people have little patience with information on goal setting. Too visionary, they complain, and too vague. You'll hear them say, "Let's get started, and I'll figure out exactly where I'm going later." But I believe it's important to have a clear goal in mind before you begin. Starting a company, building a house or figuring how to become faster and more skilled on a bike—the principles are the same.

YOUR VISION STATEMENT

Start with a vision statement. It doesn't have to be visionary (often a derogatory term meaning vague and mush-minded). Rather, good vision statements are the basis for your goals, helping you identify your destination. In the process, they save many false steps.

Listen to Chris Carmichael: "Forget the touchy-feely stuff. You want a long-term vision to direct your actions and emotions. If you were to drop dead tomorrow, what would you want people to say about you? That's your vision statement." When Carmichael coached the U.S. National Team, they had this vision statement: "We're 100 percent prepared, physically and mentally, to race to the full potential of the entire team." Here are some examples to guide you:

- **Fitness rider**: "I am making a mid-life transition from being sedentary and unhealthy to becoming fit and strong, and my love of cycling is helping me accomplish this."

- **Strong recreational rider**: "I train hard but I don't neglect the really important things—spending time with my family and having fun on my bike."

- **Masters racer**: "I'm an aggressive-but-sporting rider, not the most talented cyclist among my age-peers but I work hard and ride smart so I can be competitive."

Write your own vision statement. Don't agonize over it. Think about what's important to you, on the bike and in the other facets of your life. Then put those priorities into one strong sentence.

> **TIP!** If you've thought long and hard and still can't find the right words, go for a ride. Often our best thinking is done subconsciously while we're doing something else—and there's no better "something else" than the simple act of pedaling along with your mind wandering. Suddenly, solutions to vexing problems appear, seemingly without conscious effort. Want to be sure you remember your mid-ride epiphanies? Carry a small tape recorder in your jersey pocket and capture them before they vanish.

DREAM ON

From your vision statement spring specific goals. They're unique to you and your situation. But an intermediate step is often useful, so many riders start by listing their dreams.

That's right, the kind of dreams that we had when we were young, beginning life and discovering something that we really liked to do. Remember those? Big dreams, dreams that were so unachievable when looked at rationally that adults would shake their heads and laugh if they knew what we were thinking.

When we're young, we don't share our dreams with other people very often. They're too personal. They're often unrealistic, too, but in that resides their charm and their power to help us achieve great things. Maybe not the things we dreamed in our innocence, but more realistic goals that suit our talents and our personalities.

Perhaps you aren't young any more, at least not that young. I'm not. But we can still have dreams, regardless of our age. Having something to shoot for keeps life worth living. So take some time and daydream about cycling. When you do, what do you see? A warp-speed sprint? Climbing ability that puts the best Tour de France anti-gravity men to shame? Time trial power like a Harley? Go ahead—indulge your fantasies.

FOUR KEYS TO SETTING GOALS

Okay, now come back to Earth. Dreams are a necessary precursor to goals. But unlike dreams, goals must be realistic. They should be set high but not out of reach. Here are 4 simple guidelines you can use to set up your own seasonal objectives.

1. **Goals should be achievable**. Base goals on your current performances. It's obvious that a top-10 finish in the Skunk Hollow Criterium last summer doesn't mean you should aim for the world road championship next season. (In your dreams!) Goals should be based on dreams, but they're not the same thing. For instance, if you rode the local 10-mile time trial in 26 minutes, don't set your goal for next July at 22 minutes. Unless you're genetically gifted and weren't really riding your best, you won't improve by 4 minutes. That's unrealistic. It'll be depressing when you fail despite hard training. Instead, set your goal at a reasonable level, say 24:30. With proper planning, a modicum of smart training and a good day at the event, you'll reach this goal and may even surpass it. Then, after glowing in the accomplishment, you'll be fired up to set a more aggressive mark.

2. **Goals don't need to be quantifiable**. Goals aren't just for racers and they don't have to be timed or measured. Here's a perfectly reasonable goal: "This year I finished the cross-state tour exhausted and demoralized. Next summer I want to do the same ride and finish strong." Beware, however, of goals that are so vague as to be meaningless. "I want to climb better," is one example. Better than what? In this case, numbers help. Aim to improve your time up the local killer hill.

3. **Goals should be independent**. Don't set goals that compare your performance to someone else's. For example, "I want to stay with Steve in the Thrilly Hilly Century Ride." What if Steve rides badly for physical or mechanical reasons? Your achievement is lessened. What if he doesn't even show up? All the work toward your goal becomes fruitless. Goals should always be aimed at improving what *you* can do, independently of others' achievements or failures. For similar reasons, avoid goals that depend on an exact placing at an event, such as, "I want to win the district time trial championship." Winning or placing depends on your performance, of course, but it also depends on who else rides. No matter how strong you are, there's always someone, somewhere, who can beat you on a given day. If that person is home ill, or racing in a different event, or mowing the lawn, you win. If he shows up,

you lose. In the final analysis, every winner is lucky. When his performance gets him on the top step of the podium, it's because no stronger rider competed. As novelist Joseph Conrad said, "Your strength is just an accident arising from the weakness of others."

4. **Goals should not be too easy**. Finally, don't undersell yourself. It's as bad to set goals too low as to set them too high. Cycling is a sport that rewards consistent, moderate and well-planned effort over a relatively long period. If your goals are realistic, you can get from here to there even if the gap at present seems unbridgeable. For example, let's take this worst-case scenario: Suppose you're overweight, just quit smoking, a clumsy bike handler, and have no discernible athletic talent. You're slow on the flats and get off to walk even on mild climbs. You have the power of a 3-toed sloth. But hey—you have the whole off-season to get better. That's 5 months to turn things around. Economies have rebounded, dynasties have been overturned and scientific theories formulated in less time than that. You can do it!

LIST YOUR STRENGTHS & WEAKNESSES

In order to set specific cycling goals, you must isolate the skills that need improvement. There's no reason to work on climbing if you drop everyone on hills, while on the descent you tend to fly over the handlebar into roadside bushes at the first hint of a turn. In this case, maybe you should focus on cornering. On the other hand, if you can sprint like a cheetah but get dropped on highway overpasses, a goal to improve your climbing is appropriate.

Cycling coach Joe Friel, in his excellent book, *The Cyclist's Training Bible*, calls weaknesses "limiters." I like this term because it's so descriptive and useful. Deficiencies in any cycling skill limit not only your performance but also your enjoyment of the sport. You don't have to be a racer to benefit from better climbing ability or faster cornering. Doing these things well makes cycling more fun.

What are *your* limiters? Where are your weaknesses? It's often hard to be objective about shortcomings. Here are 6 ways to discover yours. When you have them pinpointed, you can develop a plan to turn limiters into strengths during the off-season.

1. **Consult your training diary**. You do keep a diary, don't you? A simple log of each day's physical activity is the best way to see trends in your fitness and spot shortcomings that need work. For instance, if you suffer on climbs during weekend group rides but your training diary confirms that you rarely ride hills during the week, it's pretty obvious that you're not climbing often enough to improve.

2. **Get feedback from fellow riders**. Training buddies are a good source of knowledge about weaknesses. They see when you ride strongly and in what conditions you falter. After all, if you lag behind they have to wait. If your bike-handling skills are suspect, they must be extra alert.

3. **Analyze when you leave your comfort zone**. If you ride with a compatible group (meaning you can stick with the pace nearly all the time), pay attention to what happens that makes you struggle. Do you get dropped on short, hard climbs that other riders sprint over in the big chainring? Then your limiter is explosive power. Do you hang fine on short climbs but lose contact on long ones? You probably have an unfavorable power-to-weight ratio. Do you always win the sprint to the city limit sign in the early going but fade near the end of the ride? Endurance is a probably a weakness. Many sprinter-types, endowed with

plenty of fast-twitch muscle fibers, often lack endurance. This problem may be more than just physical. There seems to be a "sprinter's mentality" that loves speed and short-term bursts but lacks patience for the long, steady rides that build endurance.

4. **Analyze your technical skills.** Physical prowess such as power or endurance is important, but so are skills like bike handling, closely following a wheel and holding your position in the pack.

> **EXAMPLE!** You'll waste energy if you can't ride behind another cyclist smoothly. Here's a typical technique problem: In a paceline you let a gap open through inattention, pedal hard to close it, then brake so you don't ride into the wheel in front of you. Repeated numerous times during a ride, it's amazing how much energy yo-yoing wastes. And this sort of squirrelly riding certainly won't make you welcome in a group.

5. **Get physiological testing.** I discuss testing in the next chapter. It's the easiest way to discover your physical abilities (and liabilities). Testing the physiological parameters that impact endurance can tell you a lot about your genetic ceiling—how good you can become if your training is optimum.

6. **Get a coach.** A coach is crucial to performance improvement. He or she can set up a solid program, keep you from overtraining and monitor your results. But a coach's most important function is to identify your limiters and figure out how to remedy them.

> **EXAMPLE!** A masters rider I know was self-coached for his whole career. He prided himself on objectively monitoring his fitness and his skills, devising training plans that addressed his weaknesses. He often won races. But one season he began to falter. He could stick with the lead group to the finish but couldn't sprint fast enough. So, he worked on his sprint exhaustively—and still didn't improve.
>
> Finally, in desperation, he hired a coach. After some analysis, the coach determined that this rider's sprint was fine when he wasn't tired. His problem was that accumulated fatigue from the early stages of the race was blunting his sprint at the end. He shouldn't have been working on speed—he had plenty of speed—he needed to work on endurance at race intensities. Then he could get to the finish with some freshness still in his legs.

TRAIN, OR RIDE LIKE YOU FEEL?

Once you've determined your limiters, the next step is to develop a plan to remedy them. The rest of this section will tell you how to get better during the off-season, no matter what kind of limiters you've identified. I'll also suggest specific training to help you address your weaknesses.

But maybe you're like some riders who don't like structured training plans. If they're given a schedule that tells them to do intervals on Tuesday, they protest that while those intervals may be the appropriate training routine for that day in theory, in practice the world gets in their way. It's raining, or the boss wants them to stay late, or the windows need caulking, or their child is sick.

These riders solve this problem by riding like they feel. If Tuesday comes and they feel like hammering, they do intervals or hit hills hard. On the other hand, if they aren't recovered from the weekend or suspect that they're coming down with a cold, they may take an easy 45-minute spin instead. When the responsibilities of life intervene and they're forced to miss a Tuesday ride, they shrug it off and tend to the other things.

Because life happens, training plans that are set in stone are doomed to failure. "You must plan to meet a goal," says training guru Tudor Bompa, "but the plan doesn't need to be rigidly applied. The plan must be flexible." This is why my 18-week training schedules for 3 broad categories of riders in chapter 28 are only suggestions. The final decision on what you do each day is up to you. It's this individual fine-tuning of workouts that makes physical improvement such a fascinating game.

CHAPTER 20

Physiological Testing

No training program is truly useful unless you can monitor its results. Why train hard all winter without a means of tracking improvement—or identifying stalled progress? In the weight room, it's easy to see if you're getting stronger. Simply record pounds and repetitions for each exercise. On the bike (outdoors or in) it's more difficult to precisely chart improvement. In this chapter, we'll look at several valuable self-testing procedures you can do.

WHY TEST?

Because the bottom line for any off-season program is improved riding ability, it's absolutely vital to generate quantifiable information. That's the only way to know when to change your program and when to stay the course. As Chris Carmichael says, "Evaluation is important so you can see if you're improving. A good test has to be easy to administer, not invasive, and quick so you don't lose training time."

WHAT KIND OF TESTS?

There are 2 types of on-bike tests. The first starts at low resistance and takes you to maximum effort. The resistance is cranked up at set intervals (usually 3 minutes) until you simply can't continue to turn the pedals at a reasonable cadence. Sometimes only wattage and heart rate are recorded for each 3-minute segment. If you go to a sports medicine facility, you'll also usually get an EKG and figures for maximum oxygen consumption (VO$_2$ max), lactate levels and blood pressure.

> **CAUTION!** Maximal tests are exhausting so should be administered only once or twice a year. Tests that require extreme effort shouldn't be taken without a physician's permission.

The other test requires only a sub-max effort, usually around 90 percent of your heart rate potential. Because a sub-max test isn't so strenuous, it can be done more frequently and even as part of regular training. Usually, coaches suggest that you undergo a diagnostic test every 4 to 6 weeks. It takes at least a month for any training program to generate results, so more frequent testing isn't useful.

Dr. Max Testa suggests this pattern: "In a four-week training cycle, test for improvement in the last part of the fourth week, the week you decrease your volume and intensity of training. The test should be like a race. Get psyched up and mentally involved to do your best." Chris Carmichael, on the other hand, likes his riders to be tested only every 6 weeks. You can use the schedule that works best for your program.

> **TIP!** Test only when you're rested, well hydrated and ready for a strong effort. Treat the test like a race. Get psyched and round up some friends to cheer you on. Dedicate yourself to making an eye-bulging, teeth-gnashing, full-out effort. That's what it takes each time to get the most accurate and useful results.

PERFORMANCE TESTING IN A LAB

Once a season, usually in the middle of summer, it's useful to go to a sports medicine facility for a test that measures your VO₂ max, heart rate at lactate threshold (LT) and wattage at LT. These things are good to know so you can chart your progress from year to year.

> **CAUTION!** It's tempting to compare your results to other riders in your age category. Don't do it! Use performance testing only as a way to chart your own improvement.
>
> VO₂ max (a measure of how much oxygen your muscles can use) is often considered the best indicator of endurance potential. A relatively low number has ended the careers of promising riders. Even though they were performing well on the bike, they thought that their test meant they'd never reach higher levels in the sport. Because VO₂ max is highly heritable and hard to improve significantly, they simply gave up. Now we know that VO₂ max is a relatively poor indicator of actual performance on the bike.
>
> One example: My colleague Ed Pavelka has an unspectacular VO₂ max in the mid 50s, whereas top cyclists are in the 70s and even 80s. Even with this genetic limitation, he's had some impressive performances. In fact, 2 of them came after age 50 when he rode 100 miles solo in 3:59 and a 40K time trial in 55:30. You can't tell Ed that VO₂ max counts for much.

Far more important than VO₂ max are 2 other parameters easily measured with a lab test:

1. The percentage of maximum heart rate that you can sustain at your lactate threshold. LT is the highest heart rate you can ride at before the nasty effects of lactic acid accumulation in your muscles make you slow down. Most top endurance athletes can maintain a heart rate of 90-92 percent of their LT for 30-60 minutes. This ability can be trained and improved significantly.

2. The amount of power (watts) you generate at your LT heart rate. This, too, can be improved with progressive workouts.

LAB TEST PROTOCOL

I've taken a number of tests at facilities around the country. The protocol can differ slightly, but typical is the procedure used at the renowned Boulder Center for Sports Medicine in Boulder, Colorado, directed by Andy Pruitt (www.bch.org/sportsmedicine).

Lab testing takes place on a special stationary bike (ergometer) integrated with a computer. The ergometer should be set up with a racing-style saddle and a drop handlebar so you can duplicate your position on your own bike. This is crucial to getting accurate results, so insist on it. An unfamiliar position means you won't be working at your optimum level. Incorrect saddle height can injure knees even in a short-duration test because you turn the pedals with so much force.

In some facilities you can be tested on your own bike. It's mounted on a trainer with wattage and speed read-outs. But it's simpler to use an ergometer as long as it can be adjusted for your position. Another plus: You won't sweat all over your good bike—and you will be sweating! When testing at the BCSM, riders bring their pedals, shoes and shorts so they feel at home on the ergometer.

When you sign up for a test, the BCSM sends instructions on how to prepare—taper workouts the week before, and don't eat during the 3 hours preceding the test. It's important to have an empty stomach because the test requires all-out effort. It's okay to sweat on the ergometer but not decorate it with your breakfast.

Before starting, the lab technician attaches electrodes to your chest to monitor heart rate and EKG. They're held in place with a stretchy piece of gauze shaped like a sock that you pull over your upper body. It's tight and uncomfortable but you get used to it. The technician also checks your blood pressure periodically throughout the procedure. Testing is stopped if it rises excessively.

The most unpleasant part for most cyclists is the plastic mask you have to breathe through. It's designed to collect and analyze expired air. The mask goes over your nose and mouth. It's uncomfortable and a little claustrophobic for some people, at least at first. Don't worry—soon you'll be working so hard you won't even think about it.

The test starts with an easy warm-up. Then pedaling resistance is increased 20 watts every 3 minutes. Heart rate is monitored continuously. At the end of each 3 minutes, the technician draws blood from a fingertip. It's relatively painless compared to the effort you must make. Each blood sample is analyzed to see how much lactate it contains. When the amount rises abruptly, you've reached your lactate threshold. Your heart rate and wattage output are recorded right then.

After you reach LT, the technician decreases the resistance and lets you pedal easily until you recover. So far, so good. But now comes the fun part.

To measure VO_2 max, the resistance is repeatedly and rapidly cranked up (usually every minute) until you can't pedal at a reasonably high rpm no matter how hard you try. It feels like racing up a steep hill in the big chainring. The computer automatically analyzes the gases you're breathing in and out to determine your maximal oxygen uptake.

It's tough! Then you're given time to pedal slowly and recover before you head to the shower.

After the test, a physiologist sits down with you to go over the computer-generated charts and graphs that define your performance. He makes recommendations about training zones and workout plans to help you improve. This data also helps your coach set up a year-long training program with appropriate intensity levels in each season. The key, as always, is to work hard enough to reach your potential but also avoid overtraining.

OTC TEST PROTOCOL

If you have an indoor trainer with watts-measuring capability (such as a CompuTrainer), it's easy to duplicate the protocol used at a sports medicine facility. It's done this way at the Olympic Training Center (OTC) in Colorado Springs.

> **CAUTION!** Don't administer any performance test to yourself without a physician's approval. These tests require you to reach maximum exertion. If you have an undetected heart condition, they could be fatal. Always have someone on hand to help in an emergency.

After you have medical clearance and a spotter, the test is done by pedaling for as long as you can maintain a cadence of 90 rpm while resistance is increased every 3 minutes. In the OTC protocol, the workloads are equal to progressively greater percentages of the power required to maintain a speed of 35 kph (21.6 mph) up a 1-percent grade. The percentages are set at 30, 50, 70, 90, 110 and 130.

The actual wattages are height- and weight-based. For example, a 70-kg (154-pound) rider between 69 and 72 inches tall would ride for 3-minute periods at workloads of 113, 188, 264, 339, 416, 490 and 566 watts. The figures are usually rounded off because most devices can't be set with such precision. So, a common sequence would be 110, 190, 260, 340, 420, 490 and 560 watts.

For any but young, elite riders destined to spend July in France, this test gets very hard very quickly. Many strong masters-age recreational riders can manage to get through 3 minutes at 260 watts but can't last for another 3 minutes at 340 watts. If they get to 420 watts, they blow up quickly. Those last 2 jumps are huge!

> **TIP!** If you want to take this test and you're not an elite rider in your 20s, it's better to uniformly reduce the wattage by 10 or 20 percent. This way, the test will last a bit longer and give you a more useful picture of your fitness.

HOME MAX-TEST PROTOCOL

If you have a CompuTrainer or other watts-measuring device, you may find the following simple testing protocol easier to self-administer than the OTC method just described.

1. Wear a heart monitor and ask a friend to record your heart rate at the end of each 3-minute "ramp" in the test.

2. Warm up with 15 minutes of easy pedaling at a low wattage. Build from 80 watts to approximately 120. When you're breathing steadily and have broken a light sweat, pedal easily for 5 more minutes.

3. Begin the test by pedaling at 90 rpm and 100 watts for 3 minutes. Record your heart rate at the end of this ramp.

4. Increase resistance by 30 watts (to 130) and pedal for another 3 minutes. Keep a 90-rpm cadence. Again, record heart rate at the end of the ramp.

5. Increase resistance by 30 watts 3 more times (160, 190, 220 watts) and ride for 3 minutes at each setting. Make subsequent increases 20 watts, again riding at each successive setting for 3 minutes. Continue recording heart rate at the end of each 3-minute ramp.

6. The test is over when you can't maintain 90 rpm no matter how hard you try. Record your final heart rate and how long you lasted during the concluding 3-minute segment.

This test is extremely demanding, but it's worth the effort because it tells you how much power you can maintain at a given heart rate. Because it's an all-out test, it should be done only twice a year. Schedule the first test in early January to give you baseline numbers. Re-test in the middle of the season to get results when you're at peak fitness.

> **TIP!** Always taper training for several days before testing to make sure you're fresh and results are comparable.

HOME SUB-MAX-TEST PROTOCOL

Every 4-6 weeks, schedule a simpler, less exhaustive test. Simply repeat the Home Max-Test Protocol but don't actually max it (pedal to exhaustion). Stop the test when you reach your lactate threshold heart rate—the rate you can maintain for a 30-minute time trial. In a well-trained cyclist, this is usually about 90 percent of maximum heart rate. So, if your max heart rate (as revealed in the all-out effort of the primary test) is 185 bpm, your LT heart rate should be near 165.

Obviously, it's much less stressful, both physically and mentally, to raise your heart rate to 165 bpm than to 185. That's why it's no problem to take this second version of the test more frequently.

With the data from these tests, you'll learn how much wattage you can push at a given heart rate. After training effectively for 6 weeks, you should be able to ride a given 3-minute test segment at a lower heart rate than you achieved in the previous test.

WHAT? NO WATTS?

What if you don't have a CompuTrainer or other method of determining wattage? Simply use your basic indoor trainer. You don't need a specific wattage number, just a consistent resistance from one test to the next. Use the same bike, the same tires and the same trainer each time you test. Inflate the tires to the same pressure (100 psi is good). Turn the crank that tightens the roller against the rear tire an identical number of turns each time.

Start in an easy gear (say 39x19-tooth) and shift to a harder gear at the end of each 3-minute segment. Use the same size cassette so you have the same gear progression each time. Ideally, cogs will have a consistent difference or 1 or 2 teeth so that there are consistent jumps in effort from one 3-minute ramp to the next. Stop the test when your heart rate reaches LT. Record the gear and how long you lasted before reaching LT in the final 3-minute segment.

You can also do this test outside on a flat road by shifting through the gears every 3 minutes. But wind, traffic and other variables make it tough to get consistent results.

TIP! Always remember, you're not competing against anyone when you test. Instead, you're comparing your fitness this month with next month or next year so you can chart your improvement.

There's no standard protocol you must use. The only requirement is to use the same protocol each time. Then you can accurately compare yourself to yourself.

CHAPTER 21

Whipping Winter Weather

Unless you live in temperate climes where winter means slipping on a sweater in the cool of the evening, you probably equate off-season training with cold weather. Sure, you can retreat to the indoor trainer and weight room to escape the arctic blasts. But what fun is that? Cycling is an outdoor sport. Even at its January worst, cold weather shouldn't limit your riding (or crosstraining). As you'll hear the Scandinavians say, the weather isn't too cold, you're just underdressed!

What about your precious bike, subject to the perils of gritty slush and road salt? I have a solution for that problem, too. If you know how to handle winter, both with clothing and equipment, you can ride into spring with all the fitness you need to begin a great season. So, let's see how to beat the Big Chill.

IT'S A COLD WIND BLOWIN'

Before you venture outside in frigid conditions, it's important to know about windchill. Wind decreases effective temperatures enormously. For instance, at a balmy 40F degrees, a 25-mph headwind means that the cold you feel is equal to only 16 degrees.

Remember that even on a dead calm day, riding a bike creates its own headwind. If you're riding at 15 mph, it's equivalent to standing still and being buffeted by a 15-mph wind with its accompanying chilling effect. If you're riding 15-mph into a 10-mph headwind, it's the same as a headwind blowing at 25 mph. This has a huge impact on how cold you feel—and how to dress.

Dress for duress: It's the key to riding through winter.

TIP! To lessen the effect of windchill, plan winter routes so you travel into the wind on the outward leg. You'll get the coldest part of the ride done early before your clothes become moist with sweat. When you're damp and getting tired, the frigid blasts will be at your back, blowing you home.

Windchill below about 10 degrees can make cycling dangerous. It's hard to stay sufficiently warm to ride long enough for worthwhile training, though an hour of pedaling in winter's crisp air and sunshine certainly has other benefits.

The faster you go, the greater the windchill. So, it makes sense to reduce your ground speed while still keeping resistance high enough for a good workout. One way is to ride a mountain bike on the road. You'll go slower, but the fat tires and wind resistance of a more upright position guarantee productive pedaling. As a bonus, you'll spare your good road bike a soaking in the slush and salt.

Another benefit of knobby tires: They provide much better traction in any snow you might ride across.

DRESS IN LAYERS

You've probably heard about layering your clothes in cold weather. The idea is to trap body heat in several lightweight garments, which also sequentially wick sweat away from your skin to keep it drier. For cycling, layering works much better than wearing a heavy, bulky jacket over a sweatshirt.

On your upper body, start with a thin base layer. Most are made of a synthetic material. Although synthetics can smell like a hibernating bear after one wearing, they do a great job of wicking moisture from your skin. If they get damp—from sweating on a climb, for instance—they feel dry again quickly. Dry skin stays warmer than damp skin.

Some riders like wool base layers because wool has great insulating properties without accumulating the objectionable odor. Wool garments are harder to find but worth the effort. Modern wool base layers don't itch or shrink.

> **TIP!** Turtlenecks are nearly essential for winter cycling because it's so easy to lose heat from your unprotected neck. An icy wind on your throat or the back of your neck can make you feel cold no matter what you're wearing. If the high top irritates your skin, lube the affected areas with petroleum jelly or a skin cream.

Over the base layer, add a short-sleeve jersey for moderate temperatures or a long-sleeve jersey or light fleece vest if it's below freezing. On top, wear a lightweight windbreaker (often called a "shell"). It should block the wind but have underarm or back vents that allow some airflow. It should also have a full-length zipper for ventilation.

If it's significantly below freezing, wear a second base layer or jersey. In arctic conditions, use a winter cycling jacket. It should have windproof panels on the chest, shoulders and front of the arms. The material on the back should breathe to let excess heat escape. Again, there should be a full-length front zipper.

> **CAUTION!** Never wear a cotton garment next to your skin. Cotton doesn't wick sweat. Instead, it gets soaked, then feels clammy and cold. It's one fiber that doesn't belong in a cyclist's winter wardrobe.

LEGS

Legs are easier to keep warm than your trunk or extremities. Most riders are comfortable in leg warmers down to about 45F degrees. Lightweight tights work from there to about freezing. Wear heavier winter-specific tights with windproof front panels, especially on the knees, when the temperature is in the 20s or colder. Don't make the mistake of wearing too little on your legs even if they feel okay. You risk knee injuries if they aren't appropriately covered. Also, your body will shunt blood from your feet to your under-protected legs, leading to a serious case of frozen pups.

> **CAUTION!** Men—beware of penile frostbite! A cold wind can penetrate your tights and cycling shorts, freezing tissue that's near and dear to you. Wind-front tights help. So do special windproof briefs designed for cycling. Tuck your base layer down around everything. You can also stuff an old polypro glove, sock or piece of fabric down the front of your shorts.

HEAD

Lots of warmth can be lost through the head because the scalp is networked with blood vessels. A thin polypro skullcap under your helmet is usually enough to prevent excessive heat loss. Ears are a different story. They can become uncomfortably cold even in air that's above freezing. A fleece-lined ear band will keep them warm without making the rest of your head too hot. Excess heat will still escape from the crown of your head.

When it's colder, wear a thin balaclava under your helmet. This covers everything but your face and can be pulled up under your mouth or nose. Tuck it into your turtleneck or a neck gaiter to prevent air leaks. If the balaclava is properly thin, it won't make you too hot or even require you to change the thickness of your helmet pads.

Speaking of helmets, it takes very cold conditions before you need to cover the vents. Otherwise, let the airflow keep your head from becoming too hot. If your head starts sweating, you'll start sweating all over.

FEET

There's an old saw in cycling that says: You can only be as warm as your hands and feet. When your extremities get cold, your core is next. When your core gets cold, your hands and feet can freeze because minimal blood will go there. Your body fights to keep vital organs warm by reducing blood flow from your torso. So, let's keep your feet toasty first, then warm up your hands.

> **TIP!** For frigid temperatures, or if you want to stay out for more than 90 minutes around freezing, you need extra foot insulation. Consider buying cycling shoes one size larger so you can wear thick wool or wool/synthetic socks. Don't try to cram thick socks into your regular summer shoes. The tightness will restrict circulation, making your feet feel colder than if you wore thinner socks.

Cold feet are probably the biggest complaint of winter cyclists, and for good reason. Few things are more painful than feet thawing after a frigid ride. But it's not hard to keep your tootsies toasty even in subfreezing temps, at least for rides up to 90 minutes or so. Shoe covers ("booties") are the key. They come in 2 types: neoprene rubber, or fabric with a fleece lining.

Neoprene is heavier, bulkier and stiffer than fabric, but it costs less. It does a good job of blocking wind, but it's only fair against water. It holds in body heat pretty well. In fact, too well in one respect. Neoprene can cause condensation that dampens your shoes and socks. Dampness and cold are never a good combination.

Fabric booties are light and floppy. Most models can be rolled up and stuffed in a jersey pocket or seat bag. Wind resistance is good, and so is water resistance, depending on the outer material. Fleece lining helps insulate and is less likely than neoprene to cause condensation.

When shopping, choose booties that extend high up your ankle and have a snug top. You want plenty of overlap with your tights to keep feet heat in, not vented like a chimney. Make sure there are reflective stripes. It's smart to wear things that can catch a driver's eye. In the low light of a dank winter day, bobbing booties that shine in headlights make you safer.

If you ride in cleated shoes, you may need to cut a hole in each bootie's sole. Make it just large enough to expose the cleat. Any more will let in cold air.

It's hard to overheat feet, so wear booties even on days that are merely chilly. Remember, when your feet are warm, you've got a much better chance of feeling comfortable all over.

HANDS

If it's cold in the morning but will warm during the ride, wear regular short-finger cycling gloves under lightweight long-finger gloves. These gloves should be made of a stretchy woven fabric with a gripper material on the palm so your hands won't slip on the handlebar. They'll keep your hands comfortable on the cold metal brake levers. Simply strip them off and stuff them in your jersey pocket when it gets warm.

Lightly insulated gloves work fine to the mid 30s. Below freezing, go for so-called "lobster" mitts (photo, page 77). These put your fingers into 3 compartments—one for your thumb and one each for your first 2 and last 2 fingers. This pools finger heat for more warmth, but unlike with full mittens you still have the dexterity to operate a bike.

Winter gloves should have a tall, stretchy, snug-fitting cuff for plenty of overlap with your long sleeves. An air leak at your wrist will make your hands feel cold no matter how well insulated the gloves.

> **CAUTION!** Don't overdress your hands. Unlike with your other extremities, feet, there's such a thing as too warm. If your hands begin to sweat and gloves get damp inside, your fingers can become uncomfortably cold real quick. It's better to err on the side of cool but dry.

In a cold rain, good luck. Shell gloves may keep your insulated gloves drier, but hands are susceptible to getting wet and chilled because they're so exposed as you ride. Your best bet may be insulated lobster mitts, which still work fairly well when wet. Neoprene gloves are supposedly designed for the rain but still get wet inside, and the models I've seen lack insulation.

HYPOTHERMIA IS NO HYPE

Hypothermia is an insidious killer of the unprepared. It's often associated with raging blizzards and treks to the North Pole. But hypothermia is more likely to strike in relatively mild weather when an unprepared cyclist or backcountry traveler gets stuck in an unexpected cold rain or wet snowfall. The body's core temperature gradually falls to a level that can be fatal.

Symptoms progress from mild to uncontrollable shivering as the body tries to warm itself. Victims become fatigued, lose their sense of time and distance, and gradually become so confused that they make irrational choices like abandoning gloves or parkas. When shivering stops, a sense of profound apathy takes over and many victims die, unable to find their way to safety or perform simple survival tasks like starting a fire.

Avoid hypothermia by dressing in layers. Always wear moisture-wicking clothing instead of cotton. Be aware of weather patterns in your area and dress or pack your bike bag accordingly.

If you're getting cold and begin shivering, especially if you're wet, seek shelter immediately. Because victims are often unaware of hypothermia's onset, watch for symptoms in your companions. Find a convenience store and buy something hot to drink. Eat enough to produce some body heat. Don't set out again until you've added enough clothing to stay warm.

EXAMPLE! The closest I've come to hypothermia on a bike didn't take place on a frigid Colorado ride. Instead, it was in Arizona in March, on the final day of a PAC Tour Endurance Training Camp. I was riding the 90 miles from Sierra Vista to Tucson and got caught in a wind-whipped 38-degree monsoon.

With me were 2 friends, Ed Pavelka and Pete Penseyres. It was raining so hard that we couldn't see the pavement clearly, and we were worried that overtaking vehicles couldn't see us. Every time one passed, it kicked up a tsunami of spray that concealed us from other traffic. It was like riding in an icy waterfall. I was wearing tights, shoe covers, 2 layers of fleece, a balaclava, winter gloves and a shell zipped up tight. I was soaked and freezing.

Then Pete flatted. We huddled by the roadside, 3 of us trying to force a wet tube into a sodden tire with fingers too numb to feel. Picture the Keystone Cops changing a flat. Our skin was literally turning blue. Without pedaling to generate body heat we immediately started shivering. When we finally got the flat fixed, we tore off down the road as fast as our stiff legs would move, riding as hard as we could to warm up.

It didn't help much because the chill was core deep. Another flat would have meant true disaster. Eventually, we came to the camp support van. Piling inside, we sat shivering and dripping and eating till the heater worked its magic. The rain let up. We put on dry base layers and continued to Tucson with an epic-ride memory that has yet to fade.

SLICK ROADS

Running or cycling in cold weather can be dicey if you come upon an icy spot unexpectedly. The most dangerous condition occurs after the sun melts snow slightly. A thin layer of water spreads over the pavement, then freezes in late afternoon, creating a barely visible film of incredibly slippery "black ice." When the roads are mined with such skating rinks, it's far safer to choose an indoor fitness activity.

Even on a warmer day, you need to be careful anytime you ride through a shadow, especially in a turn. Without direct sunlight, icy patches often won't melt. To make it worse, they're hard to see when your eyes are trying to adjust from bright light.

If you brave slick roads—or the surface begins icing over because of falling temps—ride gingerly. In corners, slow way down, take a wide line and don't make abrupt movements. If you're losing traction in turns, use a mountain bike downhiller's trick by unclipping your inside foot so you can use that leg like an outrigger.

Remember, it's no disgrace to phone home or hitch a ride when the road becomes dangerous. It's preferable to hitting the deck and breaking something. Drivers may not be fully in control of their vehicles, either, making it risky for them to maneuver around a cyclist.

> **TIP!** Snowy, icy roads are best tackled on a mountain bike with studded tires or chains. The upright riding position is better for control. Studs or chains grip like a limpet, even in skating rink conditions.

EARLY DARKNESS

Even if winters are not icy where you live, it still gets dark early after the autumnal equinox. Just about the time you get off work, aching for a ride, the sun goes down. And Old Sol sinks with a thud in winter—there's no extended twilight to give you a safety margin if a ride runs long.

The solution is a good lighting system. Bike shops and cycling catalogs are full of models in a wide price range. For short jaunts on lighted roadways, opt for a simple headlight that operates on replaceable batteries. You don't need to pay more than $25. Because there's ambient light to see by, the headlight's main purpose is to make sure that drivers spot you. Combine the headlight with a rear flasher and plenty of reflective material on your frame and clothing.

If you plan to ride much on dark roads, consider a high-end lighting system with a rechargeable battery. I'm partial to models that have both a low and high beam. This extends the battery charge because you can use the low beam much of the time. But when you're going fast enough to outride it, the high beam provides a safety margin of illumination.

> **TIP!** Don't be too frugal when buying a lighting system. After all, your riding enjoyment and safety are at stake. Pay enough for dual beams, weatherproofness, and a NiCad or NiMH rechargeable battery. The latter, nickel metal hydride, is lightweight and requires minimal care for long life. Steer clear of lights that use sealed lead acid (SLA) batteries. They may be cheaper, but they're also heavy and short-lived if the light is kept on after it dims. NiCad and NiMH batteries thrive on deep discharges.

THE BEATER BIKE

Riding in the off-season means you'll be riding in sloppy weather. Rain and melting snow can make a mess of streets and highways. On rural roads, mud tracked onto the pavement by farm equipment turns idyllic country lanes into something resembling muddy singletrack.

Ride your good bike in these conditions? Forget it. The thought of risking your favorite mount on roads that look like the trenches of World War I is guaranteed to send you scurrying back to the comfort of the couch.

The solution? A bike for all seasons, a "beater" that laughs at the worst that winter has to offer. This is a bike that you can ride in the worst conditions imaginable, then simply hose off once the grime gets so bad that you can't remember the frame's color.

Now I'll tell you something that you may not believe: You're gonna love this bike! It might be old, it might be dirty, it might be fitted with a mismatch of cheap and discarded parts, but it's the reason you can ride in winter and through spring rain, too. Almost no conditions can stop it. Bad-weather rides tend to be among the most memorable, so it won't be long before you look at your beater fondly, remembering the challenging—even epic—rides that it made possible.

If you don't already have an old bike that you can turn into your beater, look for one in bike shops, yard sales, or classified ads. Check bulletin boards and bike club newsletters. Ask other riders what's gathering dust in their garages. Sure, you can buy a new bike built for touring or cyclocross and outfit it for winter. But it makes sense to economize and buy something that's already scratched and dented. It won't break your heart the first time it gets filthy.

You'll love it: Set up like your summer bike, a fendered beater is the ticket for training in any weather.

> **EXAMPLE!** When writing this chapter I did some research at my local shop, Cascade Bicycles in Montrose, Colorado. I wanted to see if they had any used bikes in stock that might make good winter steeds. (Hey, any excuse to hang out at the shop!)
>
> Cascade owner Alan Ardizone had just acquired an old Motobecane Grand Jubilee in good condition. It was equipped with 1970s-era components that seem like museum pieces now but are perfect for winter training because they're simple and reliable: Weinmann centerpull brakes, SunTour Cyclone derailleurs with Power Ratchet down-tube shifters, plenty of clearance for wide tires and fenders, and eyelets on the rear dropouts and fork for attaching rack or fender struts. That's the kind of bike to look for when you're beater hunting.

Of course, there's one critical requirement when picking a beater: It must allow you to have the same riding position as on your good bike, using simple tweaks to the saddle and stem/handlebar locations. If you train all winter in one position, then jump on your summer scoot that's set up differently, you're asking for injuries. That said, here are 2 exceptions:

1. If you wear thick tights over your cycling shorts, you should lower the saddle a couple of millimeters to compensate. The added material between your crotch and the saddle has the effect of reducing your leg length. In effect, it makes the saddle higher than on your summer bike.

2. Raise the handlebar slightly in relation to the saddle if you regularly ride in lots of clothing. Layers around your midsection may make it harder to bend over in your regular riding posture. A higher bar also helps bike handling in slick conditions.

MECHANICAL MATTERS

To keep a beater running well, recycle old components. Toss them in a box when they come off your summer bike during upgrades. Then when your beater needs a part (or a part of a part), you can get several thousand more miles out of things that you might have thrown out.

EXAMPLE! Ed Pavelka pretzeled his front wheel on a cross-country PAC Tour when he rode into the biggest man in Jessup, Georgia, just 2 days from the finish. This human brick wall suddenly stepped into the street from between parked cars. The crash even splintered Ed's helmet.

While Ed was being patched up, tour director Lon Haldeman stomped on the wheel to remove the biggest bends, then finished the job with some rough-and-ready truing. Amazingly, the wheel held up for the last 2 days of the tour. After getting home, Ed decided to put it on his circa 1986 Bridgestone RB-2 beater bike to milk a few more miles from it. Now, 11 years and some 50,000 miles later, that wheel is still on the bike.

The rest of Ed's beater is a collection of parts saved from the scrap heap, too. Other than the frame, seatpost, down-tube shifters and brake calipers, nothing is stock. Look closely under the grime and you'll see components like a Dura-Ace crankset and D-A derailleurs—still working reliably even though they were once "too old" to keep on his Litespeed.

My beater just happens to be a Bridgestone, too—an XO-1 retrofitted with road bars (photo, page 83). In 8 years of winter training and summer dirt road abuse, it has gone through a number of different derailleurs and drivetrains. Now it has bar-end friction shifters mated to an old mountain bike cassette, components I scrounged from my spare-parts box in the garage.

It looks like something ridden by a 1950s English tourist—as his second bike. Would Ed and I use such archaic equipment for important events or racing? Of course not. But for winter training, these old Bridgestones (a Japanese brand sadly no longer available) are perfect.

TIP! Don't worry about your beater's weight. Ed's RB-2, fully outfitted for winter riding, is 33 pounds. My XO-1, with fenders and a seat bag containing 2 spare tubes and a mini-tool, comes in at 30 pounds. It's a tank. But when I'm riding it on flat or rolling courses, I don't notice the weight at all. Of course, on long climbs I'm slower on this bike than on my sub-20-pound Litespeed. But in winter it doesn't matter because I'm not trying to drop anyone. And if I'm the one who gets dropped, well, I know the way home.

I believe that a heftier winter bike is actually a training advantage. Come spring, a regular bike feels like a feather. Pedaling extra pounds all winter can even be viewed as "weight training."

One thing a true beater must have is fenders. You gotta have fenders in winter. Without them, water, mud and grit kicked up by the front wheel coats the bike and soaks your feet and legs. A rooster tail of grunge wets your fanny and stripes your back. Road crud enters the headset and trickles inside the bike's frame tubes via the seatpost.

Install fenders, however, and most of that grime and water is caught and directed back to the road where it belongs. Your body stays much drier (if it isn't actually raining) and your bike stays cleaner. You won't have to wash and lube it as often. Fenders also protect your riding companions from wheel spray. In wet climates like England, Ireland and the U.S. northwest, you aren't welcome on group rides without fenders. No one wants to suck gritty water flying up from your rear wheel.

The best fenders are plastic and have mud flaps. The one in front is vital for keeping water off your feet. If your fenders don't have flaps, fabricate them from a large plastic detergent bottle. Make them about 6 inches long and several inches wider than the fender itself. Drill through and attach with small bolts. Be sure to use lock washers.

TIP! Fenders may fit better and won't rattle if you use a tip from Grant Petersen at Rivendell Bicycles (www.rivendellbicycles.com). He recommends attaching fenders with zip-ties rather than the metal or plastic brackets they come with. Simply drill small holes in the fenders so you can zip-tie the front one to the bottom of the fork crown and the rear one to the chainstay bridge and rear brake bridge.

No dropout eyelets on your frame for attaching fender struts? No problem! Simply zip-tie the struts to the fork or the rear dropouts. Wrap electrical tape where there might be metal contact with the bike's finish.

Three final beater bike tips:

- **Use wide tires.** Winter is no time for skinny rubber. Thicker tires give you more protection against punctures and better traction. For even more flat resistance, use tires with a Kevlar belt under the tread. Remember, when you have to stop to fix a flat, you may catch a chill that you can't shake for the rest of the ride.

- **Use strong wheels.** Your beater bike is a great place to install those heavy-but-tough 36-spoke wheels that are now outmoded for performance riding. A well-built wheel should last for years of winter riding. My Bridgestone XO-1 is still rolling on its original wheels after 7 years of hard use. I've replaced a couple of spokes and re-trued occasionally, but even after miles on dirt roads and some singletrack, these old wheels are going strong.

- **Use reflectors.** Decorate your beater like a sixth grader with bad taste. Even if you don't plan to ride after dark, the sun may set on you occasionally. In winter, a puncture or wrong turn can transform a late-afternoon ride into a night ride real quickly. With reflectors and reflective tape on your frame, wheels and crankarms, you'll still show up in car headlights. For the same reason, it's smart to have a high-intensity, battery-powered taillight on your seatpost. You can reach down and click it on anytime you feel that dim daylight may be making you less visible to drivers.

CHAPTER 22

Reaching Ideal Weight

If enthusiastic cyclists have one predominant obsession, it's the endless quest to lighten up. We shave needless weight from the bike by scouring catalogs in search of gram-saving components. But that fixation is minor compared to our dreams of looking as light as Lance Armstrong in July.

The off-season is the ideal time to shuck extra pounds, as we'll see. But before you pass on dessert for the rest of the winter, let's look at the facts about body type and weight loss.

IS HEREDITY DESTINY?

Elite road riders are almost uniformly thin. Body fat percentages for top male cyclists average 4-10 percent. Elite women, because of their sex's childbearing demands, range about 5 percentage points higher.

In addition to low body fat, these athletes are typically quite small. The average Tour de France competitor (male) is about 5-foot-9 and 150 pounds. However, because the bike equalizes physical differences, elite cyclists vary in size more than, say, elite runners. The biggest rider in the 2001 Tour was 6-foot-5 and 190 pounds. Put him on a weight program and you've got an NFL linebacker. In contrast, the shortest rider was 5-foot-4, and the lightest was 116 pounds—jockey material. But big or small, none of these top-rated cyclists pack much fat.

So, it's easy to look (and ride) like our cycling role models, right? Simply shed that excess avoirdupois. Now here's your dose of reality: You can train at pro levels and restrict your diet to anorexic levels in an attempt to get that greyhound look. It ain't gonna happen.

While a sensible training regimen, coupled with a moderate and nutritious diet, will in most cases cause body fat percent to decline, it won't change your body type significantly. Let's see why great endurance athletes are so thin—and how you can improve the body you have even though you can't become a waif regardless of your training and nutrition.

THE TRUTH ABOUT BODY TYPES

Elite cyclists chose their parents carefully. Young athletes naturally gravitate to sports where they're successful. Muscular, fast people become football players. Those gifted with outstanding vertical jumps and eye-hand coordination become basketball players. In the same way, small, wiry athletes with great endurance capacity tend to become runners or cyclists. The sport doesn't mold the body in its image. Rather, the athlete chooses (often unconsciously) the sport for which he or she is most suited. It's a form of natural selection, not training.

Elite cyclists are trees, not V's. I owe that one to Eddie Borysewicz, the legendary cycling coach. Eddie B means that top riders generally have a similar circumference from their hips to their shoulders, not the V-shape upper body we generally consider the athletic ideal. Top cyclists carry only appropriate muscle. Their legs are strong but still lean. Their upper bodies, which do little to propel a bike, are extremely light. If you naturally have substantial muscle in your upper body, training only the legs through cycling will cause arm and torso muscles to get smaller, but only proportionately.

Cycling depends on body mass. To be a successful road racer, you need to climb well. It's on hills that the selection in many races takes place. And because light cyclists generally have a better power-to-weight ratio than heavier ones, they are almost always better climbers. The old adage, "You can't race if you can't climb," is demonstrated in local events as well as the Tour de France.

Ideal endurance athletes have the least amount of body fat they can tolerate and still retain general health. Even so, some relatively hefty people are quite talented cyclists. The pro ranks contain the occasional 190-pound rider who excels on flat courses. But because heavier cyclists generally can't climb well enough to challenge in mountainous races, they're often among the first victims of the selection process.

It's tempting to think that even if you're a bit heavy, you can compensate on climbs by working harder than the competition—or even developing a greater ability to suffer. But there's no way to beat the laws of physics. As race commentator Paul Sherwen noted during a Tour de France telecast, "Courage doesn't make you into a climber."

NOW HERE'S SOME GOOD NEWS

Is there any hope that a recreational athlete can get leaner? Of course. Work with what you have, accept the body type you were given, and enjoy cycling. You may never reach the extreme leanness of elite athletes, just as you can't equal their achievements. But you can improve your health, shed excess body fat, ride closer to your potential—and enjoy a common bond with others who have an interest in fitness. Here's how to do it without starving or riding 10 hours a day.

- **Avoid winter pigouts**. First, don't let winter set you back in your quest for ideal cycling weight. Many riders finally are fit and lean by October, only to pack on 20 pounds in the cold months due to inactivity and plentiful helpings of holiday grub. (See: Jan Ullrich.) The maximum amount it's safe to gain in winter, according to coach Chris Carmichael, is 10 pounds. "If you gain more than 10 pounds over your in-shape summer weight, it costs you too much time and effort to lose the excess when the season starts," he says. "You'll have to focus on losing weight rather than on the training that helps you get better." Push some iron in the weight room this winter and push the pedals, too. But also push back from the kitchen table.

- **Eat fewer calories**. Instead of adding pounds from October to April, those months are the best time to lose excess weight. Why?

  - You aren't training as much so you don't need to consume as many calories.

  - With no events to taper for, you have several uninterrupted months of steady training—ideal for a consistent weight-loss program.

  - You're lifting weights to help burn calories. Weights won't cause you to bulk up unless you're genetically programmed for a Rock-like physique and you spend hours doing multiple sets. A good resistance program will increase your muscle mass slightly but lead to an overall weight loss. The reason? Muscle burns calories but fat doesn't. So the more muscle tissue you have, the more active your metabolism. Also, a vigorous weight training workout raises your metabolism that day, so you continue to burn calories at a heightened rate for several hours after you leave the gym.

- **Know how much you should lose**. Unless you're positive that you're porcine, get a body fat analysis from your doctor, health club or a sports medicine clinic. Using one of several methods—skinfold calipers, electrical impedance, underwater weighing—you can learn the precise percentage of your body weight that's fat. Remember, elite male riders carry 4-10 percent fat; elite women about 5 percentage points more. In contrast, sedentary American males are about 20 percent fat and American women are around 25 percent.

> **CAUTION!** If your body fat percentage is already at an elite level, don't undertake a weight-loss program. You may be heavier than you'd like to be, but if it's muscle weight rather than fat weight, it's unhealthy to reduce.

- **Commit to a long-term plan**. Successful weight loss isn't a quick process. Crash diets don't work. You go down fast and then you go back up, sometimes to an even higher weight. The steady loss of about one pound per week is more likely to permanently reshape your body. Start in midwinter and you can hit your target weight in March or April—just in time for the new cycling season.

WEIGHT-LOSS PLAN

Although human metabolisms are quite variable, shedding pounds is essentially simple: Burn more calories than you ingest, and weight loss must follow.

STEP 1: Cut calories painlessly. Review chapter 16 for my tips on how to eliminate unnecessary calories—especially those from excessive fat, which also come with health risks.

STEP 2: Increase your metabolic rate. Exercise burns calories while you're working out, of course, but it also elevates your metabolic rate for a time afterwards. You continue to burn calories faster than normal. Studies show that intense exercise increases and prolongs this effect. To take advantage, include 2 or 3 interval training workouts each week (heart rate at least 85 percent of your maximum). They can be done on the bike indoors or out, or with crosstraining activities such as running, snowshoeing or cross-country skiing. Weight training is important, too, because only muscle mass burns calories. Lifting produces more calorie-consuming potential and less useless fat.

STEP 3: Increase your burn rate. If you can increase your total weekly exercise time by 1-2 hours, you'll consume as many as 1,500 additional calories, depending on the activity. Ride outside on weekends when weather permits. Add hour-long indoor trainer workouts twice a week. Run an additional 8 miles. Lift weights 3 times per week instead of 2.

STEP 4: Periodize your nutrition. You don't do the same training in winter that you do at the height of the cycling season. By the same token, it makes sense to change your nutritional patterns in the off-season. "Periodize your nutritional program just like you periodize your training," says Chris Carmichael. "You aren't doing the long rides in winter that you do in summer. You don't burn as much glycogen, so you don't need to eat as much carbohydrate. In the summer, 60 to 70 percent of your diet should come from carbohydrate. But in the winter, you can safely reduce it to 50 or 60 percent. This allows you to eat more protein [around 30 percent of total calories] to help rebuild muscle tissue and increase strength."

Above all, be consistent. Schedule daily nutritional planning like daily workouts and any other obligation. You can do it if you are willing to treat exercise (and eating) like a job.

CHAPTER 23

Resistance Training

This is a heavy chapter (sorry, couldn't resist). Read it carefully because the activity it covers—weight training—is potentially the most important part of your off-season program. I say "potentially" because in spite of its widespread acceptance in other sports, resistance training for endurance athletes is still a controversial subject.

It seems logical that greater strength would improve endurance performance. After all, don't many pro cyclists have bulging quads? Shouldn't the fast route to better cycling go directly through the weight room? What could be better than pumping iron all winter, then showing up at the first race of the season not only faster but buff as well?

It isn't that simple. As we'll see, there are important reasons for endurance athletes to strength train, especially in the off-season. But while authorities differ, it's becoming increasingly obvious that toiling in the weight room, by itself, probably won't directly improve your cycling performance—unless you're a novice for whom any physical improvement will pay off. In fact, too much lifting, especially for the legs, can negatively affect your training on the bike.

As Chris Carmichael points out, "Lifting and cycling are like oil and water—they don't mix well. When you're lifting heavy weights, you have to reduce cycling volume and intensity. And when you're riding hard, you can't do much in the weight room."

What's the solution to this conundrum? Once again, it's the P word. Says Carmichael, "It's a question of periodization. You must find a balance in the off-season. Make your strength gains over the winter and then convert that strength to cycling-specific power." To understand this crucial idea, you need to know the difference between strength and power.

STRENGTH VS. POWER

Strength is the ability to move a certain amount of weight without regard to the time it takes to do so. A weightlifter who needs 2 seconds to get 400 pounds from the floor to an overhead position is just as strong as another lifter who takes only 1 second. They both moved 400 pounds the same distance. In the same way, a cyclist who, together with his bike, weighs 180 pounds and rides a century in 7 hours has done the same amount of work as another rider with the same combined bike/body weight who scorched the century in 5 hours. They both moved the same amount of weight the same distance, so they're equally strong.

Power is different. It's defined as work over time. So, riding the century in 5 hours takes much more power (measured in watts) than hauling the same amount of weight 100 miles in 7 hours.

Obviously, to be a better cyclist you need more power. So why worry about strength of the grunt-and-groan, weight-room variety? Why not just train for power instead by riding intervals and hard climbs? The answer is that strength is a precursor to power. Power is built in a continuum that progresses all the way from low-repetition strength in the weight room to high-cadence pedaling. You need strength to build power.

WHAT STUDIES SHOW

It makes intuitive sense that you can't make a strong cyclist out of a weak person. In practice, however, there's a tremendous gap between the physiological abilities needed to perform a few repetitions with a heavy weight compared to the thousands of low-resistance repetitions that characterize endurance activities such as cycling or running. A quick look at lab studies shows why this issue is so confusing.

RESEARCH! In one study, previously untrained men cycled to exhaustion, then did a 3-times-weekly resistance program consisting of standard lower-body exercises (leg presses, hamstring curls, calf raises) in sets of 10-12 repetitions. After 8 weeks, cycling performance in the test improved, even though VO_2 max, a key endurance indicator, didn't.

However, in a study using experienced riders, a similar weight training regimen caused their performances to slow by nearly 2 minutes in a 40-kilometer time trial.

Why the discrepancy? Experts theorize that the sedentary subjects improved their cycling performance with weight training because, due to their lack of fitness, any physical improvement would result in faster riding. But the experienced cyclists got worse because when their regular training on the bike was combined with the added stress of resistance training, they became over-trained and too tired to perform well.

EMPIRICAL EVIDENCE

Experienced coaches differ, too. Chris Carmichael recommends building leg strength with low repetitions and heavy weights in winter, then switching to the bike for high-repetition power work in the form of intervals up steep hills. Conversely, cycling physician and trainer Max Testa counsels riders to begin winter leg work with 3-4 sets of 12-18 reps with medium resistance, then progress to 3 sets of 25 reps followed by 2 sets of 50 reps with light weights. His reason for high-rep/low resistance leg training: "When you pedal you use a very small percentage of maximum strength on each stroke."

To further confuse the issue, there's the case reported by legendary researcher Tudor Bompa, Ph.D. He chronicled a pursuit cyclist who weighed 154 pounds and left cycling to become a power lifter. After 3 years in the iron game, this athlete was able to do full squats with 585 pounds. Then he returned to cycling and shaved 5 seconds from his best time in the individual pursuit. As Bompa told me in a letter, "Because he applied the 'periodization of strength' concept of training, he was able to recruit more fast-twitch fibers and, as such, display more power. Cyclists can improve their performance if they improve their power output."

EXAMPLE! Case histories are fraught with problems, but my personal experience is illuminating. In college, I was an undersized but enthusiastic football lineman who was able to compete because I gained nearly 50 pounds through a combination of weight training and conscientious overeating. When I started bike racing, the pounds melted away and I returned to my normal weight. But the experience sold me on the benefits of weights.

One winter, after a disappointing bike racing season, I determined to return to my athletic roots. For 4 months, I did exhausting squat and leg press workouts—as many as 50 reps of squats with 200 pounds and sets of 10-15 reps with more than 700 pounds in the leg press.

I couldn't wait until spring. I had visions of not only blowing everyone away on hills but also cracking crankarms and tearing spokes out of my rear hub. But instead, I learned that all that work had made me pretty good at squats and leg presses but not so good at cycling. I got dropped like a rock in the early races and it took several months of riding before I came around.

The moral: The physiological law of specificity can't be avoided. Weight-room strength has to be converted to cycling-specific fitness before it's of much use on the bike.

THE 'WEAK LINK' THEORY

To make sense of this phenomenon, consider what Steve Johnson, Ph.D., calls the "weak link" theory. Steve is the CEO of USA Cycling, an exercise physiologist and a masters cycling world champion. He maintains that there's always at least one weak link in any person's power production mechanism. It might be strength, aerobic capacity, lactate tolerance or endurance. If you lack strength, weight training is necessary. But if you're a former football player who can leg press half a ton, the weak link is probably in the aerobic system and it makes sense to spend the majority of training time riding rather than lifting.

Does this mean that most cyclists are better off skipping weights and riding instead? No. Endurance athletes should strength train even if it won't make them faster. Here's why:

- **Use it or you'll lose it**. The body has a disturbing tendency to lose muscle mass as we age. According to some authorities, strength stays relatively high till age 50, then begins a precipitous decline of as much as 10 percent a year. If the slide continues unabated, we face a lengthy period of physical decline and worsening performance. Eventually we can't even perform simple tasks of daily living, such as getting out of chairs or carrying groceries. As we age, we need to lift to keep all the muscle that it's possible to keep. Chris Carmichael has this advice for masters-age riders: "You need year-round resistance training, including exercises for the legs. Leg work should be lighter during the cycling season but it should still be done." Coach Joe Friel agrees with year-round weight training, noting that "older athletes seem to have more trouble gaining and maintaining muscle strength."

- **You'll look better in a skinsuit**. Well, at least a little better. It's a myth that if you lift, you'll automatically bulk up. People who get big, rippling muscles from weight training must be blessed with advantageous hormones and train using specific regimens. Most people make much more modest gains in weight and size. If you're an endurance athlete who doesn't want to gain weight, you can develop a routine that will increase your strength significantly but not your size.

- **Weight training is social**. At the local health club, you'll meet people who share your fitness interests. It's easy to strike up a friendly conversation. Gyms used to be macho and competitive testosterone dens, but now in most cases they're friendly and welcoming to everyone.

- **Weight training is solitary**. Okay, I just said weight training is social. But some people like to train at home because they get a better workout when they don't have to wait for a bench or a machine. Scheduling is easier, too. They can fit training into any open slot and don't waste time driving to the health club. Another option: Visit the gym on weekends when you have more time, and lift at home during the workweek.

- **Weight training is simple**. Weight training is more properly termed "resistance training." It doesn't really matter what provides the resistance. It can be fancy exercise machines, free weights or simply body weight. Time-tested exercises such as pull-ups, pushups, dips and body-weight squats work great. So does using gravity as resistance—like jamming up short hills in a big gear (more on this later).

- **Strength prevents injuries**. A strong athlete is a more injury-resistant athlete. In cycling, an upper body with good muscle tone is less likely to get hurt in a crash. Think of it this way: Resistance training keeps your chassis strong so you can work on your motor.

So here's the bottom line: Weight train not just for next season but to ensure that you're still exercising—and independent—decades down the road.

THE EXERCISES

The specific exercises you choose—and the way you set up your resistance training program—should depend on:

- your strengths and weaknesses
- your goals on the bike
- your time available for training
- your interest in pursuing strength development

I suggest a general approach here. Because it's generic, it won't work for everyone. In fact, it may not work for you. But because its principles are sound, you can use it to customize your own program. Better yet, find a cycling coach, physical trainer or strength coach certified by the National Strength and Conditioning Association who knows cycling. He or she can help you design an appropriate program.

Begin with the number No. 1 rule for resistance training for cyclists: *Do only those exercises that help improve your riding ability*. This minimalist approach saves time better spent turning the pedals. There's no need to do certain exercises that are staples of most weight programs. Take bench presses, for example. That movement isn't necessary when you ride your bike. Upper-body pushing exercises are important only to balance pulling exercises and to give you sufficient strength to support yourself on the handlebar. Simple pushups will do the job. By the same token, dead lifts and power cleans might make it easier to put your bike on the roof rack, but they don't directly affect your pedaling. Next are the exercises that will help your cycling.

> **TIP!** I suggest the number of sets and reps in the training schedules found in chapters 23 and 28. But don't be afraid to do your own thing. For instance, when I'm using the standard recipe of several sets of 8-15 reps in most exercises, every fourth or fifth workout I'll use half the weight and do only one set of 30-50 reps. It's a great way to add variety and endurance capacity.

UPPER-BODY PULLING

These exercises strengthen the muscles that help you pull on the handlebar powerfully during sprints or hard climbing. Choose one or 2 per workout:

Pull-Ups
- Grip the pull-up bar with your hands about shoulder width apart and palms facing away.
- Pull your chin to the bar, hold for one second, then lower slowly to the hanging position.
- If you can't do at least 5 reps, place your foot on a chair and "cheat" with one leg to help push you up.

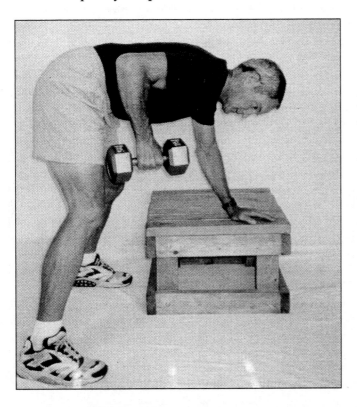

Dumbbell Rows
- Bend at the waist and put your left hand on a bench. Keep your back flat.
- Hold a dumbbell in your right hand with arm extended straight down.
- Pull up the dumbbell till it touches your waist. Keep your elbow in. Pause for one second at the top of the movement, then lower slowly to the starting position.
- After the requisite number of reps, do the same with your left arm.

Upright Rows
- Stand with your feet shoulder-width apart.
- Hold a barbell slightly below waist level with your hands about 6 inches apart, palms facing your thighs, and arms straight.
- Pull up the barbell to collarbone height, hold one second, then lower to the starting position.
- Don't cheat on this exercise by bending your knees. Use a weight sufficiently light to allow 10-15 reps with proper form.

Lat Pull-Downs
- Hold the bar with palms facing away and slightly more than shoulder-width apart.
- Pull the bar down to the front of your chest, pause one second, then return it slowly to the starting position.
- Don't pull the bar down behind your neck. This could injure your shoulders.

Seated Rows
- Sit at the machine with your legs braced and knees nearly straight.

- Place your hands on the rowing handle about a foot apart with palms down.
- Pull the handle to your stomach, pause one second, then return to the starting position.
- Keep your back straight and a 90-degree angle between upper and lower body. Don't bend forward.

UPPER-BODY PUSHING

These exercises strengthen muscles that are used when leaning on the handlebar for long periods during extended training rides or events. Choose one per workout.

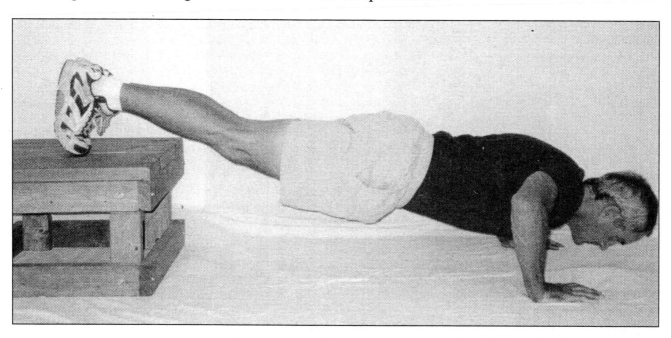

Pushups
- Stretch out in a prone position and support your body on shoulder-width hands and toes. Keep your back straight and head up. For additional resistance, elevate your feet as pictured.
- Lower your chest to within 3 inches of the floor, pause, and push up to the starting position.
- Don't dip your head or let your back bow.

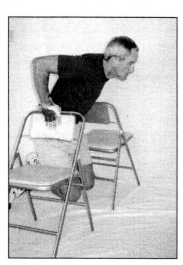

Dips
- Position a pair or chairs or a dip rack so the supports are shoulder width apart.
- Support yourself on your hands with your arms straight.
- Bend arms to lower yourself till your upper arms are parallel to the floor. Keep your elbows in. Push back to the starting position.
- Don't do this exercise if you have a history of shoulder injuries.

Triceps Extensions
- Stand facing the lat machine with the bar near shoulder height.
- Hold your elbows to your sides and grip the bar with hands about a foot apart.
- Press the bar downward to groin level, hold, and return slowly to the starting position.

LEG EXERCISES

These strengthen the prime movers of the cycling motion. Choose one exercise per workout.

Squats
- Face the squat rack, step under the barbell and position it on your upper shoulders about 2 inches lower than the base of your neck. You'll probably be more comfortable if you pad the barbell with a towel or foam pipe insulation.
- Lift the barbell off the rack and step back about 3 feet.
- Stand with feet shoulder-width apart and pointed either straight ahead or angled the same way they are on the pedals. If you toe in or out slightly when pedaling, reproduce that foot angle when you squat.
- Squat down until your thighs are approximately parallel to the floor. Don't go lower. Pause slightly, then return to the starting position.
- Keep your back straight and upright. Don't lean forward.
- You need a spotter when doing squats. Without one, you could lose your balance and get injured, or you might get stuck in the down position when trying to squeeze out a final rep.

> **CAUTION!** Squats are the most dangerous exercise in this list when done incorrectly. Get a demonstration from a strength training professional if you don't know how to do them.

Step-Ups
These are done one leg at a time, just like pedaling. They're easier on your back than squats because you don't need much weight for resistance.

- Face a sturdy bench or platform that's about 14 inches high (slightly below knee level).
- Put your right foot on the platform.
- Step up so you are standing on the platform on your right leg. Don't push off with the left leg. Use it only for balance so your right leg does all the work.
- Step back to the starting position. Do the number of reps called for in your program with the right leg.
- Repeat with the left leg.
- For more resistance, hold a barbell across your shoulders or a dumbbell in each hand.

Leg Presses
These are done on a "hip sled" found in health clubs. Leg presses are excellent for cycling strength. You can use as much or more weight as in squats, but there's less risk of injury because you're seated. Because proper technique varies with different kinds of apparatus, please consult a staff member at your health club before you try this exercise. Generally, you should place your feet about the same distance apart as they are on a bike, and your knees should bend no more than they do at the top of the pedal stroke.

CORE EXERCISES

These strengthen your torso, your core. They're crucial because a strong midsection stabilizes your body on the bike while your legs whirl below. Include crunches and back extensions in every workout.

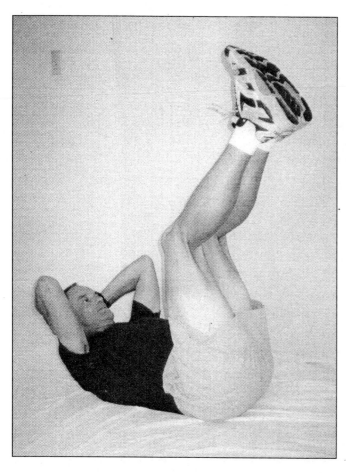

Crunches

- Lie on your back with knees bent and legs propped up on a chair or held up in the air with the knees slightly flexed.
- Put your hands to your ears or fold your arms on your chest.
- Curl your upper body up until your shoulder blades leave the floor. Hold one second and lower slowly. Relax a moment and repeat.
- Don't interlace your hands behind your neck. You will have a tendency to pull up and possibly strain your neck. Make your abdominal muscles to all the work.

Back Extensions

- Lie face down on the floor with your hands behind your head.
- Lift your heels and shoulders simultaneously, pause for one second, and relax to return to the full prone position. Repeat.

Don't neglect **neck exercises**. A helmet can save your head in a crash but only strong muscles can save your neck. Isometrics or a "4-way neck machine" found in clubs are the safest ways to strengthen neck muscles. Get instruction before you use the machine.

DON'T FORGET TO RIDE!

Weight training should never be done in isolation from riding. After all, you're pumping iron so you can lay a foundation for better cycling performance, not to become a power lifter. Chris Carmichael sums it up best: "Build strength in the off-season with relatively low-rep leg work. While you're doing this in the weight room, you'll be riding with a high cadence and working on your spin, maybe using a fixed-gear bike. Then, when you've developed the strength base, convert it to cycling power with low-cadence, high-resistance work on the bike." In the next chapter we'll see how to combine weights and cycling.

THE LEAST YOU CAN DO

Little time or inclination to lift weights, but you still want to get stronger? Here's a quick-and-convenient resistance program that'll help. It's also great for strength maintenance during the cycling season. This program takes only about 15 minutes twice a week. It's done at home, immediately after easy recovery rides. And you can do it in a hotel fitness room when you're traveling.

At home, all you need are a pull-up bar, a light barbell set and several dumbbells. Do these exercises with body weight:

- crunches
- pull-ups
- pushups
- squats

Do these with weights (or with your suitcase if no iron is available):

- dumbbell rows
- upright rows

This is a minimalist program. Do only one set of each exercise and you'll still get lots of benefit. Some studies show that one set provides most of the benefit of multiple sets. As for reps, aim for sets of 12-20 dumbbell rows and upright rows, 5-10 pull-ups, 15-50 pushups, 50-100 crunches and as many as 100 bodyweight squats. These are like deep knee bends, but don't go lower than where thighs are horizontal.

That's it! This routine is very quick. When done twice a week it will increase your strength in winter and maintain it in summer.

CHAPTER 24

Strength Conversion

Lance Armstrong has revolutionized cycling in several ways. Of course, he has shown that it's possible to come back from cancer and regain top form in a very hard sport. Also, unlike more traditional European racers who try to be competitive from February to October, Lance focuses intently on the one race that matters to him—the Tour de France. He skips other events to train, or uses them to achieve peak form for the Tour.

But Lance's most important contribution to modern cycling practice is his ability to generate great power at pedaling speeds 15-20 rpm higher than most of his contemporaries. When Lance pedals, it appears as if he's turning the crank almost too fast. Watching him on TV, it's hard to resist the urge to yell "Shift! Shift!" as he spins his legs into a blur. It looks like he could go faster by using a bigger gear.

High-rpm riding has long been a tenant of Lance's coach, Chris Carmichael. In the early 1990s when Chris was the U.S. National Team coach, he was preaching the merits of a high cadence and I passed along his ideas in several magazine articles. But high-cadence riding didn't catch on. Lance wasn't sold on its merits and hadn't trained himself to spin fast. Then cancer interrupted his career. When he returned, he displayed both greater pedaling speed and lighter body weight. The result was an improved power-to-weight ratio. The muscular classics rider was transformed into a lean, agile climber who could still time trial as well as anyone. That's the formula for Tour success.

Want some of the same? You can improve your pedaling speed—and power production, too. This transformation doesn't happen overnight, but the off-season provides a 4-month opportunity. And because increased power production is a combination of strength and fast pedaling, it makes sense to work on this skill in the winter when you're in the weight room. That's why I've placed this chapter here, right after the one on resistance training.

TIP! Before you dive in, get a more complete perspective on high-cadence pedaling by reading chapter 44. It's based on the latest research and recommendations. It doesn't conflict what's said here, but it just emphasizes the importance of being sure that fast pedaling is compatible with your physiology.

WHY HIGH CADENCE MAKES SENSE

First, let's see why fast pedaling in a moderate gear is more efficient than slow pedaling in a larger gear.

EXAMPLE! If you climb a hill in a gear of 39x25-teeth at 100 rpm, and then climb the same hill in a much bigger gear of 53x17 at 50 rpm, your road speed will be exactly the same. The rear wheel turns 1.56 times with each pedal revolution in 39x25. It turns 3.12 times with each pedal revolution in 53x17.

So if speed is identical, why is 39x25 at 100 rpm better than 53x15 at 50 rpm?

The reason has more to do with physiology than gearing. It requires the identical

---

amount of work to get up a hill at, say, 10 mph no matter whether you pedal rapidly or slowly. But when you grind that big gear, your leg muscles do a large percentage of the work on each pedal stroke. Your quads are taxed almost like you're doing squats.

When you spin the small gear with a fast cadence, the work is divided into more pedal revolutions. Each quad has to work more often but at a lesser resistance. As a result, your cardiovascular system is stressed but your quads are spared.

Bottom line: It's easier to train your body to tolerate a high aerobic load than a high muscular load. So pedaling fast makes sense. As a bonus, it's also easier on your knees.

Lance has learned this secret. His cardiovascular fitness is superb, approaching that of elite distance runners whose legs have to turn over very quickly against minimal resistance.

There's an important caveat to this approach, however. Lance does pedal low gears fast, but they're not as low as the rest of us use. On a very steep grade where the average recreational rider struggles out of the saddle to keep a 39x27 turning over at 60 rpm, Lance uses a 39x23 and pedals at 95 rpm. (His pro competitors would use 39x19 and pedal at 75 rpm.)

It's not enough to twiddle a tiny gear fast. The trick is to turn a moderate gear fast. Lance is dominant because he combines fast, agile pedaling with considerable strength. Here's what these insights mean for your training:

– There are big benefits if you can learn to pedal quickly.

– You must build strength in the weight room with leg exercises such squats, leg presses and step-ups.

– In the spring, you must convert weight room strength to cycling power with low-rpm repeats on hills.

Chris Carmichael isn't the only cycling coach to recommend these workouts. Max Testa likes them, too. This was his prescription for the Motorola pros: "Ride climbs of four-to-six minutes at 50 to 60 rpm to build strength and muscle mass." Alternate high-gear climbing (to increase strength) with low-gear climbing (to increase cadence). As your important events come near in the spring and summer, continue intervals at your normal cadence. After a winter of working on your spin, you'll be able to pedal a larger gear faster.

Below, I suggest an off-season sequence based on these ideas.

FIXED-GEAR CYCLING

Lance works on leg speed the old-fashioned way with fixed-gear training in the winter. A fixed gear is the same as the drivetrain on a track bike. There's only one chainring and one cog, and you can't coast because there's no freewheel. When the rear wheel rolls, the crank turns. You're forced into a smooth, round, fast pedal stroke—especially when going down hills.

According to Chris Carmichael, after Lance's short end-of-season break from training, "He uses a fixed gear during the first four weeks of off-season workouts. During this time, he's also lifting fairly heavily, so the fixed gear acts as a kind of governor. Ninety minutes or so on a fixed gear is quality training because you have to pedal the whole way. You're forced to keep the cadence high so you're more aerobically active."

Fixed-gear road bikes were used for winter training and even racing for decades. British riders did time trials as long as 24 hours on them because of the efficiency of the drivetrain and weight saved by eliminating derailleurs, shifters and all but one cog and chainring. It's a training method that still has value today, as proven by Armstrong and Carmichael.

Interested? The next trick is to get a fixed-gear bike. Here are 3 ways:

1. Buy a used track bike and convert it to road use by installing brakes. Be sure the seatstay bridge and the fork crown are drilled for caliper attachment.

2. Buy a fixed-gear bike designed for road riding. At this writing, moderately priced models from Fuji and Surly are available. They're drilled for brakes and ready to go.

3. Turn an old road bike into a fixed gear.

EXAMPLE! Here's how Rob, a subscriber to the weekly *RoadBikeRider.com Newsletter*, did a fixed-gear conversion:

"For less than $150, I got a rear wheel, cog, front chainring and chain from my local bike shop. I'm not wasting the old bike, and I get a great fixed-gear bike. It certainly makes familiar routes exciting. No matter how many times you say to yourself 'don't coast,' you (or at least I) eventually forget. Yee hah!"

Because this conversion is somewhat technical, ask your shop to set it up if you don't have the tools or expertise.

In addition to improving your pedaling, a fixed-gear bike has another nice advantage for off-season training: It's easy to clean and maintain because the drivetrain is so simple. You won't suffer malfunctions because derailleurs or cables get icy or clogged with road grit.

When learning to ride a fixed gear, the biggest obstacle is the ingrained tendency to coast—as Rob just noted. You get an instant reminder that it isn't possible. Don't ride in traffic until you've overcome this habit. Practice first in an empty parking lot or the vacant streets of an industrial park on the weekend. It shouldn't take long to feel confident enough to move to the road. Ideally, you can ride relatively flat courses. Steep climbs mean pedaling at a potentially knee-wreckingly low cadence. On steep descents, you have to pedal very quickly and brake to keep the bike's speed under your cadence redline.

PUTTING IT ALL TOGETHER

Okay! You're ready to begin the 3-part program to build greater cycling power. A review:

1. Improve pedaling speed (maybe with a fixed gear).
2. Build greater strength in the pedaling muscles.
3. Convert strength to cycling-specific power.

Here's a sample program that accomplishes these objectives.

OCTOBER

Weight Room
- If you've lifted all year, take October off. Don't lift. You need a break. Do other activities that exercise your upper body—mountain biking, swimming, hiking with poles.
- If you didn't lift last summer, begin with the maintenance program in chapter 23. Gradually add a few barbell exercises. Don't strain. Just accustom your muscles to the movement.

> **CAUTION!** If you want to do squats or leg presses in winter, start light. Use no more than your body weight. Squats can make your hamstrings extremely sore if you begin with substantial weight.

Cycling & Crosstraining
- Ride for fun.
- Do other aerobic activities for fun (see chapter 25).

NOVEMBER 1 TO DECEMBER 14

Weight Room
- Gradually increase sets from 1 to 3. Reps should remain at 12-20 for most exercises.

Cycling & Crosstraining
- Focus on fast, supple, easy spinning. You might choose to use a fixed gear.
- Once a week, do a longer aerobic workout on the bike or with crosstraining.

DECEMBER 15 TO JANUARY 31

Weight Room
- Work on strength. Increase sets to 3-5. Increase resistance and reduce reps to 6-12.

Cycling & Crosstraining
- Once or twice a week do short, hard efforts in a large gear at a low cadence of 50-60 rpm. Ride hills or use an indoor trainer.

> **CAUTION!** These efforts can hurt your knees. Warm up thoroughly. Don't attempt them in freezing air or if you have a history of knee problems. Do at least 500 miles of easy spinning before you ease into big gear/low cadence workouts.

FEBRUARY 1 TO MARCH 14

Weight Room
- Begin the all-important process of converting strength to cycling-specific power by reducing sets to 1 or 2, reducing weight dramatically and increasing reps to as many as 50.

Cycling
- Introduce longer, faster intervals. For example, repeats of 3-5 minutes at 90 rpm.
- Gradually build cadence until you're doing intervals at 95 to 110 rpm.

MARCH 15 TO MAY 1

Weight Room
- Scale back your resistance training to maintenance level. The program on page 97 is sufficient.

Cycling
- Now's the time to introduce a full range of interval work into your cycling program.

> **CAUTION!** Be careful when adding high-intensity cycling or strenuous weight training workouts. It's easy for enthusiasm to get you into trouble. Too much work without sufficient rest will lead to overtraining rather than improvement. As training guru Tudor Bompa warns, "Intensity is a dangerous game if you play it too much."

CHAPTER 25

Crosstraining

Exercise physiologists say that to be a better cyclist, you have to ride. The law of specificity states, not surprisingly, that we get better at those activities we practice. Muscles that pedal are better at pedaling than muscles that run or swim or do squats.

Still, because riding every day all year is a sure way to burn out on cycling, crosstraining with other activities is an important part of a productive off-season program. The pros, with their 9-month seasons, love to crosstrain because it's a vacation from the bike and an excuse to venture into a different sport.

"Crosstraining is unstructured for the pros I coach," says Chris Carmichael. "It's more supplemental training than base training [for cycling]. They do whatever sport they like for the first four to six weeks after they come off their rest period and begin to train. Some like to do mild running, especially on trails, or swimming. George Hincapie likes basketball. Others ski."

> **EXAMPLE!** In the 1980s, Andy Hampsten was one of the brash Americans who were breaking the European cycling mold. Instead of knuckling down to a traditional off-season program, he hung out in Boulder, Colorado, with other upstarts such as Ron Kiefel and Davis Phinney.
>
> "I had a great time training in the off-season," Andy remembers. "I skied, I hiked for hours, climbed rock faces, mountain biked and ran up mountains. It got me psyched for the next season. While I was doing this, my buds in Belgium were riding in the rain."

Crosstraining for fun and regeneration is important for us recreational riders, too, even though we don't rack up the 25,000 miles a year that the pros routinely endure.

MENTAL AND PHYSICAL BENEFITS

- **Crosstraining gives us a mental timeout**. We tend to fall into a psychological rut when we do one sport for months at a time. Sure, cycling is our passion. But just as lovers need some time away from each other to make the flame burn brighter, so we need to be unfaithful to the bike for several months each year. (Well, maybe the metaphor is a little forced—but you get the idea.)

- **Crosstraining gives us physical variety**. Cycling is a repetitive and nearly unvarying motion. Your leg muscles get accustomed to going in circles while your upper-body muscles barely move, holding your torso steady above your spinning legs. Doing something else for several off-season months can help you avoid becoming a one-dimensional athlete. It'll wake up some sleeping muscles that you didn't remember you had.

It's important to be a bike-riding athlete, not simply a bike rider. If all you do is ride, your other athletic capabilities will erode. So keep your general athletic skills honed with running, basketball, skiing, weight training, swimming or any other activity you enjoy. It's even helpful to have goals in different sports to give more direction to your off-season training.

- **Crosstraining helps us use and enjoy winter.** It's possible to ride outside in very nasty weather as we saw in chapter 21. But running, snowshoeing and cross-country skiing are much better sports in frigid climes because there's less speed and, therefore, less windchill. Crosstraining is a great way to rack up high-quality aerobic hours when the weather precludes riding. Running is particularly useful when time is short or darkness threatens.

RULES FOR CROSSTRAINING

- **Pick a compatible activity.** The key to surviving winter with your aerobic fitness intact is to choose a crosstraining activity that you enjoy and can do with a minimum of fuss. Running and fast walking are great choices for weekdays (when you're busy) because they are quick and don't require special equipment. On weekends, consider snowshoeing or skiing. If you don't have snow, roller skis or inline skates are a great change of pace.

- **Use gravity.** Colorado cycling coach Mike Devecka was a 4-time Olympic biathlete and a bike racer. In 1986, the World Road Championships were held in Colorado Springs. Many of the European stars rode a local race in Crested Butte shortly before the worlds to acclimate. Devecka decided to see what he could do. Although he was 15 years older than most of the pros and he trained primarily as a cross-country skier, he made the top 10. With results like that, it's important to listen to Devecka's rule for off-season training: "I don't care what you do, as long as it's uphill." Run, ski, hike or snowshoe on inclined surfaces and good things happen. Your quads come into play, and they're the same muscles that power your bike. You'll breathe hard, taxing your aerobic system. And you'll stay warmer because climbing is slow going so it reduces windchill.

- **Remember muscle memory.** When you're crosstraining, don't forget the bike. Perform 2 moderately intense cycling workouts each week to retain "muscle memory." You don't want your legs to forget how to pedal. These workouts can be done indoors, if necessary (see the next chapter). When spring comes and you get back on the road, you'll be much farther ahead compared to riders who didn't ride at all during the winter.

> **CAUTION!** When your muscles are accustomed to pedaling, injuries can result when you switch to another sport with different demands on your joints and connective tissue. Begin all alternate activities slowly and gently to avoid injury.
>
> "The danger in crosstraining is injury," warns Chris Carmichael. "Pros become so specialized on the bike during the season that it's easy for them to get hurt when they do something different."

Cyclists have such well-developed cardiovascular systems that it's easy to run a relatively long way the first time out. Fight that temptation. Your knees and Achilles tendons aren't used to pounding the pavement. They'll be the first links in your biomechanical chain to complain. You've never experienced soreness like the kind that'll grip your screaming leg muscles if you start your off-season running program with a 5-mile trot up and down hills. Instead, you might begin with a 5-mile run/walk. Jog only 100 yards out of every half mile the first time out. Then gradually increase the distance of the running sections. Make it your goal not to get sore muscles during the changeover from cycling to running.

STRETCH (WHETHER YOU LIKE IT OR NOT)

Stretching is a controversial topic for endurance athletes. Some studies show that it reduces injuries while others have found that it increases them, especially among runners.

Lance Armstrong is a recent convert to stretching. According to cycling injury expert Andy Pruitt, Ed.D., Lance once had a terse comment to suggestions that he needed to improve his flexibility: "I don't stretch," accompanied by a steely-eyed stare. However, according to a number of sources, Lance changed his attitude and stretched as much as an hour a day in preparation for the 2001 Tour de France. The nature of his program hasn't been revealed.

Stretching may even improve cycling ability. According to Max Testa, "One study shows that cyclists increased their quad power five percent just by stretching their hamstrings. Greater flexibility in the hamstrings created better utilization of the quads."

Good stretching programs are highly individual. If you have significant hamstring and low-back tightness, these areas should be targeted. The best single source for a wide variety of stretching routines is the bountifully illustrated book called *Stretching* by Bob Anderson (www.stretching.com). Another approach is to consult an athletic trainer or physical therapist who can evaluate your flexibility and create a personalized stretching program.

The key stretch for cyclists works the hamstrings. It's simple. Just sit on the floor with your legs straight in front of you about 2 feet apart. Keep your knees slightly bent. Lean forward over your right leg and lower your chest toward your thigh until you feel a slight stretch in the low back and hamstring. Hold that position for 15-30 seconds, then sit up. Do the same over the left leg. Then do each leg 2 or 3 more times, gingerly increasing the amount of bend at your waist. Never stretch to the point of pain.

> **TIP!** Many cyclists dislike stretching because it's so inactive. They think it's a waste of precious time, so they don't schedule any for it. If this sounds like you, simply flop on the floor and do your routine while watching a TV program. Get stretching's benefits instead of lying inertly on the couch.

TWO WAYS TO USE SNOW

The 3 simplest crosstraining activities are also the most useful because they're aerobically demanding and impact many of the same muscles used for pedaling. There's just one catch: You need good snow for 2 of them. I know this leaves out a good number of you. But for those blessed with plenty of the white stuff like I am in western Colorado, great crosstraining is at hand. Don't grumble about the snow, use it to your advantage.

Snowshoeing is the fastest-growing winter sport, and for good reason. It's easy to learn, fun to do and it lets you enjoy your favorite hiking trails in winter as well as summer. Snowshoeing is also a tremendous workout whether you tramp along through unbroken snow or run on packed trails. By using ski poles, you can involve your upper body, too. (Actually, you don't even need snow if you don't mind some strange looks. Snowshoeing on a grassy field or the beach has plenty of aerobic benefits, too.)

Cross-country skiing needs better snow than snowshoeing. It can be done using the classic diagonal stride or the newer skating technique. Both involve the upper body and work the quads almost like pedaling. A packed track is necessary for skating and it makes the classic style more fun. Or, simply break trail through fields and woods. It's guaranteed to get your heart rate up. Once you've packed out a track, retrace it so you can kick and glide.

To hone your endurance in either of these activities or when running, include some interval training by going harder on up-hill sections, then recovering on the downhills—just like on the bike.

HOW TO RUN RIGHT

Plenty of studies show that while cycling can improve running performance, running does very little to make you a better cyclist. Main reason: The pedal stroke is powered by the quads and glutes; running depends on the calves and the hamstrings.

Still, pro teams have experimented with off-season running. In 1996, Nicholas

Fun & effective: Snowshoeing works the whole body.

Torrados, M.D., then medical director for Spain's pro ONCE team, said that the riders' early-season training included one hour of walking in the morning before they got on the bike. Further, "They also do uphill running on a treadmill or outside." Note that Torrados' athletes practiced the key to making running helpful to cycling—they did it uphill. Remember Devecka's rule!

Running on the flat doesn't engage the same muscles that are used in the pedal stroke, but running uphill uses the quads and glutes in a similar fashion to pedaling. If you don't have hills in your area, stairs are a great substitute. Run some twice a week. Look for a tall building with stairwells that are uninterrupted for at least 5 floors. Run up, walk down, and repeat several times. Stadium steps are just as useful and get you outside, too.

> **TIP!** To lessen the chance of injuries that sometimes accompany running, wear high-quality shoes that are designed to work with your type of foot strike. People at the running store can advise you, perhaps after watching you run briefly on a treadmill.

Combine uphill running with 2 rides or trainer sessions per week to retain your cycling muscle memory and convert running fitness into cycling fitness. Always walk down hills or steps to avoid pounding your knees and hips. In fact, you can eliminate the danger of descents if you "run uphill" on an inclined treadmill. Advantages include a softer and uniform running surface. You can "climb" all you want, then just step off the treadmill when you're done.

Running has another clear advantage over other aerobic crosstraining activities: It's quick. Pull on running shoes and appropriate clothing, and go. Darkness, snow or cold rain are a lot easier to handle while running than on the bike. You can get a great running workout in less than 60 minutes from shoes to shower. This ease makes running the exercise of choice when traveling.

DRESS FOR DURESS

Running, snowshoeing and cross-country skiing are "hot and wet" sports. Because they're so physically demanding, you'll quickly work up a sweat. It gets even wetter if you're on snow and falling once in a while.

Dress in layers for all of these sports. The principles are the same as dressing for cycling in cold weather (see chapter 21). In fact, you can use the same clothing. Next to your skin, always wear a moisture-wicking synthetic or wool base layer, rather than cotton. Put on tights, a light fleece insulating layer on your upper body, and a wind shell with a full-length front zipper for ventilation. Wear a knit hat and gloves.

If you'll be venturing into the backcountry, carry a pack containing another layer of fleece, warm mittens and standard survival gear including matches, map, compass, water, food, a space blanket and a first-aid kit.

ENDURANCE WORKOUTS

Four-hour rides are hard to do in cold weather. The trick is to build endurance by combining training modes. For example, ride the indoor trainer for 30 minutes, run for 45 minutes, then get back on the trainer for another 45 minutes. Or cross-country ski for a couple of hours, then do an hour on the trainer.

HYDRATION AND SUN PROTECTION

We don't associate winter with dehydration and sunburn. But the cold, dry air sucks the water out of you with each breath (especially at higher altitudes). Performance decreases significantly when you lose as little as 2 percent of your bodyweight as fluid, so make a concentrated effort to stay hydrated. Drink plenty every day, and keep a bottle next to your bed so you can drink at night if you wake up. Pre-hydrate for workouts by downing 16 ounces of sports drink an hour or 2 before exercise. Its carbohydrate will increase your energy level, too.

When snowshoeing or skiing, use a fluid source such as a back-mounted hydration pack under your jacket. For running, a single-bottle holster that attaches around your waist prevents bouncing on every stride.

Sunburn is another danger, especially when the sun's rays are intensified by reflection off snow. Snowshoers and skiers have been known to suffer severe sunburn under their noses or chins. Protect yourself by using plenty of sunscreen. Reapply periodically if you're out for long.

CHAPTER 26

Indoor Cycling

Most cyclists love to be outdoors, even in winter. After all, fresh air, sunshine and scenery are big attractions of the sport. If we wanted to exercise inside, we'd all become gym rats.

Pedal pounder: Do hard workouts to make the most of trainer time.

Indoor cycling is usually considered a last resort when weather makes it unpleasant to ride outside. But many coaches recommend trainer workouts even if the sun is shining. "I'm a big fan of indoor trainers," says Chris Carmichael. "Indoor training is a necessity in winter, but I prescribe it to my riders all year round."

The benefits can be great, but there's a big problem: boredom. Watching sweat drip off your nose while hammering in your basement isn't quite as much fun as a spirited training ride in midsummer. But if you know a few tricks, indoor training is not only bearable but close to enjoyable. Because the trainer makes workouts predictable and repeatable, it's a great workout tool as well.

ADVANTAGES

- **Train at any hour, day or night.**

- **Ride despite rotten winter weather.**

- **Save time.** Dressing and undressing for outside rides takes precious minutes. Then you may have to spend more time washing and lubing your bike.

- **Be safer**. When you ride indoors, there's no treacherous ice or traffic to pose a threat.

- **Seize control**. Riding a trainer allows you to precisely monitor each workout. That's why coaches love it. It's controllable and predictable so you can duplicate workouts and find out exactly how much you're improving. You determine the time and intensity of every session. Outside, all sorts of things can interfere. Plus, it's difficult and even dangerous to ride vigorously in frigid air. Winter clothes are restrictive. It's hard to warm up well in order to reduce the risk of injury. Once you do work up a sweat, a cold chill can set in to make the rest of the ride uncomfortable.

- **Remember how to pedal**. Spinning on a trainer after a crosstraining workout of weights, running, skiing or any other activity helps you retain your pedal stroke. It loosens leg muscles, too, reducing the soreness that can result from launching into unaccustomed, weight-bearing exercise.

TIPS FOR SUCCESSFUL INSIDE RIDES

Does it sound like I'm trying to talk you into something? Despite all the advantages, I know (like you probably do) that indoor training can be terminally boring. Time passes at a snail's pace because your mind isn't occupied with everything necessary to keep a 2-wheeled vehicle upright and on course. Indoor riding creates sensory deprivation equal to any devised in a psychology experiment. However, with the right approach, time on the trainer can be coaxed to flow along at normal speed. Here are some effective ways.

- **Limit your riding time**. An indoor trainer isn't for off-season endurance workouts. I'll bet most riders try at least once to ride their nowhere bike for 3 hours while watching football or reading *War and Peace*. They find out that once is more than enough. It's not very effective training, either. Crosstraining is a much better way to get off-season aerobic conditioning. So on the trainer, limit each workout to 60 minutes. Get on, warm up, do your workout, cool down and call it good. A trainer works great for short, intense, structured workouts. It becomes a torture machine for long steady-state rides.

- **Vary every workout**. Never do the same thing on a trainer for more than a few minutes at a time. Shift gears, stand up, pedal with one leg, go hard, go easy—anything to give your body and mind a break.

- **Keep your mind occupied**. On a trainer, your brain wants to dwell on time and discomfort. Stimulate it with music, movies, TV sports or even, if you're really desperate, soap operas or quiz shows. I like watching bike races. I tape the Giro, Tour and spring classics to use during the winter.

- **Stay cool**. Without a cooling wind, you'll heat up quickly while riding in your own stale indoor air. So, put a large fan a few feet in front of your face to create an artificial headwind. The stream of air will help evaporate the quarts of sweat you produce, keeping your core temperature down for a better, more comfortable workout. This is important, as indicated by the result of a recent lab study: Endurance time on a cycle ergometer at an intensity that could be maintained for 92 minutes when the temperature was 52 degrees decreased to 83 minutes at 70 degrees and to only 51 minutes at 86 degrees. The cooler you can make the indoor cycling environment, the more work you can do—and the greater fitness you can gain.

> **EXAMPLE!** Steve Johnson, now head of USA Cycling, used to do his winter training in a janitor's closet at the University of Utah, where he headed the Human Performance Lab. Without air flow, his body heat would have quickly turned the closet into an oven. But with 2 big box fans blowing directly in his face, he kept his cool—and was able to build on his winter fitness to win the masters world road championship.

- **Drink up**. Down at least one big bottle per hour while on the trainer, just like outside during a hot summer ride. Sports drinks work better than water because they replace carbohydrate, extending your energy.

- **Train with others**. Sign up for a cycling class at your local health club. Generically called "spinning" classes, these group hammer-fests are a great way to add variety and interest to your indoor riding and meet other fitness enthusiasts as well. Another approach is to start a "trainer night" at your home. San Diego cycling coach Arnie Baker, M.D., invites up to 70 members of the CycleVets club to his house one evening per week. They set up trainers on the patio and go through a specific workout. Then they order pizza and socialize.

> **TIP!** This chapter is devoted to making the most of indoor cycling, but you should know that experienced riders usually don't get on their trainer frequently in the winter. They know that stationary cycling can be mentally taxing. If they use up their store of enthusiasm in January, they'll hate getting on the trainer in spring when bad weather interferes with riding the road. Instead, they crosstrain in winter and save the trainer for spring. Then when they need a hard workout but can't get outside, they don't mind climbing on their nowhere bike.

ONE-LEG PEDALING

Leg isolation: Superior strokes next season.

One-leg pedaling is an extremely effective way to work on strength and add variety to your indoor training at the same time. When you pedal with both legs, the leg that pulls the foot through the bottom of the stroke, up the back and over the top gets lazy. That's because the other leg is pushing the pedal down, a much more powerful and natural action than pulling the pedal up.

Now think about it. If your leg doesn't help bring the pedal up and over the top, it's just dead weight. It increases the resistance your muscles must overcome to move your bike down the road. This is why learning to pedal a complete, 360-degree circle with each leg makes you a better rider. One-leg pedaling drills teach your muscles and nervous system.

– Warm up on the trainer for 20 minutes by pedaling with both legs.

- Unclip your left foot from the pedal. Hook it back over the trainer just to the left of where it connects to the rear hub. Or, rest it on a chair or stool just outside the left pedal circle.

- Pedal at about 90 rpm with your right leg. Use an easy gear until you get accustomed to the unusual feeling. You'll probably find it difficult to pedal for more than 2 or 3 minutes the first time. The muscles that lift your thigh and push the pedal over the top will fatigue quickly. But you'll improve rapidly.

- After a few minutes of using the right leg, switch to the left and pedal for the same amount of time.

- As you improve, increase the gear and the amount of time you pedal with each leg.

INDOOR RIDING + WEIGHTS

You don't need to stay on the trainer for an entire workout. For example, you can alternate 2- or 3-minute cycling intervals at about 85 percent of your max heart rate with leg presses, squats or step-ups. The weight workout improves strength. The pedaling intervals remind your legs and nervous system that you're a cyclist, too. This workout is a great way to create strength and begin the process of converting it to cycling-specific power. (See chapter 49.)

TRAINER WORKOUTS USING SEGMENTS

I use a segmented approach to indoor cycling workouts. Here's how it works:

- Each segment below is a self-contained workout spanning 15-20 minutes.

- Segments are designed to accomplish a specific training objective, such as warming up, improving speed or increasing power.

- Segments can be combined to fill the amount of time you want to spend on the workout.

- Segments can be chosen to pinpoint specific skills you want to improve.

Remember that these segments are samples. Each workout suggests several variations—and variety is the key to enjoying (not just surviving) your time on the trainer.

> **TIP!** Gear suggestions are expressed as, for example, 39x19. This means a 39-tooth chainring (a size found on many bikes) combined with a 19-tooth cog.
>
> You don't have to use the gear I list. More important is using whichever gear is easy or hard for you in the context of the segment. The right gear will change as your fitness develops during the course of training.

Trainer workouts are limited only by your imagination. In fact, it's possible to train indoors 3 times per week for several months and never duplicate a workout. Make it your goal never to do the same one twice. Be creative!

SEGMENTS: *Warm Up and Cool Down*

Always do these 2 segments. Warm up to begin a trainer workout and cool down before climbing off. Most cyclists use the same warm-up and cool down each time to simplify the workout. But you can vary the approach as long as you work gradually into and out of higher intensities.

- **Warm up** (15 minutes). Start in a low gear of about 39x19, depending on the resistance of your trainer. Spin easily at about 70 revolutions per minute. Monitor your rpm by counting every time your right foot comes around during 30 seconds and multiply by 2. Each minute, increase cadence by several rpm. After 5 minutes, increase the gear. At the end of 15 minutes, you should be sweating lightly and your heart rate should be about 80 percent of max. Finish the warm-up with several 10-second sprints in a large gear.

- **Cool down** (10 minutes). When the main workout is complete, decrease cadence and gearing on 1-minute intervals until you're spinning an easy gear at about 70 rpm. Then get off.

SEGMENTS: *Leg Speed*

- **Spin-ups** (20 minutes)

  1. In a low gear (39x19), spin at 70 rpm for 60 seconds.

  2. Each minute, increase cadence by 5 rpm. You'll know when cadence gets too fast to sustain for 60 seconds because your butt will bounce on the saddle.

  3. When you start bouncing, reduce cadence by 5 rpm every minute to the end of the 20-minute segment.

- **One-leg speed** (20 minutes)

  1. In a low gear (39x19), spin at 90 rpm for 15 seconds. Then pedal slowly for 45 seconds.

  2. Repeat 4 more times, but increase your cadence during the first 15 seconds by 5 rpm each time.

  3. Unclip your left foot. In a low gear (39x21), spin with your right leg for 60 seconds at about 100 rpm.

  4. Do the same with the left leg.

  5. Repeat steps 3 & 4 4 times.

  6. Using both feet, repeat steps 1 and 2.

- **Stand and sprint** (20 minutes)

  1. In a moderate gear (53x19), stand and sprint at about 100 rpm for 15 seconds.

2. Sit and spin the same gear gently for 45 seconds.

3. Repeat steps 1 & 2 four times.

4. In a fairly large gear (53x17), stand and sprint hard for 10 seconds.

5. Sit down, shift to a fairly low gear (39x17) and spin easily for 50 seconds.

6. Repeat steps 4 and 5 nine times.

SEGMENTS: *Climbing Power*

> **TIP!** To simulate riding uphill, put a block of wood under the front wheel to tilt the bike. A 4- or 5-inch block will do it.

- **Minute on, minute off** (20 minutes)

  1. In the saddle using a fairly large gear (53x17), pedal at 90 rpm for 60 seconds. This should raise your heart rate to within 5 bpm of your lactate threshold (LT). It should feel "hard."

  2. Shift to the small chainring and spin easily for 60 seconds.

  3. Repeat 9 times. During the final 3 efforts, your heart rate will climb to your LT or slightly above as you near the end of 60 seconds.

- **Stand and ascend** (20 minutes)

  1. In a big gear (53x13), stand and pedal rhythmically for 2 minutes. Your heart rate should rise to about 5 bpm below your lactate threshold. It should feel "hard."

  2. Sit down, shift to the small chainring and spin easily for 2 minutes.

  3. Repeat 4 times. During the final 3 efforts, your heart rate will climb to your LT or slightly above as you near the end of the 2 minutes.

- **Up and down** (20 minutes)

  1. In a moderate gear (53x19), pedal for 5 minutes at a cadence around 90 rpm.

  2. Stand and shift to a cog that's 2 or 3 teeth smaller than you were in while sitting. For example, if you pedal seated in 53x19, shift to the 17 or even the 15 when you stand. Intensity should feel "hard." Your heart rate should rise to your LT in the last 2 minutes.

  3. Sit down, shift to the small chainring and spin easily for 5 minutes to recover.

  4. Repeat once.

SEGMENTS: *Time Trial Power*

> **TIP!** If you have a time trial bike, use it for these workouts so you get accustomed to the position. Or, put clip-on aero bars on your trainer bike.

- **TT "threes"** (20 minutes)

  1. Ride for 3 minutes at a steady pace. Choose a gear that allows a cadence of 90-100 rpm but does not drive your heart rate past LT. It should feel "hard" but not exhausting.

  2. Shift to the small chainring and pedal easily for 2 minutes.

  3. Repeat 3 times.

- **TT ladder** (20 minutes)

  1. Choose a gear that lets you maintain a cadence of 90-100 rpm and a heart rate not exceeding your LT. It should feel "hard" but not exhausting.

  2. Do a "ladder" like this:

     - 1 minute hard, 1 minute easy
     - 2 minutes hard, 2 minutes easy
     - 3 minutes hard, 3 minutes easy
     - 4 minutes hard, 4 minutes easy

- **TT "eights"** (20 minutes)

  1. Choose a gear that lets you maintain a cadence of 90-100 rpm and a heart rate not exceeding your LT. It should feel "hard" but not exhausting.

  2. Ride at time trial cadence and intensity for 8 minutes. Check your cyclecomputer to see how far you go. Check your heart monitor to determine average heart rate.

  3. Pedal easily for 4 minutes.

  4. Repeat the 8-minute TT and re-check distance and average heart rate. If you cover substantially less distance the second time, or your heart rate is more than 5 beats higher, it says you did the first effort too hard.

SEGMENTS: *Intervals*

- **Interval ladder** (20 minutes)

  1. Choose a gear that allows a cadence of 90-100 rpm for the length of each interval. Intensity should be "very hard" at the end of each work period.

2. Do a "ladder" like this:

- 2 minutes hard, 2 minutes easy
- 1:45 hard, 1:45 easy
- 1:30 hard, 1:30 easy
- 1:15 hard, 1:15 easy
- 1:00 hard, 1:00 easy
- :45 hard, :45 easy
- :30 hard, :30 easy

- **Interval "threes"** (18 minutes)

1. Choose a gear that allows a cadence of 90-100 rpm for the length of each interval. Intensity should be "very hard" at the end of each work period.

2. Ride hard for 3 minutes.

3. Shift to the small chainring and pedal easily for 3 minutes.

4. Repeat 2 times.

THREE SPECIAL SESSIONS

For variety, these workouts are in a different format. Use them for the benefits listed as well as to keep your indoor sessions as interesting as possible.

- **Blue Collar Special** (basic workout for overall fitness)

Minutes 1-15	Warm up.
Minutes 16-25	Pedal with one leg for 1 minute, then switch legs. Use a moderate gear that lets you maintain a cadence of about 80 rpm. Hook the non-pedaling foot on the trainer.
Minutes 26-35	In a moderate gear, pedal steadily at an effort level of about 8 on a scale of 10. Work hard but not all-out.
Minutes 36-40	Spin easily in a low gear to recover.
Minutes 41-50	Alternate 1 minute of hard pedaling with 1 minute of spinning.
Minutes 51-60	Cool down.

- **Time Trial Terror** (develops ability to maintain high speed)

Minutes 1-15	Warm up.
Minutes 16-25	Pedal with 1 leg for 1 minute, then switch legs. Use a moderate gear that lets you maintain a cadence of about 80 rpm. Hook the non-pedaling foot on the trainer.
Minutes 26-30	Pedal for 5 minutes at a heart rate of about 85-90 percent of your max. Use a gear that allows a cadence over 90 rpm. Don't overgear!
Minutes 31-33	Spin easily in a low gear to recover.
Minutes 34-49	Repeat the 5-minute interval and the 3-minute recovery 2 more times.
Minutes 50-60	Cool down.

- **Climb!** (tilt your bike by putting a block of wood under the front wheel)

Minutes 1-15	Warm up.
Minutes 16-25	Shift to a relatively large gear, stand up, and pedal at about 80 rpm for 1 minute. Then sit and spin a low gear for 1 minute to recover. Repeat for 10 minutes.
Minutes 26-50	In a large gear, stay seated and pedal at about 85 percent of max heart rate for 3 minutes. In the same gear, stand and pedal at a low cadence (about 50 rpm) for 3 minutes to recover. Repeat 3 times.
Minutes 51-60	Cool down.

CHAPTER 27

Better Bike-Handling Skills

The off-season is a great time to increase fitness, so in much of this section I focus on strength and power. But winter is also the best time to become a better bike handler.

Many cyclists never feel totally comfortable on their bikes, especially around other riders, so they don't enjoy the sport to its fullest. After all, it's hard to have fun when you're nervous about falling! Let's see how you can increase your skill and confidence on the bike with a few simple off-season activities and drills.

CYCLOCROSS

Cyclocross in the fall and winter will significantly hone your bike-handling ability. It will boost your fitness, too. You don't need special equipment, and you don't need to race. Merely hammering around a half-mile loop in the local park will do it.

If you're not familiar with cyclocross, the concept is simple. You ride a road bike on a course that's mostly unpaved. There are steep uphill sections and obstacles that require dismounting and running while pushing or carrying the bike. It's a combination of riding, running and bike handling with some weight lifting and agility drills to boot. That's a combo that's hard to beat. Plus, it might just save your skin.

EXAMPLE! When I was the training/fitness editor for *Bicycling* magazine, the editorial staff gathered in Moab, Utah, for an October mountain bike festival. Technical editor Jim Langley also brought along 2 cool road bikes to test (a Waterford and a Litespeed).

We wound up riding the La Sal Loop, a 65-mile course into the mountains above Moab that features 6 miles of steep climbing. The descent's a doozy—half a dozen tight switchbacks spiraling down the valley's headwall. The road is narrow and steep, the pavement frost-buckled and speckled with potholes.

And on this day, it had an additional surprise for us, courtesy of a recent storm that had dumped snow in the high country. The road was dry on the climb, but as we descended I came around a shaded corner and was confronted by a 300-yard stretch of packed snow—with a tight bend in the middle. It looked like a crooked skating rink!

I braked as much as possible while still on dry pavement, yelled a warning to Jim, then rode it out using the cyclocross skills gained in the workouts described below (along with a little luck).

Here's how to make cyclocross drills part of your off-season routine:

- **Use your beater bike**. An old road bike is the best choice for cyclocross. Just add knobby 'cross tires to the beater described in chapter 21. You'll probably need to remove fenders to fit the bigger rubber. It's helpful if the beater has cantilever brakes for more mud clearance, but this isn't vital. Lower the saddle about 5 mm from your normal position. This makes dismounts easier.

- **Cleat your feet**. You can ride cyclocross in running shoes and platform pedals. But cleated mountain bike shoes and clipless pedals are better. An off-road pedal system gives you more security and control while riding, and it allows you to get off and run well, too. The shoe soles have pockets that put the cleats just below sole level.

- **Find a loop**. Scout out a park or vacant lot. You need a half-mile loop that's mostly dirt. The ideal location is about 5 miles from home so you can warm up on the way there and cool down as you spin back. The course should include a couple of short, steep hills and several things that force you off the bike—benches, parking barriers, low fences, fallen logs and so on.

- **Mix technique with intensity**. Hit the 'cross course once or twice a week during November and December. Total about a dozen workouts. For the first 3 or 4, simply ride around the course 2-5 times, working on the techniques described below. Don't force either the pace or your skill level. Then you should add laps but hold intensity to about 80 percent of max heart rate. During the last 4 workouts, reduce the number of laps but increase the intensity to about 90 percent. As former pro team physician Max Testa, M.D., points out, "Work on technique at low intensity, but do it at high intensity, too. It's at high intensity that technique falls apart."

FOUR 'CROSS SKILLS YOU NEED TO KNOW

1. **Dismount**. As you approach a steep hill or obstacle, judge your speed and distance so you don't get off needlessly soon or so late that you stumble. A little practice will allow you to judge the correct velocity every time. Place your hands on the brake lever hoods for the best bike control. Unclip your right foot and swing your right leg back and over the rear wheel. Then put your right foot between your left ankle and the bike and step forward. As your right foot hits the ground, click out of the left pedal and begin running.

2. **Lift the bike over low obstacles**. When you come to a low obstacle, dismount as above but move your right hand from the brake hood to the middle of the top tube. Pick up the bike as you run and carry it like a briefcase as you step over the obstacle.

3. **Shoulder the bike up steep hills**. When scrambling up a steep pitch, it's best to carry the bike on your shoulder. As you dismount, place your right hand on the top tube as just described. As you begin the hill, flip the bike to your right shoulder. The top tube should rest near your neck. Steady the bike with your right hand on the right handlebar drop.

4. **Remount**. Place the bike on the ground with both hands on the brake hoods. You're still on its left side. Smoothly swing your right leg over the rear wheel and onto the saddle, making initial contact with the inside of your right thigh, not your crotch (*ouch!*). Spring smoothly off the left foot (don't leap). Then slide to the right until you're on the saddle. Locate the pedals and clip in. This is where a clipless pedal system is a big advantage over clips and straps. Off-road pedals can be engaged from either side.

BIKE-HANDLING DRILLS

Cyclocross teaches you balance and how to stay upright when your tires don't have good traction. These are solo skills. Next, you need to learn to ride with other cyclists in close proximity. This skill isn't useful only for racing elbow-to-elbow in a mass sprint. Century rides often feature several hundred (or thousand) adrenaline-charged cyclists packed together, especially in the early going. The starts of El Tour de Tucson and the Hotter'n Hell Hundred are good examples. When I rode these big events, I was reminded of a land-rush scene in an old Western. Even if you only ride with a few friends, pacelines necessitate getting close, so it pays to learn to be comfortable in company.

For these drills, you need a large grassy area. A soccer field is perfect. Don't worry if there's some snow on it. The drills will be even more fun with the extra bike-handling challenge. And if you take a tumble, your landing will be softer. Ride the same bike you use for cyclocross. Wear your usual winter garb and, of course, your helmet. Break out your protective mountain bike or inline skating gear if you have it. Get several Big Gulp-size paper cups to stuff up your jacket and carry to the field.

Recruit several similarly equipped friends into joining the fun. Warm up by riding to the field. Combined with the 'cross workouts above, you'll be amazed how quickly these drills improve your bike handling.

- **Bump and grind**. With one other cyclist, ride side by side at walking speed. Keep both hands on the bar. Bump hands and elbows. When you're comfortable with that, lean on your friend shoulder-to-shoulder. Try to push him off his line while you maintain yours. Soon you'll be aggressively bumping and pushing without fear of falling. Head butts are legal! To make it even more fun, start side by side in identical low gears and ride at a cup or water bottle placed 30 yards away. The goal is to be the first to reach the cup, unclip a foot and kick it over. Push your pal with your shoulder, throw a few elbows, lean in to push him off course—anything to keep him from beating you to the cup.

- **Bottle snatch**. Put 2 water bottles on the ground about 50 feet away and 5 feet apart. Line up with your friend side-by-side. Be in identical low gears. On "Go!" sprint to your respective bottles. While still on your bike, lean down, pick up your bottle, put it in your cage while doing a 180-degree turn and race back to the starting line. First rider to get there, with his bottle, wins.

- **Cup criterium**. Set 4 cups about 80 feet apart to form a square. With several friends, ride around this cup course as if riding a city block criterium. You should all be in the same low gear to keep speed down. Ride side-by-side to get used to bumping when the bike is leaned in turns. When you're comfortable with a controlled version of this drill, do 5-minute races around the cups. Retain the gear restriction. For variety, ride the course the opposite way or arrange the cups in an L shape so you must turn in both directions.

After doing these drills several times, riding in a bunch on the road will feel much less intimidating.

MOUNTAIN BIKING

When you ride a mountain bike off road, then get back on your road bike, the handling requirements seem so simple. Your confidence is high on smooth pavement after dealing with everything trails throw at you. So if you live in a relatively warm area and trails stay clear in winter, give mountain biking a try. You'll get many of the same bike-handling skills provided by cyclocross.

Too snowy? Not really! Deflate your mountain bike's tires to about 15 psi for maximum traction and flotation. To make icy stretches nearly as safe as dry pavement, install chains or studded tires. Check at a bike shop for these products. The secure traction they provide will amaze you. Of course, be extra careful in traffic when riding on icy or snow-packed roads. Remember, drivers have less control in slick conditions, too. Their steering is hampered and stopping distances are greater.

CHAPTER 28

Three Off-Season Programs

Now let's put it all together and set up individual, 18-week off-season training programs for 3 primary cycling interests.

- **Fitness.** Choose this program if you are new to the sport or want to achieve and maintain general cycling fitness. This program is also an excellent maintenance routine at any time of the year. Use it when your life gets too busy to devote much time to cycling but you want to retain your base fitness.

- **Fast recreation.** This program works well for more experienced cyclists who rode at least 2,000 miles last season and whose goals include centuries, multiday tours and maybe club time trials and training races.

- **Competition.** Racers and even nonracers who want to ride with speed, power and athleticism should choose this program.

This chapter doesn't provide detailed schedules with exact day-to-day workouts. I think you'll agree that doing so for a long, 18-week period would be a mistake, for these reasons:

- The principle of individualization. Because any specific schedule would be generic, it almost certainly wouldn't work for you. One size does not fit all when it comes to training. Never has, never will. Instead, I list principles to guide you as you set up weekly workouts based on your individual goals, available time and energy for cycling.

- Life is never routine. If I say to do an endurance ride on Sunday, some people can't do it because of church, overtime work, family functions or even because it's a stormy day. It's far better to tell you to schedule one endurance workout each *week*. Then you can decide the best *day* for it.

> Right off the bat, I want to say this:
>
> ## *Don't worry if you miss a workout!*
>
> No schedule should be set in stone. Family or job responsibilities, bad weather or a sudden attack of sloth can keep you from training on any given day. When it happens, simply shrug it off and pick up the program as soon as you can. It's consistency over the long haul that counts, not slavish adherence to each day's workout.

- The danger of believing everything you read. If I create a specific schedule, some people will follow it no matter what simply because it's in print. I know you wouldn't make this mistake—but in my many years of experience writing articles and books about training, I know it happens. There's a great temptation to put on blinders and follow a training plan without regard to its applicability.

Next, I lay out basic principles for each of three 6-week cycles. This totals 18 weeks of off-season training. Start in November, December or anytime you want to begin progressively improving each element of your cycling ability.

Fitness Riders

WEEKS 1-6

- **Self-test**. At the beginning of week 1, perform a cycling self-test. The results will enable you to chart your improvement over the off-season. See chapter 20.

- **Rest and recovery**. Devote 2 days each week to rest. No training. It's okay to take an easy walk or use your bike for errands. A third day should be a recovery day with mild aerobic exercise on the bike or crosstraining. Limit a recovery workout to 45 minutes. See chapter 18.

- **Bike handling**. During this 6-week period, schedule 5 bike-handling sessions. They should be separated by at least 6 days. Start with cyclocross or mountain bike trail riding for the initial 4 workouts, then follow with 2 sessions of bike-handling drills. See chapter 27.

- **Resistance training**. The goal for this 6-week period is to accustom your muscles to weight training. Lift 2 times per week, once on your recovery day and again on an easy aerobic day. Separate resistance training sessions by at least 48 hours. See chapter 23. Here's the program:

  - 1-2 sets of 12-20 reps for each upper-body pushing and pulling exercise you choose
  - 1 set of 15-25 reps for back extensions
  - 1 set of 30-50 reps for crunches
  - 1 set of 15-25 reps for each leg exercise you choose

- **Endurance training**. Do one long aerobic workout per week, either on the bike or crosstraining. Duration should start at 45 minutes and increase to 90 minutes at the end of 6 weeks. Keep intensity at the "moderate" level—65 to 80 percent of max heart rate.

- **Other workouts**. Each week, do 1-3 workouts at an easy-to-moderate aerobic pace. These can be outside on the bike, inside on the trainer, or crosstraining. Include stretching after each easy aerobic workout. See chapter 25.

> **CAUTION!** Don't do *any* hard aerobic training during this period. Keep effort no greater than "moderate." If you use a heart monitor, don't exceed 80 percent of your maximum heart rate.

SAMPLE 'FITNESS' WEEK (1-6)	
Monday	Rest day. No training. It's okay to take an easy walk or use your bike for errands.
Tuesday	Easy 0:45 aerobic workout followed by resistance training.
Wednesday	0:45 of bike-handling drills, cyclocross or mountain biking.
Thursday	Easy 0:45 aerobic workout.
Friday	Recovery day. Resistance training after very easy riding or cross-training to warm up.
Saturday	Rest day.
Sunday	Endurance training with a 1:00 ride or crosstraining activity.

WEEKS 7-12

- **Rest and recovery**. Devote 2 days each week to rest. Don't train. It's okay to take an easy walk or use your bike for errands. A third day should be a recovery day with mild aerobic exercise on the bike or crosstraining. Limit these workouts to 45 minutes. See chapter 18.

- **Bike handling**. During this 6-week period, schedule 6 bike-handling sessions. Three should be for cyclocross or mountain biking, and 3 should be devoted to bike-handling drills. Round up several friends to do these drills with you. See chapter 27.

- **Resistance training**. Your goal during this 6-week period is to build strength. Lift twice each week, once on your recovery day and again on an easy aerobic day. Separate resistance training sessions by at least 48 hours. See chapter 23. Here's the program:

  - 2-3 sets of 8-12 reps for each upper-body pushing and pulling exercise you choose
  - 2 sets of 15-25 reps for back extensions
  - 2 sets of 30-50 reps for crunches
  - 2-3 sets of 12-20 reps for each leg exercise you choose

- **Endurance training**. Do one long aerobic workout per week, either on the bike or crosstraining. Ride if weather permits. Workouts should progress from 90 minutes to about 2 hours at the end of the 6-week period. Keep intensity at the "moderate" level—65 to 80 percent of your max heart rate.

- **Other workouts**. Each week, do 1-3 workouts at an easy-to-moderate aerobic pace. These can be outside on the bike, inside on the trainer, or crosstraining. Include stretching after each easy aerobic workout. See chapter 25.

> **CAUTION!** Don't do *any* hard aerobic training during this period. Keep your effort "moderate." If you use a heart monitor, don't exceed 80 percent of your maximum heart rate.

SAMPLE 'FITNESS' WEEK (7-12)	
Monday	Rest day. No training. It's okay to take an easy walk or use your bike for errands.
Tuesday	Easy 1:00 aerobic workout followed by resistance training.
Wednesday	1:00 of bike-handling drills, cyclocross or mountain biking.
Thursday	Easy 1:00 aerobic workout.
Friday	Recovery day. Resistance training after very easy riding or cross-training to warm up.
Saturday	Rest day.
Sunday	Endurance training with a 2:00 ride or crosstraining activity.

WEEKS 13-18

- **Rest and recovery.** Devote 2 days each week to rest. Don't train. It's okay to take an easy walk or use your bike for errands. A third day should be a recovery day with mild aerobic exercise on the bike or crosstraining. Limit these workouts to 45 minutes to ensure recovery. See chapter 18.

- **Bike handling.** During this 6-week period, schedule 5 bike-handling sessions. Phase out cyclocross and emphasize bike-handling drills with friends. See chapter 27.

- **Resistance training.** Your goal during this 6-week period is to convert leg strength to power. Switch to an easier, maintenance workout for your upper body and core. Emphasize higher-repetition leg work. Lift twice per week, once on your recovery day and again on an easy aerobic day. Separate resistance workouts by at least 48 hours. See chapter 23 for exercises. Here's the program:

  - 1-2 sets of 12-15 reps for each upper-body pushing and pulling exercise you choose
  - 1 set of 15-25 reps for back extensions
  - 1 set of 30-50 reps crunches
  - 1-3 sets of 20-40 reps for each leg exercise you choose

- **Endurance training.** Do one long aerobic workout per week, always on the bike if weather permits. Workouts should be in the range of 2½ hours, depending on your goals and available time. Keep intensity "moderate" at 65-80 percent of your max heart rate.

- **Intensity**. Now's the time to convert weight-room strength to cycling power. Once a week, ride hills at a steady pace. The effort should feel "hard" but not exhausting. If you use a heart monitor, reach about 85 percent of your max by the top of the climbs. Alternate sitting and standing. Use gears that allow you to keep cadence around 90 rpm. See chapters 7 and 24.

- **Other workouts**. Each week, do a couple of rides at an easy-to-moderate aerobic pace. These can be outside on the bike, inside on the trainer, or crosstraining. Include a stretching routine after each easy aerobic workout. See chapter 25.

- **Self-test**. At the end of week 18, perform a cycling self-test exactly like the one you did in week 1. Compare the results. I know you'll be pleased with your progress! See chapter 20.

SAMPLE 'FITNESS' WEEK (13-18)	
Monday	Rest day. No training. It's okay to take an easy walk or use your bike for errands.
Tuesday	Easy 1:00 aerobic workout followed by resistance training.
Wednesday	1:00 of bike-handling drills.
Thursday	1:00 hill workout. Do 3-5 climbs of about 3 min. each at 80-90% of max heart rate.
Friday	Recovery day. Resistance training after very easy riding or crosstraining to warm up.
Saturday	Rest day.
Sunday	Endurance training with a 2:30 ride or crosstraining activity.

TIP! Although I've labeled the above program for "fitness riders," it makes an excellent conditioning program for anyone.

Let's say you want to peak in July or August for a long tour or race series. It's wise to avoid training too hard in the off-season. You don't want to burn out before your big event.

In this case, the preceding program works great. Use it for your base, then increase your training 2-3 months before the important date circled on your calendar. I discuss peaking for a key event in chapters 15 and 54.

Fast Recreational Riders

Be sure to keep your goals in mind when you design your personal program. For example, if your objective is fast centuries, make your endurance day a longer ride. If you want to hang with the group on 2-hour weekend-morning jam fests, limit endurance rides to 3 hours and include more intensity, including hill work.

WEEKS 1-6

- **Self-test**. At the beginning of week 1, perform a cycling self-test. The results will enable you to chart your improvement over the off-season. See chapter 20.

- **Rest and recovery**. Devote 2 days each week to rest. No training. It's okay to take an easy walk or use your bike for errands. A third day should be a recovery day with mild aerobic exercise on the bike or crosstraining. Limit these workouts to 45 minutes. See chapter 18.

- **Bike handling**. Do one bike-handling session each week, separated by at least 6 days. Cyclocross is a good choice for the initial 4 sessions because it builds power as well as bike-handling skills. Or, go mountain biking on hilly trails. Devote the remaining 2 sessions to bike-handling drills. See chapter 27.

- **Resistance training**. The goal for this 6-week period is to accustom your muscles to weight training. Lift twice a week, once on your recovery day and again on an easy aerobic day. Separate resistance training sessions by at least 48 hours. See chapter 23. Here's the program:

  - 1-2 sets of 12-20 reps for each upper body pushing and pulling exercise you choose
  - 1 set of 15-25 reps for back extensions
  - 1 set of 30-50 reps for crunches
  - 1-2 sets of 15-25 reps for each leg exercise you choose

- **Endurance training**. Do one long aerobic workout per week, either on the bike or crosstraining. Workouts should start at 60 minutes and increase to at least 2 hours by the end of the 6-week period, depending on your goals and available time. Keep intensity "moderate" at 65-80 percent of your max heart rate.

- **Other workouts**. Each week, do 2-3 workouts at an easy-to-moderate aerobic pace. These can be outside on the bike, inside on the trainer, or crosstraining. You may choose to ride a fixed-gear bike for these workouts (chapter 24). Include stretching after each easy aerobic workout. See chapter 25.

> **CAUTION!** Don't do *any* hard aerobic training during this period. Keep your effort "moderate." If you use a heart monitor, don't exceed 80 percent of your maximum heart rate.

SAMPLE 'FAST RECREATIONAL' WEEK (1-6)	
Monday	Rest day. No training. It's okay to take an easy walk or use your bike for errands.
Tuesday	Easy 1:00 aerobic workout followed by resistance training.
Wednesday	1:00 of bike-handling drills, cyclocross or mountain biking on trails.
Thursday	Easy 1:00 aerobic workout.
Friday	Recovery day. Resistance training after very easy riding or cross-training to warm up.
Saturday	Rest day.
Sunday	Endurance training with a 1:00-2:00 ride or crosstraining.

WEEKS 7-12

- **Self-test**. At the beginning of week 7, perform a cycling self-test. The results (compared to the identical test you took during week 1 and the identical test you'll take in week 18) enable you to measure your improvement over the off-season. See chapter 20.

- **Bike handling**. Do one bike-handling session each week, separated by at least 6 days. Two sessions should be cyclocross to continue building power. Expand bike-handling practice to include friends for competitive drills. See chapter 27.

- **Resistance training**. Strength building is the goal for this period. Lift 2-3 times per week, once on your recovery day and again on easy aerobic days. Separate resistance training sessions by at least 48 hours. See chapter 23. Here's the program:

  - 2-3 sets of 6-10 reps for each upper-body pushing and pulling exercise you choose
  - 2 sets of 15-25 reps for back extensions
  - 2 sets of 30-50 reps for crunches
  - 2-4 sets of 12-20 reps for each leg exercise you choose

- **Endurance training**. Do one long aerobic workout per week, on the bike if weather permits. Otherwise, crosstrain. Workouts should progress to as many as 3 hours, depending on your goals and available time. Keep intensity "moderate"—65 to about 80 percent of your max heart rate.

- **Other workouts**. Each week, do 2 workouts at an easy-to-moderate aerobic pace. These can be outside on the bike, inside on the trainer, or crosstraining. You can use a fixed-gear bike for the first 3 weeks (chapter 24). Include stretching after each easy aerobic workout. See chapter 25.

- **Intensity**. Once a week, do 1 hour of interval training on the bike indoors or out. Do a variety of intervals, but never exceed 90 percent of your maximum heart rate. Emphasize low-cadence, high-resistance pedaling to begin the process of converting weight-room strength to cycling-specific power. See chapters 7 and 24.

> **CAUTION!** High-resistance pedaling can be hard on your knees. If you experience any knee pain, stop doing these workouts immediately and return to easy, low-resistance spinning until the problem is resolved. If knee pain is often a problem, I recommend getting to the bottom of it with an RBR book I coauthored, *Andy Pruitt's Medical Guide for Cyclists*. In it, you'll learn how to diagnose, treat and prevent 8 different knee injuries cyclists may experience.

SAMPLE 'FAST RECREATIONAL' WEEK (7-12)

Monday	Rest day. No training. It's okay to take an easy walk or use your bike for errands.
Tuesday	Easy 1:00 aerobic workout followed by resistance training.
Wednesday	1:00 of bike-handling drills, cyclocross or mountain biking on trails.
Thursday	1:00-1:15 interval workout.
Friday	Recovery day. Resistance training after very easy riding or cross-training to warm up.
Saturday	Easy 1:00 aerobic workout.
Sunday	Endurance training with a 2:00-3:00 ride or crosstraining.

> **TIP!** Make week 10 a "rest week." You've been working progressively harder for 9 weeks. Now back off and give your body time to consolidate the gains. Cut your total workout time by 1/3. In the weight room, reduce the number of sets of each exercise by the same fraction. Reduce intensity, too. You'll begin week 11 with renewed energy.

WEEKS 13-18

- **Bike handling**. During these final 6 weeks of off-season training, do one bike-handling session each week, separated by at least 6 days. By this time, you will know whether you need to emphasize cyclocross for power or whether your bike handling needs more work. In the latter case, devote all 6 sessions to bike-handling drills. See chapter 27.

- **Resistance training**. The objective of this period is to begin converting strength to cycling power. Lift twice per week, once on your recovery day and again on an easy aerobic day. Separate resistance training sessions by at least 48 hours. Reduce your upper-body and core work to a maintenance level. Use the extra energy for harder leg workouts. See chapter 23. Here's the program:

  - 1-2 sets of 12-20 reps for each upper-body pushing and pulling exercise you choose.
  - 1 set of 15-25 reps for back extensions.
  - 1 set of 30-50 reps for crunches.
  - 2-3 sets of 25-50 reps for each leg exercise you choose.

> **CAUTION!** Combining high-rep leg work in the weight room with interval sessions on the bike can result in too much intensity. If you lack enthusiasm for this hard work, you may be overdoing it. Reduce weight room leg workouts to one per week.

- **Endurance training**. Do one long aerobic workout per week, always on the bike if weather permits. Make every effort to get on the road. Rides should progress to as long as 4 hours, depending on your goals and available time. Keep intensity "moderate"—65 to 80 percent of your max heart rate.

- **Other workouts**. Each week, do 2 workouts at an easy-to-moderate aerobic pace. These can be outside on the bike, inside on the trainer, or crosstraining. Include stretching after each easy aerobic workout. See chapter 25.

- **Intensity**. Once a week, do a 90-minute interval session on the road or a 60-minute interval session on the trainer. Only rarely exceed 90 percent of your maximum heart rate. Gradually progress from the low-cadence, high-resistance pedaling you did in weeks 7-12. Now you want to do higher-cadence intervals at higher heart rates for added power and acceleration. See chapters 7 and 24.

- **Self-test**. At the end of week 18, repeat the cycling self-test you did in weeks 1 and 7. Compare the results to the 3 tests to get an objective view of your improvement. See chapter 20.

> **TIP!** Plan weeks 14 and 18 as "rest weeks" to let your body consolidate the gains you've made. As you did in week 10, cut your total workout time by about 1/3. In the weight room, reduce the number of sets of each exercise by the same fraction. Reduce intensity on your hard day. This tapering is especially important in week 18 so you're rested for your final self-test.

SAMPLE 'FAST RECREATIONAL' WEEK (13-18)	
Monday	Rest day. No training. It's okay to take an easy walk or use your bike for errands.
Tuesday	Easy 1:00-1:15 aerobic workout followed by resistance training.
Wednesday	1:00 of bike-handling drills, cyclocross or mountain biking on trails.
Thursday	1:00-1:15 interval workout.
Friday	Recovery day. Resistance training after very easy riding or cross-training to warm up.
Saturday	Easy 1:00 aerobic workout.
Sunday	Endurance training with a 2:00-4:00 ride.

Competitors

If you want to race next summer, off-season planning becomes more difficult than for fitness or fast recreational riders. Performance is more important, for one thing. Racing demands time, energy and money, so you certainly want positive returns. Committing to competition is likely to mean time away from other parts of your life, too. It's essential to train smart. Here are 3 key guidelines:

1. **Plan your program to reflect your goals**. If you're aiming for criteriums that won't exceed an hour, don't do 4-hour endurance rides twice a week. Instead, concentrate on speed. Conversely, if you want to do well in road races, endurance should be a priority.

2. **Know your strengths and weaknesses**. If you need climbing power, plan extensive weight room work and include cyclocross early in the off-season. Gradually begin to ride hills fairly soon. If your sprint is weak, work on leg speed on the indoor trainer.

3. **Take it personally**. Any off-season program I devise for competitive riders can't cover all goals. You need to evaluate my suggestions, then modify them for your unique individual situation. Be flexible. Pay attention to your self-tests. Their results will tell you if your training is working or if it has taken you down a dark alley to stalled progress and fatigue.

WEEKS 1-6

- **Self-test**. At the beginning of week 1, perform a cycling self-test. The results help you evaluate the effectiveness of your off-season program. See chapter 20.

- **Rest and recovery**. Devote one day each week to rest. No training. It's okay to take an easy walk or use your bike for errands. A second day should be a recovery day with mild aerobic exercise on the bike or crosstraining. Limit these workouts to 60 minutes. See chapter 18.

- **Bike handling**. Do one bike-handling session each week, separated by at least 6 days. Cyclocross is a good choice for the initial 4 sessions because it builds power as well as bike-handling skills. Or, ride a mountain bike on hilly trails. The remaining 2 sessions should be devoted to bike-handling drills. See chapter 27.

- **Resistance training**. The goal for these 6 weeks is to accustom your muscles to weight training. Lift 2 or 3 times per week, once on your recovery day and again on easy aerobic days. Separate resistance training sessions by at least 48 hours. See chapter 23. Here's the program:

  - 1-2 sets of 12-20 reps for each upper-body pushing and pulling exercise you choose
  - 1 set of 15-25 reps for back extensions
  - 1 set of 30-50 reps for crunches
  - 1 set of 15-25 reps for each leg exercise you choose

- **Endurance training**. Do one long aerobic workout per week, either on the bike or crosstraining. Workouts should start at 90 minutes and increase to at least 2:30 at the end of the 6 weeks, depending on your goals and available time. Keep intensity "moderate"—65-80 percent of max heart rate.

- **Other workouts**. Each week, do 2 or 3 workouts at an easy-to-moderate aerobic pace. These can be outside on the bike, inside on the trainer, or crosstraining. You can use a fixed-gear bike for these workouts (chapter 24). Include stretching after each easy aerobic workout. See chapter 25.

- **Intensity**. Don't do any hard aerobic training during the first 3 weeks of this period. Keep your effort "moderate." If you use a heart monitor, don't exceed 80 percent of your maximum heart rate. In the last 3 weeks, gradually increase effort on the bike or indoor trainer by including some 5- to 10-minute time trial efforts at about 85 percent of max heart rate. See chapters 7 and 24.

> **TIP!** Make week 4 a "rest week." You've been working progressively harder for 3 weeks. Now back off and give your body time to consolidate the gains. Cut your total workout time by 1/3. In the weight room, reduce the number of sets of each exercise by the same fraction. Reduce intensity a notch, too. You'll begin week 5 with renewed energy.

SAMPLE 'COMPETITOR' WEEK (1-6)	
Monday	Rest day. No training. It's okay to take an easy walk or use your bike for errands.
Tuesday	Easy 1:00 aerobic workout followed by resistance training.
Wednesday	1:00-1:30 of bike-handling drills, cyclocross or mountain biking on trails.
Thursday	Easy 1:30 aerobic workout.
Friday	Recovery day. Resistance training after very easy riding or cross-training to warm up.
Saturday	1:00 of aerobic riding or crosstraining.
Sunday	Endurance training with 1:30-2:30 of riding or crosstraining.

WEEKS 7-12

- **Self-test**. At the end of week 8 (a "rest week"), perform a cycling self-test with the same protocol as the one you did to start week 1. Then you may want to modify your program, depending on how the tests compare. See chapter 20.

- **Bike handling**. Do one bike-handling session each week. Each session should be separated by at least 6 days. Cyclocross is a good choice if you need to build power as well as bike-handling skills. If your power is solid but riding skills aren't, do bike-handling drills. For at least 3 sessions, have friends join you in grass criteriums so you get a feel for bumping shoulders and handlebars in a tight pack. See chapter 27.

- **Resistance training**. Strength is the goal for these 6 weeks. Lift 2 or 3 times per week, once on your recovery day and again on easy aerobic days. Separate resistance training sessions by at least 48 hours. See chapter 23. Here's the program:

  - 2-4 sets of 6-10 reps for each upper-body pushing and pulling exercise you choose.
  - 2 sets of 15-25 reps for back extensions.
  - 2 sets of 30-50 reps crunches.
  - 3-5 sets of 12-20 reps for each leg exercise you choose.

- **Endurance training**. Do one long aerobic workout per week, on the bike if possible. If not, crosstrain. Workouts should start at 2 hours and increase to 4 or more by the end of this period (depending on your goals and available time). Keep intensity "moderate"—65-80 percent of max heart rate.

- **Other workouts**. Each week, do 2 or 3 workouts at an easy-to-moderate aerobic pace. These can be outside on the bike, inside on the trainer, or crosstraining. You can use a fixed-gear bike for weeks 7-9 (chapter 24). Include stretching after each easy aerobic workout. See chapter 25.

- **Intensity**. Once a week, do intervals on the bike or indoor trainer. See chapters 7 and 24.

> **TIP!** Plan weeks 8 and 12 as "rest weeks." You've worked progressively harder for 3-week periods. You need to back off to let your body consolidate gains. Cut your total workout time by about 1/3. In the weight room, reduce the number of sets by the same fraction. Reduce intensity a notch, too. You'll enter each 3-week "build" period with renewed energy.

SAMPLE 'COMPETITOR' WEEK (7-12)	
Monday	Rest day. No training. It's okay to take an easy walk or use your bike for errands.
Tuesday	Easy 1:15 aerobic workout followed by resistance training.
Wednesday	1:30-2:00 of bike-handling drills, cyclocross or mountain biking on trails.
Thursday	1:30 aerobic workout.
Friday	Recovery day. Resistance training after very easy riding or cross-training to warm up.
Saturday	1:30 of aerobic riding or crosstraining.
Sunday	Endurance training with a 2:00-4:00 ride or crosstraining activity.

WEEKS 13-18

- **Bike handling**. Do one bike-handling session each week, separated by at least 6 days. Eliminate cyclocross because you'll be doing intervals on the road or on the trainer to develop power. Instead, devote this session to honing your bike-handling skills. Have friends join you in grass criteriums so you get a feel for bumping shoulders and handlebars in a tight pack. See chapter 27.

- **Resistance training**. The goal for these 6 weeks is converting strength to cycling-specific power. Lift twice each week, once on your recovery day and again on an easy aerobic day. Separate resistance training sessions by at least 48 hours. See chapter 23. Here's the program:

  - 1-2 sets of 12-20 reps for each upper-body pushing and pulling exercise you choose.
  - 1 set of 15-25 reps for back extensions.
  - 1 set of 30-50 reps crunches.

— 1-2 sets of 25-50 reps for each leg exercise you choose. Consult chapter 24 for additional, specific ideas.

> **CAUTION!** Combining high-rep leg work in the weight room with interval sessions on the bike can result in too much intensity. If you lack enthusiasm for this hard work, you may be overdoing it. Reduce weight room leg workouts to one per week.

- **Endurance training.** Do one long aerobic workout each week, always on the bike unless the weather is abysmal. Rides should reach 4 hours or more at the end of this period, depending on your goals and available time. Most of each ride should be done at a moderate, steady pace of about 70-85 percent of your max heart rate. But also include some hill jams, sprints for city limit signs and time trial-like efforts to chase down frisky riding companions.

- **Other workouts.** Each week, do 2 or 3 workouts at an easy-to-moderate aerobic pace. These can be outside on the bike, inside on the trainer, or crosstraining. Include stretching after each easy aerobic workout. See chapter 25.

- **Intensity.** Once a week, do intervals on the bike or indoor trainer. See chapters 7 and 24

- **Self-test.** At the end of week 18, perform your cycling self-test. Compare the results to the previous 2 tests to get an objective view of your off-season improvement.

> **TIP!** Plan week 16 as a "rest week." You've worked progressively harder, so it's time to back off and let your body consolidate the gains. Cut your total workout time by about 1/3. In the weight room, reduce the number of sets by the same fraction. Reduce intensity a notch, too.

SAMPLE 'COMPETITOR' WEEK (13-18)	
Monday	Rest day. No training. It's okay to take an easy walk or use your bike for errands.
Tuesday	Easy 1:15 aerobic workout followed by resistance training.
Wednesday	Up to 2:00 of bike-handling drills.
Thursday	2:00 interval workout.
Friday	Recovery day. Resistance training after very easy riding or crosstraining to warm up.
Saturday	1:30 of aerobic riding or crosstraining.
Sunday	Endurance training with a 3:00-4:00 ride.

Happy campers: The Saturn pro team collects base miles during pre-season training in California.

TRAINING CAMPS

One final thing to consider when planning your off-season training: a spring cycling camp. Riders on pro teams routinely meet in a warm-weather location in January to log miles, get to know each other better and plan strategy. Recreational riders can enjoy spring training camp benefits, too.

- **Learn from coaches**. Most camps combine skull sessions with daily rides. You get to hear experienced coaches and ask questions about everything from riding position to nutrition to peaking for your big events.

- **Escape winter**. After several months of spending as much time dressing for riding as actually riding, you get to be in warm weather again.

- **Meet other cyclists.** Riders from all parts of the U.S. (and other countries) come to training camps to jump-start their seasons. It's a great way to meet people and develop a network of cycling friends. It might pay off with a place to stay when you travel to an event.

- **Build base miles**. A week of cycling in early spring provides a solid mileage foundation for the new season.

> **CAUTION!** I've seen riders let their enthusiasm overcome good judgment at early-season camps. After several months of crosstraining and pedaling indoors, when they finally get on the road with their leg warmers off they pile up a huge mileage week. Sometimes this results in an injury and a forced layoff just when they're eager to begin the season. Most camps offer optional daily distances. All you need is the self-control to resist doing the long loop every day.

Heed the words of coach Chris Carmichael one more time: "Training camps are great. But there's a tendency to do too much too soon. Don't jump from 150 miles a week at home to 600 miles during a camp week. Mileage increases of over 20 percent can cause problems. If you have to ride more miles than you're accustomed to, do some days extremely easy."

PART 3

SPRING TRAINING

Introduction

In part 2, I said that winter is perhaps the most important time of the training year. This opinion is shared by Lance Armstrong's coach, Chris Carmichael. Remember his revelation: "Lance wins the Tour de France in November, December and January."

But April and May are just as important. For recreational riders as well as pros, spring represents a crucial transition between winter's foundation and the summer season. Much of your off-season work can be wasted in these 8 weeks if you do too little—or too much. This section is about doing it just right.

Without the proper approach in spring, you won't build on the crosstraining and strength work you did from December through March. You won't be any faster, stronger or more skilled in July than you were at Christmas. But if you get carried away with enthusiasm and train too hard and too long in the 8 transition weeks, you'll be tired when the season arrives. The fervor that fueled your training in April will be long gone. You'll hate your bike.

Don't let either awful fate befall you.

HOW TO USE THIS SECTION

The goal is to use spring to develop strength, power and speed that's ready for prime time—no matter what "prime time" means for you. I've arranged the information in the order you need it to set up your most-effective spring training program.

Start by reviewing the material in chapter 29 about goal setting, measuring intensity and proper nutrition. Even if you think you know about these subjects, this review is important for understanding my approach.

Chapters 30, 31 and 32 are about foundation work—long rides, muscular endurance and lactate threshold workouts. You worked on these abilities in winter. In spring, they must be improved.

I cover the specific skills of climbing and sprinting in chapters 33 and 34. Winter fitness allows you to climb competently and sprint a little. By focusing on these skills for 8 spring weeks, you can get significantly better.

Spring is also when group training rides begin in most areas of the country (as opposed to winter social rides). Everyone is eager for the season, so group rides often get competitive. You'll improve by joining in. But you must be careful. Chapter 35 tells you how to use these rides for your own needs while still contributing to the goals of the group.

It's important to kick up the intensity a notch in spring, but increased training volume and effort can lead to overtraining and injuries. Chapters 36 and 37 show you how to fix problems so your season isn't compromised.

And because spring training is often defined by spring weather—chilly and wet—chapter 38 covers dressing correctly, which can mean the difference between shrugging off the rain or being miserable. Also included are bike-handling tips for slick conditions.

In part 2, *Off-Season Training*, I give guidelines for setting up a program divided into three 6-week blocks. I include a sample week's schedule for each block. In chapter 39, I'll be even more specific about training plans. That chapter includes 8-week schedules for the 3 divisions of roadies we've established:

- **Fitness cyclist**. Choose this if you are just getting started in the sport or want to achieve and maintain general cycling fitness.

- **Fast recreational cyclist**. This is the program for more experienced riders who want to perform well in group rides, in centuries and on multiday tours.

- **Competitive cyclist**. This is for licensed racers. And it's for those who want to ride athletically with speed and power in club training rides and events.

Remember that my schedules are flexible. Everyone has different goals, varying amounts of training time and disparate abilities. Use my schedules as starting points for devising your own optimum plan.

Also, recognize that you don't have to start this "spring program" in the spring. What you'll read works during any 2-month period if your goal is to convert general fitness into cycling-specific speed, power and endurance.

CHAPTER 29

Setting the Stage

I had a short and inglorious basketball career, marked mostly by broken bones in my foot for 2 consecutive years. (Those canvas basketball shoes in the '60s didn't provide much support.) But my predominant hoop memory is of the coach harping endlessly on the importance of what he called "fundamentals."

We spent most of our practices drilling on free throws, passing and dribbling. I was bored. I wanted to play basketball, not practice its parts. We even mocked his endlessly repeated mantra: "Fundamentals come first."

But you know what? Coach was right. We'd have been a much better team if we'd concentrated on those basic skills as much as he wanted us to. In the same way, before you can begin a training program for cycling, you need to know the fundamentals. I discuss these issues in part 1, *Foundation Information*, but we need to review them here in the context of beginning the season with spring training.

Even if you think you know all about setting goals and determining intensity, please read this version of the information again. Coach would be happy!

CHOOSE YOUR GOALS

Your cycling objectives probably are based on summer events. Maybe you're aiming at a best-ever century or a PR in the local 10-mile time trial. Maybe you want to be strong every day on a week-long tour. Before you set up your spring training schedule (or follow one of the programs in chapter 39) take a few minutes to write out the goals you want to achieve this summer. You need to establish them in order to shape your training.

When setting goals, remember the basic rule of fitness—you can't be your best for everything all the time. If your endurance is high, your sprint speed probably won't be. If you can outsprint everyone on the local club ride, your long-distance stamina is likely to be lacking.

Think of fitness as a geometrical figure with power, speed, endurance and recovery as the 4 corners. If all are equal, you've got a square—and none of these attributes will be developed more than the others. You'll be an "all rounder," which is fine if you don't mind not being exceptionally good at anything. On the other hand, if you work hard on one trait—say, endurance—then the square will get pulled into an elongated form. Endurance will be prominent but the other traits will recede. Your task is to decide which ability you want to emphasize, then design a spring program that enables you to meet that goal.

To get you thinking, here are sample goals and a glance at the training you'd need to meet them:

- **A century PR**. You need the endurance to last 100 miles, a good sense of pacing and a heightened "cruising speed"—the ability to ride relatively fast for hours without using excessive energy.

- **A time trial PR**. You need to maximize the speed you can maintain at or slightly above your lactate threshold. If the course is hilly, you need some anaerobic power, too, so you can go slightly into oxygen debt on the climbs and recover on the descents, thus keeping your average speed high.

- **Short road races and criteriums**. Endurance isn't a major factor in these races. Instead, the key is speed to close gaps and hang with a fast pack. This speed also needs to be repeatable, especially in criteriums with their dozens of accelerations out of corners.

- **Tours of 5-10 days**. Once you have the endurance to ride 75-100 miles during a one-day event, you need to develop the endurance to do it day after day on a tour.

FOUR WAYS TO MEASURE YOUR INTENSITY

Now the question becomes: How should training effort be measured? This is crucial, especially in spring when ride intensity increases.

Train too easily and you won't stress your body enough to improve. Train too hard without adequate recovery and your performance will deteriorate. You won't even have enough energy to take out the trash. You'll get grumpy and unpleasant to be around.

Here are 4 methods for determining how hard you're working on the bike:

1. Speed. For runners, there's a strong correlation between speed and effort. A track offers controlled conditions. A 75-second lap one week probably takes the same effort as running that speed the next week. Things aren't as simple on a bike. Because you're riding on roads exposed to the elements, external factors such as wind have a large effect. It's easy to go 20 mph with a strong tailwind but much harder—maybe impossible—to ride back into the gale at that pace. And, of course, riding in the draft of a group of cyclists is much easier than time trialing on your own. Speed on a bike rarely correlates well with how hard your body is working. Even so, I recommend installing a cyclecomputer for the useful data it provides for certain types of training. All computers tell you time, distance, average speed and maximum speed, and some models record elevation gain.

2. Heart rate. Heart rate monitoring has revolutionized training in the last 15 years by revealing how hard the cardiovascular system is working. But this information isn't perfect. Heart rate can vary widely for a given amount of power output. It's influenced by factors such as hydration and muscle fatigue. For example, if you ride hard for an hour, your heart rate will gradually rise even though you maintain a steady pace. This phenomenon, called *cardiac drift*, is caused by overheating and dehydration. This means heart rate isn't a number you can count on to reveal intensity. You have to know how to interpret what you see on the monitor.

3. Wattage. The best way to determine how much power you're generating is to measure it directly in watts. Some indoor trainers and health club exercise bikes have wattage readouts, but it has proven more difficult to develop lightweight, affordable and weather-sealed systems for outdoor use. One unit, the German-made SRM, use strain gauges mounted in the crankarms. Another brand, the PowerTap, puts its strain gauges in the rear hub. Heart monitor manufacturer Polar has a device that uses chain tension to produce a power reading. CicloSport's unit does it with calculations based on your weight, speed and vertical gain. In chapter 42, I go into detail about these devices and how to use them.

4. RPE. Measuring watts is the best way to judge your training load. But the old-fashioned way—listening to your body—still works, too, although we've given it a modern twist. It's called "rating of perceived exertion" (RPE). It's free, the instructions are easy and it's the method I'll emphasize for spring training.

LEARN YOUR RPE

The Borg Scale for RPE uses numbers from 6 to 20, roughly corresponding to heart rate. Judge your exertion from 6 to 20, then simply add a zero to get heart rate in beats per minute (bpm). Thus, an RPE of 18 is "very hard" and denotes a heart rate of around 180 bpm, assuming that max heart rate is about 200.

Because max heart rates differ dramatically among riders, I prefer to use a simpler RPE scale of 1 to 10. In this system, a rating of 1 means you're motionless, comatose in front of the tube. Ratings from 2 to 4 denote levels of mild activity, such as walking or raking leaves. Those numbers aren't important for training. Here are the ones that are:

RATING OF PERCEIVED EXERTION (RPE)

5 = an easy spin along the bike path

6 = light effort

7 = breathing steadily and rhythmically

8 = breathing harder but not panting

9 = beginning to gasp and can't converse

10 = riding as hard as you can

With some practice, you'll be able to stay at a given RPE level as you ride. The key transitions are from 7 to 8 (when you become aware of your breathing and conversation becomes difficult) and 8 to 9 (when breathing goes from steady and measured to gasping). When you reach 9, talking stops and your quads burn.

PUT IT ALL TOGETHER

The ideal way to gauge intensity is to combine all 4 methods. By checking heart rate, speed and wattage, while at the same time judging perceived exertion, you'll have a precise measure of your absolute effort—and how your body is reacting to it.

EXAMPLE! Suppose you're doing repeats up a hill that takes about 5 minutes to climb. When you feel good, your heart rate hits 160 bpm in the last minute of the climb. Your wattage averages 300. Your RPE is 9.

On another day, the climb feels as hard as usual, maybe a bit harder. But your heart rate won't go above 150 bpm and your average wattage is 275. This combination indicates that you haven't recovered from past training. You're tired. You should rest and re-hydrate before attempting another intense training session.

In this example, if you had relied only on how you felt, you would have thought that all was well—you were climbing as hard as you usually do. But had you keyed off the depressed heart rate and the lower wattage readout, they would have led you astray by telling you to go harder. Only by combining all these measures of intensity do you get an accurate picture.

But here's an important point: RPE alone works nearly as well. For this reason, and because you may not have a watts meter or care to invest hundreds of dollars in one, I'll base this section's training plans on RPE. In addition, because many of you probably do have a heart monitor (good ones now cost less than $100), I provide an easy way to convert RPE to heart rate training zones at the bottom of this page.

LACTATE THRESHOLD REFRESHER

Lactate threshold (LT) is an essential training concept. Here's a refresher course to complement chapter 10 so we all understand it.

LT is defined as that level of exertion at which your body begins to produce more *lactate* (a byproduct of energy production) than it can use. LT is the intensity you can sustain for a time trial of at least 30 minutes. It's your maximum "steady state" intensity—you can sustain it, but just barely. In trained riders, LT is about 90-92 percent of max heart rate. An RPE on the border of 8 and 9 corresponds to your LT.

Top riders frequently train from slightly below to slightly above LT. This helps them raise the speed they can sustain without going into oxygen debt. Coach Chris Carmichael says much of Lance Armstrong's success can be attributed to his ability to climb faster than his rivals without going anaerobic. On successive climbs, Lance can cruise while others are working harder to maintain the pace. Can you guess who has more in his tank on the final climb to the finish?

LT is important for recreational riders, too. Developing a solid "cruising speed" means that you can ride faster centuries, climb better without suffering so much and keep up with strong groups on weekend rides.

FIND YOUR LT

Lactate threshold can be pinpointed with a lab test. The technician gradually increases the resistance as you pedal an ergometer. Blood is drawn every couple of minutes. The blood is tested for lactate concentrations. A lactate level of 4 millimoles per liter of blood is usually considered to be a person's LT. This can be correlated with heart rate and power output.

If you have a heart rate monitor, there's a simpler way to find LT. Do an all-out time trial of 30-60 minutes. Your average heart rate for the duration of the effort will be close to your lab-determined LT. If you also have a watts meter, average watts for the test time trial shows how much power you generate. You can use this figure to determine LT intensity, just like using average heart rate. Once you know your LT heart rate, it can be roughly correlated to RPE using this chart:

TRAINING ZONE CONVERSIONS

Zone 1: 65-74% of LT heart rate equals RPE 6

Zone 2: 75-84% of LT heart rate equals RPE 7

Zone 3: 85-94% of LT heart rate equals RPE 8

Zone 4: 95-105% of LT heart rate equals RPE 9

You can also come pretty close by feel. Gradually increase effort until you reach the point where breathing stops being regular and becomes forced. LT is the level of exertion just below where you lose control of your breathing and begin to pant and gasp. Practice treading on the edge of this threshold. Increase your pace until you start to lose control of your breathing, then back off slightly until breathing settles down. Playing on this "red line" of performance is the best way to learn about your LT—and get an intense workout.

Remember that you don't need a heart monitor for training. Once you get a feel for perceived exertion, RPE works just as well.

FOUR RULES FOR SPRING WEATHER

There's one sure thing about spring training: You're going to encounter spring weather. In most parts of the country, this means wind and rain, possibly sleet and snow—and the occasional nice day. It's depressing to think about riding into the fury of the vernal equinox. But if you're prepared, you'll be able to ride in (and enjoy) anything that April and May can throw at you. Just follow these 4 rules:

1. Get a beater bike. Nothing makes training in lousy weather more doable than having a bike set up for it. Check pages 82-85 for a full discussion. Any bike will work as long as it has:

- **Your regular riding position**. Be sure that saddle height, setback and reach to the handlebar is the same as on your summer bike.

- **An old frame and components**. It's best to ride a tough old frame and components that you don't mind getting gritty. This way, you can save your good bike for dry roads.

- **Fenders**. These keep your back, feet and bike relatively clean when roads are wet. Fenders also prevent rear-wheel spray from dousing your riding companions. You'll be more welcome in a group.

2. Get the right clothes. No matter how nasty the conditions, the right combination of base layers, insulating garments and shells will keep you warm, if not perfectly dry. I discuss specifics in chapter 38.

3. Get the right attitude. Remember the cardinal rule of riding in bad weather: Conditions always seem worse from inside a warm house than they do from the saddle of your bike. When you're lying on the couch, warm and cozy and watching the rain beat on the window, cycling is simply unimaginable. But if you get out there, properly equipped, it's not only possible, it's fun. Some of your most memorable rides will be rainy ones. And think of the psychological boost you can get from training in bad conditions. You're riding and getting fitter while everyone else is cowering inside, moaning about the weather. You're learning essential wet-road bike-handling techniques, too. As the old saying goes, you'd better train in the rain because some day you'll be racing in it (or riding a century in it, or touring in it). See chapter 38 for advice on riding in challenging spring weather.

4. Get an indoor trainer. Okay, there'll be some days when even a bombproof attitude won't get you out the door. When the gale is too nasty or roads are dangerously slippery, it's smarter to stay indoors. It's much better to sit on a trainer for an hour than on the couch all afternoon, wishing the sun would shine.

The best indoor workouts for spring are hard, intense and short. Get on the trainer, warm up for 15 minutes, do a structured interval workout, cool down for 10 minutes, and shower. In most cases, 60 minutes is the maximum you should ever spend. In chapter 26, I describe a selection of trainer workouts that fit this time frame.

> **TIP!** Don't overlook your local health club's spinning classes. Some clubs offer cycling-specific workouts led by experienced riders. My teammates in Boulder, Colorado, sometimes meet at the club on sloppy spring Sundays and treat spinning as a group ride.

NUTRITIONAL GUIDELINES

As you increase training time and intensity, you need more food to fuel your efforts.

> **CAUTION!** One of the worst mistakes riders make is cutting back on calories when they're training hard. Yes, they lose weight. But without sufficient glycogen in their muscles, high-quality workouts are impossible. Stored glycogen is directly related to the amount of carbohydrate consumed. See chapter 16.

Not eating enough has more dangerous repercussions than merely lousy workouts. According to sports nutritionists, most cases of overtraining are due to chronic glycogen depletion. Riders try to lose weight at the same time they increase their training volume. At first this strategy works, but eventually they suffer the consequences of frequently "riding on empty." Their performances suffer, they get grouchy and irritable, and finally they lose interest in exercise or competition. It's essential to eat enough to fuel your training.

Lance Armstrong is famous for weighing his food portions. He wants to eat the exact number of calories to fuel his workouts while still reaching his ideal racing weight. But for the rest of us, sports nutrition doesn't have to be rocket science and portions don't have to be precise. You don't need any complicated math to figure out how much carbohydrate to eat.

To make sure your muscles are well-stocked with glycogen, simply increase the percentage of carbohydrate in your meals. Eat more fruit, cereal, vegetables, pasta and whole-grain bread while cutting down on meat, butter, salad dressing and other fatty foods. On the bike during rides of 1-2 hours, drink at least one bottle of carbohydrate-rich sports drink every hour. On longer rides, nibble on fruit bars or energy bars at the rate of about 40 grams of carbohydrate per hour. That's about one energy bar or 6 fig bars.

After any training ride, remember to eat some carbohydrate as soon as possible. Studies have shown that muscle cells are most receptive to storing glycogen in the 2 hours after endurance exercise. Take advantage of this "glycogen window" by consuming about one gram of carbohydrate for each pound of bodyweight. A 150-pound rider, for example, needs 150 grams of carbo. This is roughly equal to washing down a banana and bagel with a glass of sports drink. Or, you can use a commercial post-exercise carbo-replacement drink such as Endurox R4.

Won't these carbo calories make you gain weight? No, not in most cases. For example, I've found that 10-12 hours a week of riding and other exercise such as hiking and weight training allow me to eat virtually anything and maintain my best weight—as long as I don't go too heavy on fat. I eat lots of carbohydrate and take it easy on cookies, muffins and ice cream. But I don't deny myself reasonable portions of these treats when I want them. Your metabolism and tendency to gain or lose weight may be somewhat different from mine, but the "10-12 hours per week" rule seems to work for many riders.

REACHING IDEAL CYCLING WEIGHT

Low body weight is an obsession with pro riders. They know that a loss of only 5 pounds can reduce their time on a 5-mile climb by several minutes, everything else being equal. That's a huge improvement that can mean better race results. So, it comes as no surprise that pros have tried medically unsound methods to lose weight. Some riders have even fallen prey to psychological problems due to their obsession with light weight.

> **EXAMPLE!** In a recent report, a Spanish pro with the ONCE team was said to suffer from bulimia. He was putting fingers down his throat so he'd vomit after meals, preventing the absorption of too many calories. He received professional counseling and the team kept him on, convinced he'd be able to recover.

Obviously, single-minded determination to weigh as little as possible can have extremely negative effects. Before you set some arbitrary weight-loss goal, make sure you really do need to reduce. The classic way to find out is with body fat analysis. It can be done using several techniques, including underwater weighing, skinfold calipers or electrical impedance. Most male endurance athletes have 5-10 percent body fat. Women with the same degree of fitness usually carry 3-5 percentage points more because of fat's role in child bearing.

These percentages aren't gospel, they're highly individual. According to Peter Janssen, M.D., in *Lactate Threshold Training* (Human Kinetics Publishing), the body fat of male endurance athletes may vary "from extremely low percentages (4-5%) to somewhat higher values (12-13%), but every athlete has his or her ideal fat percentage which does not change.... A too high or too low percentage will prevent the athlete from reaching top condition."

> **TIP!** What's the best way to tell if you need to lose weight? Your body-fat percentage can be evaluated in a lab, at your doctor's office or even at your health club. But here's a quicker, easier and cheaper technique: Get naked, stand in front of a full-length mirror, and bounce up and down. If something jiggles that shouldn't, you're carrying too much weight. Don't laugh—this is often as accurate as fancy lab tests. It won't give you a percentage, but your eyes don't lie.

SIX WEIGHT-LOSS STRATEGIES

If you're always hungry, feel out of gas and your motivation to train and race is low, you may be under-eating in an attempt to reach unnaturally low body weight. But if your energy is fine and you do need to lose weight, try these 6 proven techniques.

1. **Consume more carbo and less fat**. I don't want to beat a dead horse (much less eat one). But as mentioned, eating more carbohydrate in the form of fruit, cereal, vegetables, pasta and whole grain bread is the key. Cut down on meat, dairy products, baked goods, salad dressing and other fatty, high-calorie foods.

2. **Reduce the size of each meal slightly**. Don't eliminate a whole meal in order to cut calories. Simply eat one serving of meat instead of 2, stop at one glass of wine, eat 2 cookies instead of 3, and so on. You won't miss the lost calories this way.

3. **Snack**. That's right—snacking between meals is often discouraged in weight-loss programs, but it's actually quite helpful. Six small meals per day provide a steady source of energy, while 3 meals encourage you to stuff yourself because you arrive at the table so hungry.

4. **Get on the scale only once per week**. Weigh yourself under the same conditions—for example, upon rising and after visiting the bathroom. But weigh only once per week! Any weight loss achieved from one day to the next is probably due to dehydration rather than actual fat loss. It's misleading.

5. **Monitor your feelings of hunger and energy**. Any fit athlete who becomes tired and lethargic is probably glycogen deficient. If you're ravenous most of the time, eat! Training is hard work. In the words of renowned coach Eddie Borysewicz, you have to "eat like a farmer" in order to fuel cycling's level of manual labor.

6. **Err on the side of slightly too much body fat**. Most riders who get into trouble do so because they tried to lose "that last 5 pounds." You won't go wrong if you're a bit heavy. At worst, you won't climb quite as well as you could. That's no problem for recreational riders or even racers who compete on mostly flat or rolling courses. But the penalty for being too skinny is reduced performance, constant fatigue and perhaps serious psychological problems such as anorexia or bulimia.

CHAPTER 30

Building Endurance

Cycling is about endurance. The sport captured the fancy of Europeans late in the 19th century by serving as a metaphor of life—long struggle, tough conditions, great odds. There's no arguing that cyclists who raced hundreds of miles over dirt and gravel roads on heavy, fixed-gear bikes deserved whatever fame they won. No wonder they called these superheroes "giants of the road."

But endurance isn't an absolute. Instead, it's specific to events. For a sprinter, a 4,000-meter pursuit is a long, long race. But a Race Across America competitor considers a century a light warm-up. One of RAAM's founding fathers, Michael Shermer, said that training didn't really begin till he saw 3 digits on his computer's mileage display.

How do we define endurance? Generally, it's the ability to ride steadily and comfortably for a time equal to the duration of your longest race or event. Of course, track pursuiters do road rides that are much longer than their races. And RAAM riders don't regularly embark on 3,000-mile training rides.

Sports scientists usually agree that any ride over 90 minutes helps build meaningful endurance. Most recreational riders and masters competitors find that occasionally riding 3-5 hours provides plenty of endurance for their events. But there are 2 exceptions: First, if you're aiming at double centuries or long-distance events such as *brevets* that range up to 620 miles, you'll need to put in more time. Second, endurance over consecutive days is important for touring, so training needs to include occasional back-to-back long rides if multiday tours are your goal.

In any case, authorities agree that a well-planned schedule of endurance riding builds an essential fitness base. On this foundation, you can erect a solid structure of speed, power and technique.

HOW TO ADD MILEAGE

The rule of thumb is to increase mileage no more than about 10 percent per week. This figure refers to total weekly mileage *and* the length of the week's longest ride. So, if last week you totaled 7 hours including a 2-hour long ride, this week could be extended safely to about 7.5 hours with a long ride of about 2:15. This rule isn't absolute, of course. Some riders can increase mileage faster without any physical penalties. Others need to carefully and gradually build up or they fall prey to tendinitis and exhaustion. Know yourself, and beware of the temptation to do too much too soon.

Another important point: You don't need a long ride every week. Your body won't forget how to go long in 7 days. Many successful riders do distance only once every 10 or 12 days, using the extra time and energy for shorter, faster training.

DISTANCE *AND* SPEED

Cycling events require you to go the distance—but they also require speed and power. You need speed to stay with the pack or catch back up, and to sprint. Power is required for climbing and battling headwinds.

Think about when you get dropped. Is it when the pack is spinning along at a steady and moderate pace for a long time? I doubt it. It probably happens when the pace increases abruptly or the pack jams up a tough hill. If you have the power and speed to stick with these hard accelerations for 30 seconds or even a couple of minutes, the pace will ease and you'll still be in the shelter of the group. But if you lose contact even for a moment, you'll likely be off the back for good.

> **TIP!** Average power output during a road race is meaningless. Pros may average only about 150-170 watts—well within the capacity of recreational riders. However, watts-measuring devices such as the PowerTap reveal relentless spikes of power during races. Peak loads of more than 600 watts are common, and are repeated many times. The wattage profile looks like the teeth of a saw.

Now you see why a diet of long rides at a steady pace is fine for winter conditioning, but it's an outdated approach to be building endurance in the spring when events are much closer. It's much better to mix faster, harder efforts into long rides to simulate the demands of events you're preparing for.

Even if you usually ride solo and set your own pace in long events, developing speed and power will increase your cruising speed. This means you'll ride faster with the same perceived effort. You'll also finish more comfortably by reducing overall on-bike time.

With all of this in mind, here's the training approach I recommend: During the middle third of any long ride, push some hills, do 2 or 3 fast time trial-like efforts near your lactate threshold, and throw in a few short jumps. On group rides, sprint for road signs or other landmarks against your training buddies. Sandwich this period of hard efforts between steady spinning in the first third and last third of the ride. This is the way to build speed and power in concert with endurance.

Granted, some riders prefer a more formal schedule of hard efforts during long rides. They think about the terrain they'll encounter and plan accordingly. Here's a sample 4-hour solo ride designed for flat-to-rolling roads with a hillier section near the middle.

0 to 30 min.	Warm up on the way out of town. Settle into an intensity of about RPE 7, or about 75% of max heart rate.
0:30 to 1:30	Ride steadily at RPE 6-8. Don't go anaerobic on hills.
1:30 to 1:50	Do a 20-minute time trial at RPE 8-9, or about 85-90% of max heart rate.
1:50 to 2:00	Spin easily at RPE 6.
2:00 to 2:30	On a series of rolling hills that take 2-3 minutes to climb, ascend at RPE 8-9 and recover on the descents.
2:30 to 3:00	Do 5 sprints of about 15 seconds each, separated by 5 minutes of easy spinning. Sprinting now, near the end of the ride when you're getting tired, simulates sprinting at the end of a race.
3:00 to 3:45	Settle back into your steady long-distance pace.
3:45 to 4:00	Spin easily in the final 15 minutes to cool down.

TIPS FOR LONG RIDES

> **RESOURCE!** For the last word on endurance riding, see *The Complete Book of Long-Distance Cycling* by Ed Pavelka and Ed Burke, Ph.D. Published by Rodale, it's available in the online bookstore at RoadBikeRider.com.

- **Pre-hydrate**. Make it a point to drink at least 8 large glasses of water the day before a long ride. Put a water bottle on your desk at work and nip at it every 15 minutes. Have at least one of those 8 glasses with each meal because the sodium in food helps you retain the fluid you drink. Also, cut down on caffeine and alcohol. These are mild diuretics. You don't want to urinate away the fluid you need to store.

- **Open your legs**. Most riders go short and easy to rest and conserve energy the day before a long ride. That's fine, but take a tip from the pros and throw in 3 or 4 short sprints. These efforts "open the legs," making them feel ready the next day. Don't sprint all-out, just accelerate briskly.

- **Plan a varied route**. Are you growing weary of riding the same roads? Use long-ride opportunities to explore new areas. Ask other riders for their favorite jaunts. Check with your local bike club or shop for cycling maps or route books. Get a Delorme Atlas for your state and draw up a cue sheet. If you always ride on paved roads, don't be afraid to include some that aren't. A beater bike with beefy training tires can handle dirt and gravel. In fact, some pros ride dirt roads and even singletrack trails on their regular road bikes. It's a fun change of pace and sharpens bike-handling skills.

- **Take breaks**. It's a British cycling tradition to stop at a café for tea and a snack during long training rides. This stop is usually about 15 miles from the end so riders can meet their training objectives first, then socialize and spin easily home. A stop can be earlier, too, or there can be more than one. A long ride accommodates such breaks, and they needn't detract from training benefits.

> **EXAMPLE!** My favorite long route of about 100 miles traverses a rural area with few services. But the small town at the halfway point has a great little coffee shop with killer muffins. I ride pretty hard up the gradual climb into town and enjoy my snack on the sunny deck. The easy spin back down the hill helps the food digest. I still have 35 miles to resume my training pace before cooling down near home.

- **Make the time**. It can be hard to do a long ride during the week if you work full time. One way is to go in earlier so you can get off earlier, then ride till sunset. Or, ride 90 minutes before work and 90 minutes after. If you commute by bike, take your regular route to the office, then a longer one home. If these rides have you on the road at dawn or dusk, be sure there's plenty of reflective material on your bike and clothes. Use a simple battery-powered headlight and taillight to help drivers notice you in dim light.

- **Include the family**. Weekends are the usual time for long rides, but you also don't want to abandon your spouse and kids. So, plan your ride around family activities. For instance, get up early to ride to the lake, beach or park while your family leaves later to drive there. You meet up, spend the afternoon together, and your bike goes on the rack for the trip home. You've gotten your long ride with minimal sacrifice of family time.

- **Eat and drink**. On long rides, your endurance is often more affected by what you eat and drink than by your fitness. No matter how many training miles you've done, failing to keep fuel in your tank will doom your ride. Slug down 2 big swallows of fluid every 15 minutes and eat about 20 grams of carbohydrate (about half an energy bar) every 30 minutes. A smart way to stay on schedule is to set your watch's countdown timer to beep every quarter hour.

> **TIPS!**
> - Some energy bars have wrappers that are nearly impossible to open while riding. Tear the wrapper before the ride so it's easy to rip apart. Or, cut the bar (still in the wrapper) into 3 bite-sized pieces.
>
> - If you're fading near the end of a long ride, stop for a soft drink with caffeine. The caffeine/sugar combo can provide a noticeable lift, especially if you aren't a regular caffeine user.

COMFORT AND SAFETY

To prevent crotch numbness and undue tenderness during long hours in the saddle, stand frequently and sit in slightly different locations. Dwelling in one position and grinding away for hours is a recipe for discomfort. Use every hill and turn as an opportunity to stand and pedal out of the saddle for at least a few seconds.

Use long rides to test clothing for events. Although 2 brands of shorts may have padded liners that are comfortable for a couple of hours, one may start chafing as time wears on. Only by trying them on long training rides can you discover which pair is crotch nirvana and which is purgatory.

The same thinking goes for sports drinks and energy bars. Food or drink that tastes fine in typical conditions may gag you when it's hot and you're 4 hours into a tough century. If you have to force yourself to eat and drink certain products, it's guaranteed you won't eat and drink enough. Remember that sports drinks tend to taste sweeter as a ride wears on, especially on a hot day.

Should you carry a cell phone on rides? If you have one, why not? It's light and compact enough to tote in a jersey pocket or seat bag, and it can be a lifesaver if you fall victim to a mechanical problem or get injured when you're riding alone. However, some riders consider cell phones a crutch whose presence discourages self-sufficiency and makes it too easy to give up on a tough ride and phone for a lift home. It's your call.

> **TIP!** In most places, even a cell phone that's out of service can be used to call 911 in an emergency. If you have an old phone that's no longer in use, charge it up and take it on rides. You can't use it to call home when you bonk with 30 miles to go, but you can summon medical help if you become hurt or sick or come across another rider in distress.

Finally, is it better to ride long distances solo or with a group? It's much easier to control the intensity of your workout if you ride alone. Groups or training partners are fun, but you're governed by their pace. By yourself, you can ride at the right effort for your goals.

I recommend a mix. I do some long rides solo so I can accomplish exactly what I want. When I go with a group, I treat it as a social ride. I still get the saddle time I need, even if the intensity isn't optimum. It's also a chance to refresh bike-handling skills in a bunch. Chapter 35 has more about group rides.

CHAPTER 31

Muscular Endurance

"Muscular endurance" describes the ability to turn a big gear at a relatively high cadence for a long time. This isn't time trialing, which is done at or slightly above the lactate threshold. Instead, muscular endurance workouts take place at heart rates about 10 beats below time trial intensity. A high level of muscular endurance is a necessary precursor to TT speed because it improves strength and pedaling form.

This ability is often trained with efforts of 10-20 minutes in a gear that allows a cadence of 70-85 rpm with a heart rate about 10 beats below lactate threshold. These hard, steady efforts increase cruising speed. Soon, you'll be able to go 1-2 mph faster with no increase in perceived effort.

But muscular endurance is about more than legs, lungs and heart. Your upper body is important, too. Its muscles must be strong to stabilize your body during pedaling, especially important when you're using a slow cadence and a big gear. In addition, strong upper-body muscles are your best safeguard against long-ride discomfort and crash-induced injuries.

Building muscular endurance also involves conventional resistance training for the legs, usually with squats or leg presses. Although the time for heavy weight training is past once spring training begins, it's important to continue a twice-weekly maintenance program. So, let's begin this chapter with a simple strength-maintenance routine that's compatible with spring and summer cycling. Then I'll discuss how to improve leg-muscle endurance with specific on-bike workouts.

STRENGTH-MAINTENANCE WORKOUTS

On your 2 weekly rest or easy-riding days, do several simple upper-body resistance exercises. Here's an effective program that takes only 15 minutes:

- **Abdominals**. A strong midsection keeps your upper body steady as you pedal, the mark of a smooth and powerful rider. To strengthen your abs, do 3 sets of 25-50 crunches with your feet elevated and arms folded across your chest. See page 96.

- **Upper-body pushing muscles**. If you've ever had sore triceps (on the back of your upper arm) from leaning on the handlebar during a long ride, you know why it's important to keep these muscles strong. Use one or more of these exercises.

  - **Dips** work all of the important pushing muscles of the upper body in one exercise. See page 94. Aim for 3 sets of 10 reps.

  - **Pushups** do the job, too, and don't require equipment. Good form beats numbers—10 pushups done correctly are better than 15 done sloppily. If elevated or regular pushups are too difficult, do them from your knees rather than your toes. See page 94.

- **Upper-body pulling muscles**. Ever notice how hard you pull on the handlebar during a steep climb or sprint? Use these exercises to strengthen your pulling muscles.

  - **Dumbbell rows**. Do 10-15 repetitions, then switch arms. That's one set. Build to 3 sets. See page 93.

- **Shoulder shrugs**. These help you avoid neck and shoulder pain on long rides. Stand upright, holding a barbell or 2 dumbbells with straight arms. Keep your back straight as you relax your shoulders so they drop down fully. Then slowly hunch your shoulders toward your ears. Hold a second, then lower slowly. Don't bend your elbows. Build to 3 sets of 10-15 reps.

- **Neck isometrics**. If you have neck fatigue or pain while riding, here's how to strengthen the muscles. Stand straight and put the heels of your hands against your forehead, fingers pointing up. Push your head forward for 10 seconds while resisting with your hands. Next, interlace your fingers and put this "basket" on the back of your head, little fingers toward the ceiling. Push your head back while resisting with your hands for 10 seconds. Next, put the heel of your right hand, fingers up, on the right side of your head. Push your head to the side while you resist with your hand. Repeat on the left side. All of that is one set. Build to 3 sets.

BASE STRENGTH ON THE BIKE

The primary method is one-leg pedaling. I discuss this technique in chapter 26 and recommend it for indoor cycling. It's a great way to work on strength and pedaling form. When you're able to pull your leg through the bottom, up and across the top with greater force, it lessens the resistance felt by the opposite leg pushing down. It improves the power generated by your quads on the downstroke.

That's what one-leg training works on. It's more easily done indoors, making it a good technique when spring weather is too nasty for venturing outside. Aim for several 5-minute repeats with each leg, using a moderately big gear of about 53x17 teeth, depending on the resistance of your trainer. Keep cadence fairly low, between 50 and 70 rpm.

Outside, do this drill twice a week about 20 minutes into an easy ride. Don't let your heart rate rise above 75 percent of max. The idea is to work the muscles, not the cardiovascular system. Use a safe, lightly traveled road with few intersections. Ideally, there'll be a gentle uphill or light headwind. Unclip one foot and hold it just outside the revolving pedal. Pedal this way for several minutes, then switch feet. Keep your hips and upper body still. And keep your eyes up the road, not looking down.

MUSCULAR ENDURANCE ON THE BIKE

A few years ago, I was in Winter Park, Colorado, at the U.S. Cycling Team's high-altitude training camp. Chris Carmichael was the national coach at the time. Team members included soon-to-be-pros Tyler Hamilton, Kevin Livingston, Fred Rodriguez and Chann McRae.

When I arrived, I found the riders pounding out intervals up Berthoud Pass, a 3-mile long, 6-percent grade. But instead of using the supple pedal stroke and rapid cadence of top climbers, they were plodding in a monstrous 53x15-tooth gear at a cadence of about 50 rpm. It looked like they had broken their derailleurs and were just trying to make it home.

In reality, they were building muscular endurance using a technique that I call "grinders." That's what it feels like—low-cadence, high-resistance grinding. It's like doing weight-training squats on the bike. There are 2 basic types:

- **Grinder 1:** 3-5 minutes, moderate grade of about 5 percent, 50-60 rpm, seated. Use a cyclecomputer that counts cadence so your rpm stays in this range. Concentrate on making perfect circles with pressure on the pedals all the way around each stroke. Keep your upper body quiet—don't rock your shoulders or hips. Intensity is important. If you're breathing hard, you're doing this drill wrong. It's designed to strengthen muscles, not provide an anaerobic workout. Your heart rate should be about 10 beats below lactate threshold. You should feel the strain in your legs, not in your lungs.

- **Grinder 2:** 10-20 minutes, gradual grade of about 3 percent, 75-85 rpm, seated. These intervals are like time trialing in that you ride steadily for a relatively long time. But cadence is 10-15 rpm slower than you'd use in a competitive TT and effort is more moderate—about 5 beats below lactate threshold. Again, concentrate on your pedal stroke and overall form. Long steady grades work best because you'll be going at a steady pace and using a fairly large gear. Gravity gives you something to push against.

EXAMPLE! East of my hometown of Montrose, Colorado Highway 50 rises about 2,500 feet in 14 miles to the top of Cerro Summit. Only the final 4 miles are steep. There's a wide shoulder, no stop signs and few intersecting roads. It's a perfect venue for No. 2 grinders.

My steep hills are west of town, climbing to mesa tops. Each one is 5-8 percent and about a kilometer long. They're perfect for big-gear No. 1 grinders.

You may not have such ideal terrain, but you can make do. For instance, consider the area around Bowling Green, Ohio. I ride there when we visit in-laws. Bowling Green is aptly named—the land is dead flat. But there's a prevailing southwest wind, so I simply do grinders into it. For short climbs, there's a highway overpass just outside of town. It's not ideal, but it works.

Grinders are high-intensity workouts. The low cadence and high resistance will make your legs feel like you've done a tough weight-room workout. So, do them only once per week in the 8 weeks of spring training. This leaves room for the other workouts outlined below and reduces the risk of chronic fatigue. In chapter 30, I recommend including periods of harder efforts in your endurance rides. If you mix several grinders into your long weekend ride, count them as your once-per-week dose.

CAUTION! Grinders seem like they'd wreck your knees in short order. But if you do them right, they won't. The exception: If you have a history of knee problems such as chondromalacia or patellar tendinitis, use an easier gear and a higher cadence.

CHAPTER 32

Spring Into LT

Lactate threshold training is in vogue because it's the foundation of Lance Armstrong's training. His coach, Chris Carmichael, believes that the secret to top performance is increasing "cruising speed"—the ability to go fast while still staying within the aerobic zone. So let's expand on chapter 10 to see how this essential method for elevating performance should be used in spring training.

> **EXAMPLE!** Why is power at LT so important? Suppose Lance is capable of generating an average of 450 watts at LT while he's climbing an alpine pass in the Tour de France. His rival, Jan Ullrich, averages only 415. On the first 3 passes of the day's stage, Lance climbs at an effort equal to 435 watts. He's still under his LT, riding hard but in control. To keep up, Ullrich has to go over his LT and into oxygen debt. He's burning his glycogen stores much faster than our man. On the fourth and deciding climb, Lance will have enough left to ride away and win.

As Carmichael puts it, what's important is "the ability to produce significant power while remaining under your LT and in control." Great, that's a clear concept. But how do you increase the power produced at LT? The answer, as I've mentioned, is to do substantial training a little below, at or slightly above your lactate threshold.

Muscular endurance workouts like the grinders outlined in chapter 31 take care of training just below LT. Next, we'll see how to complete LT training. Then we'll look at some new research indicating that more-intense-but-shorter efforts increase LT even faster.

HOW TO RIDE AT LT

It's an art to ride at lactate threshold. Your body produces very specific signals that you're treading on the "red line." It's what separates a pace you can maintain for 30-60 minutes from a slightly faster pace that produces more lactate than your body can recycle. Top time trialists are masters at playing with this physiological threshold.

One way to stay close to your threshold is to ride at the LT heart rate you determined in chapter 29. So, if you average 160 bpm for a 30-60-minute all-out time trial, train your LT at 155 to 165 bpm. If you have a watts meter, you can determine average power for that same test time trial and ride near that wattage during training. But the simplest way is to listen closely to your body. Be aware of how it feels when you're riding perilously close to the threshold. The tip-off is when your breathing changes from steady and deep to panting. When you lose control of your breathing, it's a good sign you've exceeded LT.

LT WORKOUTS

- **Training time trials**. The standard LT workout mimics a time trial. Simply ride for 5-12 minutes at LT intensity, spin easily for 3-5 minutes to recover, then repeat. During the hard interval, check your upper body. Are your hands, arms and shoulders relaxed? Or are you hunching your shoulders so you look like a turtle as you ride? Tensing the upper body wastes precious energy. Strive to be fluid and elegant. Don't purposely rock your hips or torso. Allow movement that's natural, but keep it minimal.

The secret to doing hard repeats successfully is to be honest with yourself. If you plan to do 5 but can't sustain your speed during the fourth effort, that's it—end the workout. You won't get maximum benefit if you push through exhaustion merely to reach some arbitrary goal.

- **30-second intervals**. Another way to boost LT is to ride faster than your LT heart rate for short periods. Recent research by exercise scientist Veronique Billat suggests that intervals of 30 seconds hard followed by 30 seconds easy can boost LT markedly in a relatively short time—about 8 weeks of spring training!

How hard is "hard?" Billat's prescription is somewhat complicated, but essentially it's the maximum pace you can sustain for 6 minutes. The best way to find this pace is with a watts meter. Then match your all-out 6-minute wattage number during your 30-second repeats. If you don't have a watts meter, do it by feel. Duplicate the average *effort* you experienced in your 6-minute test. However, average heart rate for a 6-minute test doesn't work. Heart rate doesn't have time to stabilize at a target figure during brief 30-second efforts.

LT-boosting workouts are hard. That's why they're usually scheduled only once per week. You may wonder how you can improve such an important ability as LT when you're training it only 8 times in the spring. But studies show that nearly any hard effort gives it a boost. Climbing and sprinting during other workouts have a positive effect on LT.

TESTING FOR LT IMPROVEMENT

Twice during the 8 weeks of spring training, schedule a short time trial to test your fitness and see if you're improving. At the end of week 4, find a 3-mile section of relatively flat road with little traffic and no stop signs. Mark a starting point and a turnaround so you use the same course later. Total distance should be about 5 miles. An out-and-back format reduces the effects of wind.

After a 20-minute warm-up, roll slowly to your starting point, accelerate, and ride to the turnaround at a hard-but-sustainable pace of RPE 8-9. Carefully check both directions for traffic, make a U-turn, and ride back to the start with slightly greater intensity. Check your elapsed time and record it. Then at the end of week 8, return to this course. Ideally, the weather will be about the same. Warm up as before, ride the exact course and compare times.

Faster? Great!

Slower? Don't worry too much, especially if the wind or weather was worse. Also, 4 weeks is a pretty short period in which to make substantial gains. You're looking for improvement over the entire 8-week spring program.

Don't rely solely on your elapsed time to judge training benefits. Obviously, a faster time means better fitness, assuming weather conditions were similar. But you'll also probably notice several subtle-but-important improvements, such as feeling more at home on the bike when you're going hard and a better sense of pacing.

CHAPTER 33

Climbing

Vertical terrain is responsible for the biggest thrills—and the most intense pain—in our sport. In races, the crunch almost always comes when the road tilts up. Recreational tours such as Colorado's Ride the Rockies feature several thousand feet of climbing each day. And, of course, climbs are followed by swooping, twisting descents where the grin-per-mile quotient is literally sky high. For all these reasons, it pays to get good on hills.

Because climbing is a fight against gravity, your ultimate ability is determined by your power-to-weight ratio. Lean, small-boned riders need proportionally less power to climb well compared to big people. That's why great climbers are nearly always diminutive. The few exceptions, such as Lance Armstrong and Miguel Indurain, generate so much power that their greater size doesn't matter.

The good news is that you can improve your climbing regardless of your genetic makeup. The spring training schedules in chapter 39 include a healthy dose of hill training. In this chapter, I'll show how to use climbing days to your best advantage.

> **EXAMPLE!** At 6-foot-4 and 190 pounds, my partner at RoadBikeRider.com, Ed Pavelka, is not built for climbing. But he lived for years in Vermont and Pennsylvania, where he had to climb at least a couple thousand vertical feet on *every* ride. Over time, this improved his fitness and technique, which made him feel it wouldn't be too futile to try some hilly events. He surprised himself by finishing 9th overall in the Assault on Mt. Mitchell, which ends with a 25-mile climb. Later, he placed 2nd of 55 masters in the Mt. Washington Hill Climb, which gains 4,700 feet in 7 miles, including grades of 18-22 percent. If you think you're too big to become a better climber, work at it and you might surprise yourself, too.

HILLS FOR INTERVALS

Because you should often be training on hills in this program, it pays to scout out the best climbs within a reasonable distance of home. I hear what you're saying: "I live in Pancake, Indiana, and the biggest hill in four counties is a two-foot rise over a culvert." Don't worry. As I say in chapter 31, wind can substitute for real hills. So can highway overpasses. You could even use your indoor trainer with your bike's front wheel raised 4 inches to simulate a grade.

Assuming there are some hills in your area, categorize them for specific kinds of training. Ideally, you'll have these 3 types:

- **Sprinter's hills**. These are short and fairly steep. Highway overpasses work fine. So do abrupt climbs out of stream-cut valleys. You may find these hills in city and state parks. I know of some good ones in Cleveland's park system.

- **Hills for repeats**. The best hill for intervals takes 2-4 minutes to climb, has a steady grade of 6-8% and no traffic lights or stop signs. A road with several consecutive hills like this, separated by about 5 minutes of riding time, is ideal. It makes training more interesting. But one lone hill is fine, too. Simply climb it hard, turn around at the top and recover as you ride back down and on the approach.

- **Long climbs**. These can vary from a hill that takes 5-8 minutes to climb to real mountains. Classic examples are the canyon climbs and mountain passes of western states, and the steep grades of the Appalachian Mountains and New England.

> **TRUE CONFESSION!** I live in a western Colorado town with arguably the most varied climbing in the country within a 20-mile radius. A dozen steep, kilometer-long climbs reach the tops of mesas. Longer ascents include 6 tough miles on the entrance road to Black Canyon National Park and the fearsome 3-mile, 16-percent East Portal climb. If I want to do a century, I can climb 13-mile-long Red Mountain Pass to the south or the 30-mile, 5,500-vertical-foot grind up Grand Mesa.
>
> Guess what? All of this great climbing terrain hasn't made me into a great climber. I do okay, but smaller or more talented riders can outclimb me even if they're restricted to a training diet of predominantly flat rides. You may not live in ideal terrain, but you can still close in on your potential.

STAND OR SIT?

Is it better to be in the saddle or out when climbing? It's one of the questions asked most frequently by riders seeking stronger performance.

On short sprinter's hills, you should stand because you need to generate power. Standing produces more short-term oomph. You can use bodyweight to push down the pedals. There's a downside, though. Standing uses more energy because your legs do double duty. They support your weight while also propelling the bike forward (and up.) This is why heart rates are about 5 bpm higher for a given speed while standing.

When you're sitting, the saddle supports your weight, letting all of your leg strength be used to overcome gravity. Generally, bigger and heavier riders prefer to sit more while smaller riders like to stand more. It's essential to find which method works better for you—or whether you're more efficient when alternating sitting and standing, as many riders are. If a mix is best, you need to determine the percentage of each that leads to fast, efficient climbing. Here's how:

- **Ride 4 times up a hill that takes at least 3 minutes**. Use different methods. Do one repeat entirely in the saddle. Do another standing all the way. Do a third sitting for one portion and standing for the rest. Do the fourth by alternating stretches of sitting and standing.

- **Keep your heart rate or perceived exertion the same on each repeat**. Effort should be steady and hard, but not all out. Time yourself on each ascent and then compare times.

- **Don't do all 4 climbs the same day**. You'll be tired before the end and your times won't mean much. Instead, spread the climbs over several days or a week.

If you see more than about 10 seconds improvement in each 2 minutes, you know you're more adapted to that style of climbing. Continue experimenting. Find out how much or which part of a climb should be done seated as compared to standing. How steep does a section need to be before it's more efficient to change positions?

> **TIP!** When climbing out of the saddle, the standard hand position is on the brake lever hoods. This puts you slightly upright to see better, breathe better and use body weight to come down on the pedals. But more and more pros are seen climbing on the drops, as if sprinting. One reason is that climbing speeds have increased, making a lower, more aerodynamic position an advantage. Another is that it puts more of the shoulders, arms and lower back into the pedal stroke for greater power. At first it might feel awkward to climb in the drops, but try it for a while to see if it has advantages for you.

TRAINING TECHNIQUES FOR FASTER CLIMBING

Not all of your hill training should consist of hammering up the climb, recovering and doing it again. Variations not only boost your improvement but also add variety to training. Here's how to do the drills that are included in the schedules in chapter 39:

- **Power accelerations**. Here's a climbing drill you can do on flat roads. Shift to a high gear and roll slowly at about 5 mph. Staying in the saddle, accelerate as hard as you can for 10 seconds. Push down and pull up forcefully. Your ability to power a large gear on hills will improve dramatically. So will your uphill sprint.

- **Finish the hill**. Most attacks on climbs take place near the top when riders are easing from the effort. Use this drill to respond. During most of the climb, stay in the saddle and spin a slightly easier gear than normal. With about 200 yards remaining, shift to a bigger gear, stand and go hard. Don't slow abruptly at the summit. Instead, charge over the top for another 100 yards or until gravity takes over. This drill builds power and the positive psychology to finish climbs strongly.

- **Surges**. Good climbers don't ascend at a steady pace. Instead, they throw in surges of faster pedaling in an attempt to drop competitors. Here's how to develop the ability to hang on: Ride at a pace about 5 beats below your LT. Surge for 10-20 seconds by increasing your cadence about 10 rpm. Ease back to your cruising speed for a minute, then throw in another surge. Repeat all the way up, then accelerate over the top.

UPHILL SKILLS

Climbing is a matter of fitness, but technique counts, too. Practice the following tips till they become ingrained.

- **Move on the saddle**. As the grade wears on, push your hips to the rear and concentrate on smooth, round pedal strokes at a moderate rpm. Then scoot forward to the tip of the saddle and spin at a faster cadence. Next, slide to the middle and pedal normally. Moving and varying your stroke refreshes your legs by relieving muscle tension. You can feel the difference almost instantly. Many riders, however, lock into one location or continue moving to the rear, missing the benefits of spinning from the nose.

- **Shift to an easier gear just as the grade begins**. Most riders go too hard at the bottom of a climb and run out of steam. To counter this tendency, don't wait to shift till you begin to bog down. In fact, use a lower gear than you think you need for the first two-thirds of the climb. Keep your cadence up to keep your speed up. With about 100 yards to go, shift to a bigger gear, stand and roll briskly over the top.

> **WORDS OF WISDOM!** You'll do well to remember these quotes from 2 of America's best coaches:
>
> *"Correct climbing is a matter of increasing your gear, not decreasing it."*
> — Eddie Borysewicz
>
> *"Climb like a carpet unrolling. Get faster as the climb goes on."*
> — Chris Carmichael

- **Slide back for more power**. On steep climbs when your gear isn't quite low enough, move to the rear of the saddle. Grip the bar tops. Slow your cadence just enough to feel your legs pulling the pedals around the entire 360 degrees.

- **Monitor your breathing**. If you begin to gasp, you're going too hard. Slow your cadence slightly.

> **TIP!** Try a breathing technique from Alexi Grewal, an Olympic road race champion. When you're working hard on a climb (or anytime), exhale forcefully and inhale passively. This prevents panting and improves air exchange. Breathe in rhythm with your pedal strokes and you'll feel smoother and in control.

- **Go to the front**. If you're riding with a group and aren't the fastest climber, work your way to the front before an ascent. Then climb at the pace you can handle. If riders start passing, let them. You'll still be in contact (or close) at the top. If you avoid blowing up, you won't have a problem rejoining on the descent.

- **Keep a good attitude**. Sure, hills are hard work. But they're part of riding a bike, and nothing spikes your fitness faster than time spent climbing. Hills are good for you!

CHAPTER 34

Sprinting

Sprinting isn't just for racers. The ability to accelerate is helpful for getting out of tight spots in traffic, escaping a charging dog, or flying over short, steep hills (which is why they're known as "sprinter's hills"). And sprinting is fun—it gives you the thrill of speed.

Even so, many riders never go fast. They aren't comfortable with the bike-handling skills needed to stand, sprint and see the pavement rush by rapidly. Or, they're so locked into the long, steady distance approach to training that abrupt, hard accelerations feel foreign.

Sprints are a little like weight training. The hard efforts recruit lots of fast-twitch muscle fibers in your legs that aren't impacted in slower riding. Sprinting builds strength in your legs, low back and arms, too.

For all these reasons, the chapter 39 schedules include one day of sprint training each week Here's how to do this speedwork safely and effectively.

SPRINT TRAINING TECHNIQUES

- **Jumps**. Start any sprint workout with 3 jumps—sudden accelerations that last 10-15 seconds. After warming up, select a clear section of road, shift to a slightly higher gear, get out of the saddle and accelerate. This *isn't* a full-on sprint. Increase speed forcefully, but don't spit, snarl and violate the speed limit. The idea is to get your heart rate up, grow accustomed to how the bike handles when it's going fast and give your leg muscles some strength-building work. Ride for 5 minutes at RPE 6 between jumps.

  When you do these jumps, work on starting smoothly. Grasp the handlebar firmly in the drops, but not with a death grip. When the pedal you prefer nears the top, transfer your weight to that foot, move off the saddle and use body weight to push down. Pull up with the hand on the same side. For example, when you thrust with your right foot, pull up with your right hand to counteract the tendency of the bike to tip to the right side.

- **Sprints**. Once you're warm, you can do full-on sprints. Shift to a gear slightly higher than the one you used for jumps. Roll along on a flat, safe road at about 15 mph. Stand and accelerate hard but in control. Keep your head up for safety. Continue to accelerate for 10-20 seconds, then ease off the power but keep pedaling at cruising speed for 3-5 minutes between each sprint. In the last 10 minutes of the ride, gradually ease your effort to cool down.

- **Tailwind sprints**. Here's a variation that builds leg speed. After a good warm-up, find a flat road and ride with the wind. Using a moderate gear, get out of the saddle and sprint until your legs are spinning too fast for comfort. Then sit and increase your cadence another 5-10 rpm. Concentrate on smooth strokes. Don't let your hips bounce on the saddle.

- **Speed contests**. You can make a game of sprinting even if you train alone. For instance, see how fast you can go. Glance at your cyclecomputer at the end of the sprint to check speed. Or, let its max speed function tell you. Your fastest effort should be on the third or fourth sprint when you're well warmed up. If speed falls dramatically on the fifth or sixth effort because of fatigue, you're done. Cancel the rest of the scheduled sprints and spin easily home.

- **Speed-play sprints**. These are known as *fartlek*—a Swedish term. It's a fun way to increase intensity during a ride. Simply go faster for 15 seconds to 2 minutes whenever the mood strikes or conditions beckon. Jam up a hill, shift to a bigger gear and crank hard with a tailwind, try to catch a rider up ahead. Keep it loose and unstructured. You'll get the benefits of increased speed without the mental demands of a regimented program.

SPRINT TACTICS

It isn't the purpose of this book to explain all of the tactics that go into winning a sprint. In fact, a book could be written just about that. But for group rides or recreational racing, it pays to know several basics. The more you sprint in training, the greater control and confidence you'll have in real situations. You'll be safer for others to ride with, too.

- **Position**. In general, the best place to be is about 5 riders from the front with 500 yards to go. This lets you draft off other guys and come around in the last 100 yards for the victory. In pro races, the sprint often begins 10 miles from the finish as teams sacrifice their workers to get their sprinter into good position. In recreational races, you're probably okay to begin moving up about a mile from the finish.

- **Leadout**. Two riders working together in the homestretch are a real advantage. One rider (the leadout) starts pouring on the coals about 500 yards from the line. His partner (the sprinter) glues to his wheel. The leadout rider blows up about 200 yards out, then the sprinter jumps past and goes for the victory.

- **Gearing**. Novice sprinters usually overgear. They think it's necessary to sprint in 53x12, but they can't jump fast and quickly get up to speed in such a monstrous gear. It's better to start in a smaller gear for quicker acceleration, then shift up during the sprint. Modern brake/shift levers let you shift under power while standing, so it's not necessary to start a sprint in the ideal finishing gear.

- **Bike control**. No sprint victory is worth a crash, at least not for recreational riders. And that goes double for crashes that take down others. Keep your head up and your bike under control. Don't jerk it back and forth excessively in search of more speed. Ride a straight line. Beware of locking your arms and shoulders, which can make your bike shimmy uncontrollably at speed.

CHAPTER 35

Group Rides

Cycling is social because riding with a group is a long-standing tradition in the sport. But cycling alone is fun, too, and many riders live in areas where riding companions are scarce. If you have a choice, should you ride solo, in a group or with one training partner? Each situation has advantages and drawbacks.

- **Solo rides**. You can set your own pace and don't have to wait for companions who are slower or have punctured. The ride starts when you want it to, not when the last member of the group finally shows up. You build strength riding in the wind by yourself. You develop the self-reliance skills of bike repair and route finding. And solo riding can be safer because one cyclist takes up less room on the road and is less likely to irritate motorists. If you live where there are no other cyclists, you can still accomplish a lot alone. You won't hone pack skills or tactics, but power, speed and climbing can be developed.

- **Group rides**. Friends can encourage you to get out, even if the weather is harsh or your motivation has waned. Group riding teaches you to be comfortable in pacelines and when bumping elbows. You can ride faster than when alone. If you have an accident or serious mechanical problem, friends are right there to help. But you're also at the mercy of group behavior. One popular approach: Ride alone on weekdays when you're pressed for time and need things to happen on your schedule. On weekends, ride with a group.

- **One-partner rides**. If you don't have a full-fledged pack to ride with, there may be another like-minded rider in your area. Training with a buddy is extremely effective, and it makes rides more fun. You can take turns pulling for a natural interval session. Trade the front every 1-3 minutes. You each go hard against the wind, then recover in the draft. Such training makes the miles fly by. Just be careful not to make every ride a race. Look for training partners at work or ask at your local bike shop or cycling club. Don't forget your significant other! Riding with someone you care for can make the quest for fitness even more meaningful. Can you get a decent workout when riding with someone slower? You bet. Use your beater bike or even a knobby-tire mountain bike. You'll exert more effort at lower speeds. Or, use a low gear the whole ride regardless of terrain and work on your spin. On climbs, ride to the top, then circle back to join your friend and ride up again at his (or her) pace.

> **TIP!** Get a tandem. Nothing beats a twicer if you want to get good workouts and still ride often with a person that's slower or less fit. On the front, you can push as hard as you want. On the back, your partner only has to keep his legs going around. He doesn't have to exert to keep up, yet he can't be dropped. Tandem riding is a fun change of pace besides being a great workout. It helps keep cycling varied and interesting.

If you ride with a friend, maybe you've wondered when it's okay to ride side-by-side. Generally, it's safe and legal if you aren't obstructing traffic. On a road without a wide shoulder, switch to single file when an overtaking vehicle gets within 300 feet or so.

Ultimate group: If you want to race, training with others is the first step in learning about pack mentality.

PACELINE RULES

Paceline riding is fun, efficient and as much a part of road cycling as sprints to city-limit signs. So let's review several key dos and don'ts before getting to group training techniques.

- **Be predictable by riding a straight line**. If you tend to wobble and wander, practice this skill on a low-traffic road by riding with your wheels on the white line along the edge. You'll find that it's easier if you look ahead 30 feet rather than directly in front of your wheel. You need to keep your eyes up in a paceline, too.

- **Be responsible when at the front**. While you're leading the line, you're the eyes and ears of the whole group. It's your job to warn of obstacles in the road as well as turns and stops. Watch for vehicles at intersections.

- **Don't accelerate when taking your pull**. It's a common mistake—getting excited and going too fast because you're pulling the group. Check your cyclecomputer while you're in second place. As you take the front, maintain the speed. The former leader should slow to drop back so you don't have to accelerate. Limit your time at the front to the group's average, or less. Pull off and let someone else share the work.

- **When dropping back, stay close to the line**. This enhances the group's draft. Don't wander dangerously into the middle of the lane. Accelerate smoothly as the last rider in line comes alongside so you can move behind his wheel without a gap opening.

- **Be responsible at the back**. The last rider in a paceline should call out "car back!" when there's an overtaking vehicle. This is especially important on narrow roads when the group is in a double paceline (2 abreast). Riders need to single out and reduce the effect on traffic.

- **Never make an abrupt or abnormal move**. Smooth, steady and predictable are the bywords. Ride relaxed, especially in arms and shoulders. Elbows will get bumped. If they're relaxed, they'll absorb nudges without affecting bike control.

> **EXAMPLE!** John Allis, a national road champion in the 1970s, was a stickler for relaxed arms. On training rides, he'd unexpectedly grab a newcomer's elbow and shake it, holding on to keep the rider from losing control. The victims of this not-so-subtle tactic weren't likely to forget the importance of relaxed arms.

- **Don't let your front wheel overlap a rear wheel**. If that bike swerves, the contact will very likely knock you down. Drop back a bit more on climbs. The rider just ahead might stand and decelerate slightly—in effect, moving backward toward your wheel.

> **CAUTION!** If you have aero bars on your bike for comfort and speed on long rides, remember that they aren't to be used in pacelines. It's dangerous to ride close to others when stretched out on aero bars. Your steering precision isn't as great and your hands are far from the brake levers. Either remove aero bars for group rides or promise not to use them.

SOLO TRAINING OBJECTIVES IN A GROUP

Groups go at a certain speed—and it may not be the speed that meets your training objectives. If you scheduled an easy spin and the guys blast out of the parking lot in the big ring, you'll be unable to keep your intensity down if you want to stick with them. But when you're ready for a hard ride and everyone else is spinning to the coffee shop, it's easy to become frustrated.

For this reason, you may need different companions on different days. It depends on what you want to accomplish. If you ride with the local hammers twice a week and spin with the social cyclists on other days that might be the right mix. But even if you end up in a group with objectives far different from yours, you can still come close to meeting your goals. Let's look at the 2 common situations.

1. The group is going too hard:

- **Sit in**. Stay at the back of the paceline and let cyclists who rotate off the front drop in ahead of you. Leave just enough gap to let the rider slide in while you keep the draft. Tell the others what you're doing so there won't be any mix-ups and crashes.

- **Drop out**. Ride in the shelter of the pack during the warm-up miles and on the flats when it's easy to keep up. When the group turns toward the hills and the intensity rises, drop off and ride solo at your own pace.

- **Get help**. Let stronger riders push you up hills. A helping hand on the small of the back or the rear of the saddle makes a hill much easier. And pushing you helps stronger riders get a better workout.

2. The group is going too slow:

> **TIP!** Before using some of these tactics, tell the group what you're doing. Otherwise, it could be confusing or annoying. You won't be welcome if it looks like you're merely showboating.

- **Be the motor**. Stay at the front and tow the group. The others will be doing about 15-20 percent less work than you—a big equalizer.

- **Take longer pulls**. If you aren't appreciably stronger than everyone but simply want a hard workout, take pulls that are 2-3 times longer. You'll get more work and less rest.

- **Push willing riders**. Not everyone appreciates being pushed up hills. But if you find a willing pushee, it's a great way to build some strength on an otherwise easy ride.

- **Ride a heavy bike**. If everyone else is on their sub-20-pound superbikes and you show up on a 30-pound beater with fenders and wide tires, you'll have to work significantly harder to match their speed, especially up hills.

- **Flee and come back**. Sprint out of a slow group, then wait for them to catch up as you recover. Or work a hill hard, ride several hundred yards down the other side, then U-turn and ride back to the top to meet the group coming over.

- **Break away**. In a paceline moving at moderate speed, attack from the rear and get as much lead as possible in about 20 seconds. When this time elapses, the first person in the paceline gives the signal and everyone works together to reel you in. Even if you're much stronger than others in the group, they'll make it hard for you to stay away by sharing the chase.

- **Attack on hills**. When the group gets to a longer hill, attack in a small gear with a very high cadence. When you've gained about 200 yards, shift to a bigger gear, stand and pedal at 50 rpm to work on strength. When the group catches you, attack again in a small gear.

CHAPTER 36

Overtraining

Overtraining is especially prevalent in the spring. As the weather improves, riders let their eagerness to get back on the road overcome good judgment. Mileage is increased too much too soon.

Spring also means increases in training intensity. There's nothing wrong with training hard—it's the surest way to improve. But done wrong, it's also the fastest way to get fried. As the saying goes, speed kills. Hard training, coupled with other stresses and demands on your time, can actually make you worse.

I'm calling this a "chapter" so you'll pay attention right now. But my full discussion of overtraining is actually in the foundation information of chapter 8. In terms of the training year, spring is the first time that doing too much becomes a serious temptation, so I'd like you to turn to page 22 to review overtraining's symptoms and prevention. Should you fall victim anyway, you must know how to recover and when you're ready to resume a regular schedule.

> **CAUTION!** The spring training plans in chapter 39 are structured to help you avoid doing too much. But everyone's tolerance for hard work is different. As a result, you shouldn't blindly follow my schedules—or anyone else's. Make adjustments if you begin sensing overtraining's symptoms.

CHAPTER 37

Spring Injuries

With spring's greater training volume, the risk of injury and illness increases. Hard training can suppress the immune system, cracking the door to colds and other respiratory infections.

Here is a primer on common injuries and health problems that plague riders as they begin their seasons in earnest. Your best reference on this topic is *Andy Pruitt's Medical Guide for Cyclists* by Andrew L. Pruitt, Ed.D., director of the Boulder Center for Sports Medicine in Boulder, Colorado. He's an expert on medical problems associated with our sport. Check his book if you need more information or have questions on topics not covered here. For instance, Pruitt covers 8 knee injuries in depth as well as many other maladies from head to toe (literally). His book is available in the online bookstore at RoadBikeRider.com.

COLDS AND FLU

Nearly everyone catches a cold now and then. It's especially frustrating in the spring when you're eager to boost training. Follow these rules if you start getting the sniffles.

- **Rest**. Couch time gives your body extra energy to fight infection. Cut back on work hours, take a sick day or procrastinate on home chores to buy more down time.

- **Pump fluids**. Use them to wash down a few hundred extra milligrams of vitamin C at each meal.

- **Use cold remedies with caution**. Many contain ingredients to treat all possible cold symptoms, several of which you may not have. Alka Seltzer Plus Cold Medicine is a relatively basic formula that seems to work well for standard head colds. If you're a racer, beware of over-the-counter cold remedies that contain pseudoephedrine (most do). This is a stimulant and a banned substance. You'll probably test positive for drug use. For the rest of us, a cold medicine makes the activities of daily life considerably more comfortable.

Some riders pride themselves on "training through" a cold. I know—it's hard to stop training just when the weather is improving and you're making real progress toward your goals. But don't force it, especially in the first couple of days when you don't know the extent of the illness. A hard ride could turn an average cold into something worse. Or instead of a cold it could be the flu, a severe illness you can't afford to play with.

Certainly, if you don't feel like riding, stay home. You'll be farther ahead if you devote several days to recovery. If you try to train through, you could lengthen the cold, slow your recovery and take much longer to return to form.

> **TIP!** Use the above-the-neck rule. When cold symptoms are from the neck up (sneezing, stuffy nose), it's usually okay to exercise lightly. But when symptoms are also below the neck (coughing, chest congestion, muscle aches), don't train. Once you're feeling better again, do at least one week easy for each week you were off the bike.

Don't forget to get a flu shot each fall. It can prevent lots of physical misery as well as the mental anguish of seeing a month of your season go to waste.

KNEE PAIN

Spring is the season for sore knees. In fact, one common version of inflamed knee tendons (*tendinitis*) is known as "spring knee." When your hinges start hurting, here's a general rule from Andy Pruitt: If the pain is in the front of the knee, your saddle may be too low. If the pain is in the back of the knee, the saddle is probably too high.

In spring, however, the cause of bum knees is often overuse rather than improper saddle height. If you're still in the weight room doing squats or leg presses, your knees may protest when you add longer or harder rides. Another cause is using big gears before your tendons and ligaments are ready for the 53-tooth chainring. Not covering your knees when it's cooler than 65F degrees can inflame tendons, too.

Knee tendinitis usually takes one of 2 forms:

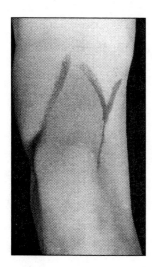

Spring Knee
This is marked by sharp pain at the top of the kneecap. The kneecap is triangle-shaped with one point at the bottom. The pain of spring knee is usually felt on the right or left points on top.

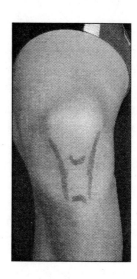

Patellar Tendinitis
Pain develops in the front of the knee, below the kneecap. It hurts while riding, perhaps when you walk up stairs, or merely when you touch the tendon. There may be swelling. Your knee may squeak when bent due to a lack of tendon lubrication.

TREATMENT

1. Apply ice (in a plastic food storage bag) 1-3 times a day for 15-20 minutes each time. Protect your skin by first laying down a washcloth or small towel. Put the ice bag on the injured area and hold it in place by wrapping loosely with an elastic bandage. Be careful. A too-tight wrap with ice could freeze your skin. Remove the ice for at least 30 minutes before another session.

> **TIP!** Buy a bag of frozen corn kernels and keep it in your freezer. When you need to ice a knee or any other injury, it's quick and effective to lay the bag on the sore spot. It can be reused many times. Corn works better than peas or lima beans, which tend to get mushy after several semi-thaws. They tend to refreeze into a hard block.

2. Take a NSAID (non-steroidal anti-inflammatory drug) with food. Ibuprofen works well for many riders.

> **CAUTION!** NSAIDs can be dangerous. Excessive doses combined with dehydration can cause kidney problems. Never exceed the manufacturer's recommended dose. This is especially important on a tour or during periods of heavy training when you might become dehydrated.

3. Apply a counter-irritant (heat rub). When you get back on the bike, consider applying hot stuff to encourage more blood flow to the area. Check with a pharmacist to see what's available over the counter. Then shield the injured knee from cool wind with a light coating of petroleum jelly. Always wear knee-protecting knickers, leg warmers or tights if the temperature is below 65F degrees. You'd be wise to raise this to 70 if you're already hurting. Use low gears and a high cadence. It often helps to raise your saddle 3-4 mm.

If you're still having problems, revise your training plan to increase mileage more gradually. Get a professional bike fit from a USA Cycling coach, reputable bike shop or a sports medicine facility with knowledge of cycling. Make sure this includes cleat positioning. As a last resort, see a physical therapist.

I.T. BAND FRICTION SYNDROME

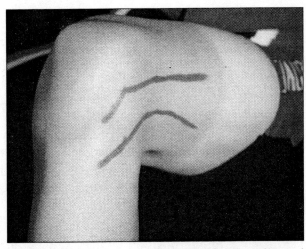

This knee injury is worth special attention because once it gets established, it's hard to correct and may even require surgery. If the following fixes don't relieve the pain in one day, stop riding.

The ilio-tibial (IT) band is the wide sheath of fibrous material that extends along the outer side the thigh from the crest of the hip bone to slightly below the knee. The lower end crosses a bony protuberance on the side of the knee. This is the area that's irritated. Symptoms are a sharp, jabbing pain around the bony bump. It can feel like someone is stabbing you with an ice pick, especially at the top of the pedal stroke.

IT band problems are usually caused by an overly narrow stance on the bike, badly adjusted cleats or a saddle set too high. Bowlegged riders and those with flat feet are susceptible too. To treat this injury, apply ice and take NSAIDs as mentioned above. Widen your stance on the bike by moving your cleats as far to the inside of the shoe soles as possible. Pedals that allow feet some free rotation usually help. Lower your saddle about 6 mm. (IT band friction syndrome is one of the few knee problems where the saddle should be lowered rather than raised.) Over-the-counter arch supports or custom orthotics usually help. Also, see a physical therapist for instruction on stretches designed to treat the problem.

UPPER-BODY DISCOMFORT

Soreness between the shoulder blades, low-back pain, neck strain and aching triceps often accompany hard, hilly or long rides in spring. Remedies:

- **Check bike fit**. Your reach to the handlebar is a crucial dimension. Stretch out too far and your triceps and low back will ache. So will your neck as you strain to see up the road. As you lean far forward, the saddle nose can press into you uncomfortably. Conversely, a reach that's too short causes you to hunch, putting stress on upper-back and shoulders. You sit excessively upright, putting too much weight on your crotch.

The rule for reach: When you're riding comfortably with hands on the brake lever hoods and elbows slightly bent, the handlebar should block your view of the front hub. This is a guideline, of course, and doesn't work for all riders. If in doubt, get a professional bike fit or consult *Andy Pruitt's Medical Guide for Cyclists* for additional self-help information. Pruitt goes into great detail on bike fit and riding position.

- **Strengthen muscles**. A basic upper-body weight training program, such as the one in chapter 31, will help prevent muscle soreness on long rides.

- **Move around**. Locking your body into one position for long periods is a sure way to make muscles seize. Stand up, sit down, move forward and back on the saddle. Change hand location frequently.

SADDLE SORES

It rarely fails. Just when spring training is going well, your crotch becomes tender, abraded or even invaded by an open wound or boil. Suddenly you're riding in pain—or not riding at all. Most medical experts think that boils are caused by skin bacteria that invade surface abrasions. Remedies have come a long way since riders put a slab of raw steak in their shorts to cushion the tender area. Of course, avoiding saddle sores is better than curing them. Here's how:

- **Check bike fit**. If your saddle is too high, your hips will rock and rub soft tissue on each pedal stroke. If the saddle is too far to the rear, you'll slide forward onto the narrow nose where your crotch bears the weight that your sit bones should be supporting. If you suffer from chronic saddle sores, have your position checked by a USA Cycling-certified coach or knowledgeable bike shop personnel.

- **Change position**. When sitting, slide to a different part of the saddle every few minutes. Stand frequently to take pressure off your crotch. Get out of the saddle on short hills or while accelerating away from stop signs. At the back of the paceline, stand and stretch. If the saddle isn't touching your crotch, it can't irritate you.

- **Wear high-quality shorts**. The liner should be large, soft, lightly padded and have no seams or at least flat ones. You'll probably need to buy different brands to find that one that your anatomy really likes. Women often do better with shorts cut for the female anatomy. If the liner isn't one piece, it should be sewn with a curved "baseball" pattern to avoid a center seam.

- **Find a supportive saddle**. Saddle choice is crucial, of course. Don't be fooled by large, cushy seats. Excessive width will rub your inner thighs. Too much padding lets your sit bones sink deep, putting pressure in the center where you don't want it. Depending on your anatomy, some narrow saddles won't support you on your sit bones. They put too much weight on soft tissue that soon becomes irritated. Trying different saddles can become expensive, so trade with other riders or find a bike shop that has a demo program.

- **Lube your chamois.** To reduce friction between the shorts liner and your skin, use Chamois Butt'r or a similar lubricant. Rub a dab into your crotch before you put on the shorts. Water washes away most lubes, so break out the petroleum jelly on a rainy day. It's greasy and stays on your skin and shorts in soggy conditions.

- **Clean up.** Always ride in clean shorts. If you're prone to problems, wash your crotch with mild soap and warm water, then dry well and lube up. After a ride, avoid hanging around in sweaty shorts. Bacteria love a damp and dirty environment. Shower as soon as possible after riding and put on loose, well-ventilated clothing. If you're at an event and can't wash, at least change out of your shorts and wipe down. Moist towelettes that pop out like tissues work well. Get an antibacterial brand.

> **TIP!** Ask your physician about a prescription for a topical antibiotic called erythromycin (Emgel). After each ride, rub a dab on any irritated "hot" spots. I got turned on to this medicine before a transcontinental PAC Tour. During 3,400 miles in 24 days, I never developed a saddle sore.

Sometimes a sore will sprout despite the best preventative efforts. A couple of days off the bike will help it heal. But if you're in a situation where you must continue riding, try these fixes:

- **Switch shorts or saddles.** Your problems are probably isolated to one small area—a boil or abrasion—so changing your saddle or shorts can change the pressure. Some people on sagged multiday tours take a spare saddle mounted on a seatpost. They switch every couple of days to avoid concentrated irritation. Or, use a thin saddle pad to increase the seat's width and softness.

- **Use a heavier lubricant.** If you're getting abraded, try a more viscous lube. A favorite of long-distance riders is Bag Balm, designed for sore cow udders but available in most pharmacies. It has healing properties, too.

- **Apply a foam donut.** You can find these in the foot department of pharmacies and department stores. About the size of a quarter, they're made to relieve pain from corns. Place one on the saddle sore so it's in the center hole. The adhesive will hold the donut in place, allowing it to prevent direct contact.

CHAPTER 38

Spring Weather

Spring is synonymous with lousy weather. If it isn't rain, it's sleet, hail, wind and the occasional snowstorm. Warm, sunny skies usually show up just when you've scheduled a rest day.

If you're serious about training and building your fitness, you'll have to ride in the rain occasionally. That's not necessarily bad. You won't have the confidence and know-how to deal with downpours and wet roads during races, tours or centuries unless you occasionally experience sloppy conditions during training. The trick is dressing right and developing certain bike-handling skills. After that, getting wet and riding through puddles can be as fun as when you were a kid. (On second thought, even kids should avoid puddles because you never know what might be underneath!)

RAINWEAR

- **Jacket**. Light windbreakers work fine in relatively warm rain. They don't keep you dry, but they do hold in body heat. For cold spring rain (or sleet) you need a waterproof jacket. Beware of overspending for one made of a high-tech fabric advertised as "waterproof and breathable." Those 2 terms don't go together. Instead, look for a jacket with completely waterproof fabric and plenty of ventilation (pit zips, full-length front zipper, back vent, cuffs that can be opened). You need airflow to reduce overheating. A poorly ventilated jacket will keep the air so stuffy inside that you'll get as wet from sweat as you would from the rain. Also, be sure there's a long tail that lets down to cover yours.

  Perhaps the most important feature for any cycling jacket is high visibility. Go for neon yellow or orange so you'll glow as you ride. If there are reflective stripes or panels, so much the better. Boycott manufacturers who produce only dark-colored outerwear. That's like wearing camouflage.

- **Shoe covers**. Neoprene booties hold in heat, up to a point. But they eventually soak through, letting your feet get wet and cold. Neoprene doesn't breathe, so even when it's cold but dry your feet will get damp from condensation. A better choice is booties made from a water-repellent fabric. They're lighter and roll up into a much smaller bundle when you want to stuff them into a jersey pocket. For spring temps above 45F degrees, consider toe covers that pull over the front of your shoes. They're enough to cut the chill, but they're not much help in rain.

- **Base layer**. Your wardrobe should contain several short-sleeve or sleeveless base layers made of a synthetic material ("polypro") designed to transport moisture. This stuff works, wicking sweat from your skin so it stays drier and warmer. Add a long-sleeve turtleneck for cold and wet conditions. Wool is another good material against the skin. Old problems with itching and shrinking have been solved.

- **Eye protection**. You can't ride safely if you can't see. In dark, gloomy conditions, clear or yellow lenses give you the best chance of spotting road hazards obscured by rain and mist. If it's raining hard, a billed cycling cap under your helmet shields your eyes. Mountain bike-style helmet visors are increasingly being worn by roadies in wet weather.

- **Head cover**. Your scalp has a rich network of blood vessels. That's why you bleed so copiously from head injuries. It's also why you lose substantial amounts of heat from your head. Anytime it's cold or wet, wear a thin polypro helmet liner "skullcap" or balaclava (also covers your neck and ears) under your helmet.

- **Gloves**. Cold hands create bike-handling problems. It's hard to work the brakes or shift with numb fingers. Most winter-weight gloves soak through in heavy or prolonged rain, but they'll keep your hands semi-comfortable for a while by virtue of their insulation. Neoprene gloves don't work any better than neoprene booties. For warmer temperatures, wear polypro gloves with gripper dots over short-finger cycling gloves. The dots in the palm and fingers are made of a tacky material that gives you a better hold on wet handlebar tape.

- **Tights or leg warmers**. You can buy waterproof nylon rain pants, but most cyclists find them floppy, noisy and unnecessary. Your legs are shielded somewhat by your upper body, and they're also working hard. If they do get wet, you may not even notice. Wool-blend tights with nylon panels over the knees and upper thighs work well when rain and cold combine. Regular polypro tights or leg warmers are fine for most wet spring conditions.

RIDING TECHNIQUES

Comfort is only part of the battle. You also need to stay upright. Nothing frightens inexperienced riders more than pavement and brake pads slickened by rain. It's tough to judge traction and easy to feel panicky when tires slip a little. When brakes are applied, nothing happens. You need to know that it takes numerous revolutions before water is wiped off and brake pads begin to grip. Use the following tips and practice so you can expand your comfort zone when it's slippery.

- **Reduce tire pressure**. Inflate tires to about 95 psi rear and 85 psi front if you weigh around 150 pounds. Run just a bit more pressure if you're heavier. Less pressure lets tires flatten more where they touch the road. A larger contact patch means better traction.

- **Relax**. If your arms are tense and you begin to lose traction, you could slide out and crash. If you're loose and relaxed, you can ride through minor skids.

- **Go easy in corners**. Slow down for turns on wet roads. Aggressive cornering will likely result in a crash. Don't make any abrupt moves. Even pros often crawl through corners when racing in the rain.

- **Beware of booby traps**. Lines painted on the road are especially slick when wet. So are metal manhole covers, railroad tracks, steel bridge decks and fallen leaves. Slow down and cross these things with your bike vertical, not angled over.

- **Be extra cautious early**. Roads are slickest just after it starts to rain. After a few minutes, oil and dust are washed away and traction improves. In fact, it may be nearly as secure as on a dry surface—except on the booby traps just mentioned.

- **Practice**. Ride in the rain. Consider it part of your cycling education. Only by experiencing braking, cornering and the limits of traction will you gain skill and confidence in wet weather. Don't take risks, but get a feel for how your bike responds.

WET-ROAD CORNERING

Brake to a safe speed *before* you reach the turn. If you grab the brakes when the bike is leaned over, crashing is almost certain. Remember that wet rims mean much less initial stopping power. Apply the brakes far enough in advance to squeegee the water. Take care to lighten your grip as soon as you feel the pads begin to grab. Otherwise, you could lock a wheel and skid.

In a turn, put even more weight on the outside pedal than you normally do, but don't lean over as much. The tires will be less likely to slip out. Take a smooth, rounded line. Use as much of the lane as traffic permits. The sharper your angle, the more likely you are to lose traction.

WET GROUP RIDES

When you're following someone on wet roads, it's easy to get blinded by the rooster tail of spray thrown up from the rear wheel. It gets into your mouth, too—not real tasty or sanitary. Here are 2 ways to avoid this spray:

1. Ride slightly to either side. This lets the spray go just past your shoulder. The problem is that you get less draft this way, and it might put you too close to the road edge or too far into the traffic lane.

2. Ride closer. This way, the rider's spray will go into your wheel instead of up onto you. Of course, this isn't a safe solution unless you and the other guy have good wet-weather riding skills.

Remember, fenders all but eliminate spray. Put them on your bad-weather beater bike. Your riding companions will thank you, and you'll stay cleaner, if not drier.

HEADWINDS

Tailwinds help you zip along effortlessly. But crosswinds and headwinds more than make up for easy breezes. A wind from the side blows you off a steady line. A headwind is just plain tough, physically and mentally.

First, the mental part. Don't fight headwinds. You'll just get frustrated. After all, a force of nature that can power huge sailing ships isn't something you can overcome with muscle power alone. Simply accept the wind and keep pedaling. In the same vein, don't overgear. Some riders try to fight headwinds with brute force in the same gear they'd use in calm conditions. They're soon laboring to turn the crank, suffering like a dog and hating the bike.

The best tactic is to treat headwinds like hills. You'd shift to the small ring and spin up a hill, right? So do the same against the wind. You'll go faster and suffer less. It also helps to get aerodynamic. If you're facing a long haul into the wind, pretend you're time trialing. Get low. Hold the handlebar in the drops or stretch out along the top tube with your hands on the brake lever hoods and your forearms horizontal. With less frontal area exposed to the gale, you'll go faster for a given amount of effort.

> **CAUTION!** Don't stay too long in an extreme aero position. Your back and neck will stiffen, and it's hard on your crotch, too. Sit up periodically. Move your hands on the bar and your sit bones on the saddle. Stand for at least one minute in every 5, just as you do when climbing a hill out of the saddle.

The best way to handle a windy day is with a little help from your friends. Riding with just one other person means you'll be at the front only half the time. A group of 5 or 6 can make steady progress into tough headwinds. It's a natural form of interval training as you push hard for a minute, then sit in for 5.

CROSSWINDS

Strong, gusty crosswinds pose a bike-handling challenge. Use a secure but not white-knuckle grip on the bar. Keep your elbows relaxed and slightly bent. Using your arms as shock absorbers will go a long way toward keeping the bike on line when gusts hit.

> **CAUTION!** Avoid using deep, V-section rims in crosswind conditions, especially for the front wheel. The wider rim will catch the wind and make handling dicey. Combine this with the speed of a descent and it's possible to lose control entirely. The same goes for composite wheels with 3, 4 or 5 wide "spokes."

CHAPTER 39

Three Spring Training Plans

Now that we've covered all the fundamentals of spring training, let's start riding. This key chapter contains 8-week training plans for our 3 levels of riders, each having different objectives.

LEVEL 1: For fitness riders who want to get in shape to ride 50 miles at a good pace, improve their climbing and do moderately paced group rides. This is the right program for cyclists who didn't ride much in winter. If in doubt, start here. You'll improve while avoiding the risk of overtraining.

LEVEL 2: For fast recreational riders whose goals include sprightly group rides, centuries and multiday tours. I'm assuming that you're coming out of winter with good fitness, hopefully from following my advice in part 2 for off-season training.

LEVEL 3: For competitive cyclists. This doesn't mean you need a racing license. You could key on competitive group rides, club time trials or club criteriums. This program works best if you established a solid base of endurance and strength during the off-season. You did if you used my program in part 2.

WORKOUT NOTES

- Daily rides are based on time rather than distance. The reason is simple: Distance traveled with a headwind vs. a tailwind, or when climbing compared to descending, can vary enormously. As a result, the number of miles you cover isn't a good measure of effort expended.

- Use the rating of perceived exertion (RPE) scale on page 141 to judge how hard you're working. My program is based on RPE. Of course, you're welcome to use a heart monitor and/or a watts meter if you have them.

- Whenever I suggest a specific workout (sprints, training time trials, hill repeats and so on), the page numbers point you to where the technique is explained or there is helpful related information. You may also see similar workouts on adjacent pages. For instance, I talk about "jumps" and "tailwind sprints" on page 160. You're welcome to substitute workouts based on your terrain, weather conditions, desire for variety or the performance shortcoming you're trying to remedy.

- What if you miss a workout—or several? Don't worry when you can't ride for a day or 2 or even 5. Simply pick up the schedule where you left off. If you miss more than a week, begin where you were, but cut both distance and intensity by about a third until you're back into the rhythm of training. That may take several days. If you miss significant time with an illness or injury, go extremely easy for at least a week when you return. Reduce mileage and intensity by half, then rebuild slowly. Carefully monitor your performance and your feeling of well-being as your comeback progresses. Don't rush it! There's plenty of time. It's a long season.

- Remember that these schedules are suggestions. They represent one good way that the disparate elements of training can be blended into an 8-week program. There are other good ways. Consider your goals, time for training, energy, motivation and other key factors in your personal situation. Please feel free to modify my recommendations to more exactly fit your needs.

> **CAUTION!** Always get a physical exam and your physician's permission before engaging in strenuous athletic training.

Level 1

This is the 8-week cycling foundation program.

By the end of 2 months, you'll be able to comfortably ride 50 miles or about 3 hours. This program works great for general fitness. If that's your goal, do the 8-week program and then repeat the final 4-week schedule to maintain your fitness. After that, you can decide whether to continue to repeat this program or advance to the next level. If your goal is to ride longer—say a 62-mile metric century or 100-mile standard century—this program will give you a solid base from which to build your endurance.

> **TIP!** The numbers in parentheses refer to chapters where you can find workouts and related information

LEVEL 1 – WEEK 1	
Monday	Rest day or weight training. (23, 31)
Tuesday	1:00 at RPE 6-7. Include 3 jumps. (11, 12, 34)
Wednesday	1:00 at RPE 6.
Thursday	1:00 at RPE 6-8. Include 10 min. of grinder No. 2. (31)
Friday	Rest day or weight training. (23, 31)
Saturday	1:00 at RPE 6.
Sunday	1:30 at RPE 6-8. Consider joining a group ride. (35)

LEVEL 1 – WEEK 2

Monday	Rest day or weight training. (23, 31)
Tuesday	1:00 at RPE 6-7. Include 4 jumps. (11, 12, 34)
Wednesday	1:15 at RPE 6.
Thursday	1:00 at RPE 6-8. Include 10 min. of grinder No. 2. (31)
Friday	Rest day or weight training. (23, 31)
Saturday	1:00 at RPE 6.
Sunday	1:30 at RPE 6-8. Consider joining a group ride. (35)

LEVEL 1 – WEEK 3

Monday	Rest day or weight training. (23, 31)
Tuesday	1:20 at RPE 6-7. Include 5 jumps. (11, 12, 34)
Wednesday	1:00 at RPE 6.
Thursday	1:20 at RPE 6-8. Include three 8-min. time trials. (32)
Friday	Rest day or weight training. (23, 31)
Saturday	1:00 at RPE 6.
Sunday	1:45 at RPE 6-8. Consider joining a group ride. (35)

LEVEL 1 – WEEK 4

Monday	Rest day or weight training. (23, 31)
Tuesday	1:20 at RPE 6-7. Include 3 sprints. (12, 34)
Wednesday	1:00 at RPE 6.
Thursday	1:20 at RPE 6-8. Include a time trial test to measure improvement. (32)
Friday	Rest day or weight training. (23, 31)
Saturday	1:00 at RPE 6.
Sunday	2:00 at RPE 6-8. Consider joining a group ride. (35)

LEVEL 1 – WEEK 5

Monday	Rest day or weight training. (23, 31)
Tuesday	1:30 at RPE 6-7. Include 5 sprints. (12, 34)
Wednesday	1:00 at RPE 6-7.
Thursday	1:30 at RPE 6-8. Do 8 intervals of 30 seconds on, 30 seconds off. (10, 11, 32, 47, 55)
Friday	Rest day or weight training. (23, 31)
Saturday	1:00 at RPE 6.
Sunday	2:15 at RPE 6-8. Consider joining a group ride. (35)

LEVEL 1 – WEEK 6

Monday	Rest day or weight training. (23, 31)
Tuesday	1:30 at RPE 6-8. Include 4 power accelerations. (33)
Wednesday	1:15 at RPE 6-7.
Thursday	1:30 at RPE 6-8. Do 10 intervals of 30 seconds on, 30 seconds off. (10, 11, 32, 47, 55)
Friday	Rest day or weight training. (23, 31)
Saturday	1:00 at RPE 6.
Sunday	2:30 at RPE 6-8. Consider joining a group ride. (35)

LEVEL 1 – WEEK 7

Monday	Rest day or weight training. (23, 31)
Tuesday	1:30 at RPE 6-8. Include 4 short hills. (33, 52)
Wednesday	1:15 at RPE 6-7.
Thursday	1:30 at RPE 6-8. Include 3 climbs about 10 min. each. (33, 52)
Friday	Rest day or weight training. (23, 31)
Saturday	1:00 at RPE 6.
Sunday	2:45 at RPE 6-8. Consider joining a group ride. (35)

LEVEL 1 – WEEK 8	
Monday	Rest day or weight training. (23, 31)
Tuesday	1:30 at RPE 6-8. Include 2 climbs of about 10 min. each. (33, 52)
Wednesday	1:15 at RPE 6-7.
Thursday	1:30 at RPE 6-8. Include a time trial test to measure improvement. (32)
Friday	Rest day or weight training. (23, 31)
Saturday	1:00 at RPE 6.
Sunday	3:00 at RPE 6-8. Consider joining a group ride. (35)

Level 2

For fast recreational roadies who want to perform well on group rides and in centuries.

You can easily modify this program to get fit for a multiday tour, too. Every other Saturday, substitute a ride of 2-4 hours at RPE 6-8 for the scheduled easy ride. High-mileage weekends will give you the stamina to ride several consecutive days.

> **TIP!** The numbers in parentheses refer to chapters where you can find workouts and related information

LEVEL 2 – WEEK 1	
Monday	Rest day or weight training. (23, 31)
Tuesday	1:00 at RPE 6-7. Include 3 jumps. (11, 12, 34)
Wednesday	1:00 at RPE 6 with one-leg training. (9, 26, 31)
Thursday	1:00 at RPE 6-8. Include 3 grinder No.1. (31)
Friday	Rest day or weight training. (23, 31)
Saturday	1:00 at RPE 6.
Sunday	2:30 at RPE 6-8. Consider joining a group ride. (35)

LEVEL 2 – WEEK 2

Monday	Rest day or weight training. (23, 31)
Tuesday	1:00 at RPE 6-7. Include 4 jumps. (11, 12, 34)
Wednesday	1:15 at RPE 6-8 with one-leg training. (9, 26, 31)
Thursday	1:00 at RPE 6-8. Include 3 grinder No.1. (31)
Friday	Rest day or weight training. (23, 31)
Saturday	1:00 at RPE 6.
Sunday	3:00 at RPE 6-8. Consider joining a group ride. (35)

LEVEL 2 – WEEK 3

Monday	Rest day or weight training. (23, 31)
Tuesday	1:00 at RPE 6-7. Include 5 jumps. (11, 12, 34)
Wednesday	1:30 at RPE 6-8 with one-leg training. (9, 26, 31)
Thursday	1:00 at RPE 6-8. Include 2 grinder No.2. (31)
Friday	Rest day or weight training. (23, 31)
Saturday	1:00 at RPE 6.
Sunday	3:15 at RPE 6-8. Consider joining a group ride. (35)

LEVEL 2 – WEEK 4

Monday	Rest day or weight training. (23, 31)
Tuesday	1:00 at RPE 6-7. Include 3 sprints. (12, 34)
Wednesday	1:00 at RPE 6-8 with one-leg training. (9, 26, 31)
Thursday	1:00 at RPE 6-8. Include a 5-mile time trial test. (32)
Friday	Rest day or weight training. (23, 31)
Saturday	1:00 at RPE 6.
Sunday	3:45 at RPE 6-8. Consider joining a group ride. (35)

LEVEL 2 – WEEK 5

Monday	Rest day or weight training. (23, 31)
Tuesday	1:00 at RPE 6-7. Include 5 sprints. (12, 34)
Wednesday	1:00 at RPE 6-8 with one-leg training. (9, 26, 31)
Thursday	1:30 at RPE 6-8. Include three 8-min. time trials at RPE 8-9. (32)
Friday	Rest day or weight training. (23, 31)
Saturday	1:00 at RPE 6.
Sunday	4:00 at RPE 6-8. Consider joining a group ride. (35)

LEVEL 2 – WEEK 6

Monday	Rest day or weight training. (23, 31)
Tuesday	1:00 at RPE 6-7. Include 4 tailwind sprints. (12, 34)
Wednesday	1:45 at RPE 6-8 with one-leg training. (9, 26, 31)
Thursday	1:30 at RPE 6. Include two 10-min. climbs or time trials at RPE 8-9. (32, 33, 52)
Friday	Rest day or weight training. (23, 31)
Saturday	1:00 at RPE 6.
Sunday	4:15 at RPE 6-8. Consider joining a group ride. (35)

LEVEL 2 – WEEK 7

Monday	Rest day or weight training. (23, 31)
Tuesday	1:00 at RPE 6-7. Include 5 tailwind sprints. (12, 34)
Wednesday	2:00 at RPE 6-8 with one-leg training. (9, 26, 31)
Thursday	1:30 at RPE 6. Include three 10-min. time trials at RPE 8-9. (32)
Friday	Rest day or weight training. (23, 31)
Saturday	1:00 at RPE 6.
Sunday	4:30 at RPE 6-8. Consider joining a group ride. (35)

	LEVEL 2 – WEEK 8
Monday	Rest day or weight training. (23, 31)
Tuesday	1:00 at RPE 6-7. Include 3 speed contest sprints. (12, 34)
Wednesday	1:00 at RPE 6-8 with one-leg training. (9, 26, 31)
Thursday	1:30 at RPE 6-8. Include a 5-mile time trial test. (32)
Friday	Rest day or weight training. (23, 31)
Saturday	1:00 at RPE 6.
Sunday	5:00 at RPE 6-8. Consider joining a group ride. (35)

Level 3

For racers and those seeking greater stamina, speed and power for group rides or events.

This 8-week program will help you reach your performance goals on an average of 7-10 training hours per week. There's even time for twice-weekly resistance training. I'm assuming that you can already ride 50-75 miles comfortably and want to compete at distances up to 75 miles. The emphasis is on intense training and enough rest for your body to rebuild after hard efforts.

> **TIP!** The numbers in parentheses refer to chapters where you can find workouts and related information

	LEVEL 3 – WEEK 1
Monday	Rest day or weight training. (23, 31)
Tuesday	1:15 at RPE 6-7. Include 3 jumps. (11, 12, 34)
Wednesday	1:30 at RPE 6-7 with one-leg training. (9, 26, 31)
Thursday	1:00 at RPE 6-8. Include 3 grinder No.1. (31)
Friday	Rest day or weight training. (23, 31)
Saturday	1:00 at RPE 6.
Sunday	2:30 at RPE 6-8. Consider joining a group ride. (35)

LEVEL 3 – WEEK 2

Monday	Rest day or weight training. (23, 31)
Tuesday	1:15 at RPE 6-7. Include 4 jumps. (11, 12, 34)
Wednesday	1:30 at RPE 6-7 with one-leg training. (9, 26, 31)
Thursday	1:15 at RPE 6-9. Include 5 grinder No.2. (31)
Friday	Rest day or weight training. (23, 31)
Saturday	1:00 at RPE 6.
Sunday	2:00-2:30 at RPE 6-8. Consider joining a group ride. (35)

LEVEL 3 – WEEK 3

Monday	Rest day or weight training. (23, 31)
Tuesday	1:15 at RPE 6-7. Include 4 sprints. (12, 34)
Wednesday	1:45 at RPE 6-7 with one-leg training. (9, 26, 31)
Thursday	1:15 at RPE 6-9. Include 6 grinder No.1. (31)
Friday	Rest day or weight training. (23, 31)
Saturday	1:00 at RPE 6.
Sunday	2:30-3:00 at RPE 6-8. Consider joining a group ride. (35)

LEVEL 3 – WEEK 4

Monday	Rest day or weight training. (23, 31)
Tuesday	1:15 at RPE 6-7. Include 5 sprints. (12, 34)
Wednesday	1:15 at RPE 6-7 with one-leg training. (9, 26, 31)
Thursday	1:15 at RPE 6-9. Include 5-mile time trial test. (32)
Friday	Rest day or weight training. (23, 31)
Saturday	1:00 at RPE 6.
Sunday	2:30-3:00 at RPE 6-8. Consider joining a group ride. (35)

LEVEL 3 – WEEK 5

Monday	Rest day or weight training. (23, 31)
Tuesday	1:15 at RPE 6-7. Include 4 tailwind sprints. (12, 34)
Wednesday	1:15 at RPE 6-7 with one-leg training. (9, 26, 31)
Thursday	1:15 at RPE 6-9. Include three 10-min. training time trials. (32)
Friday	Rest day or weight training. (23, 31)
Saturday	1:00 at RPE 6.
Sunday	3:00-3:30 at RPE 6-8. Consider joining a group ride. (35)

LEVEL 3 – WEEK 6

Monday	Rest day or weight training. (23, 31)
Tuesday	1:15 at RPE 6-7. Include 4 speed contest sprints. (12, 34)
Wednesday	1:45 at RPE 6-7 with one-leg training. (9, 26, 31)
Thursday	1:15 at RPE 6-9. Include four 10-min. training time trials. (32)
Friday	Rest day or weight training. (23, 31)
Saturday	1:00 at RPE 6.
Sunday	3:00-3:30 at RPE 6-8. Consider joining a group ride. (35)

LEVEL 3 – WEEK 7

Monday	Rest day or weight training. (23, 31)
Tuesday	1:15 at RPE 6-7. Include 5 sprints. (12, 34)
Wednesday	2:00 at RPE 6-7 with one-leg training. (9, 26, 31)
Thursday	1:15 at RPE 6-9. Include 10 intervals of 30 seconds on, 30 sec. off. (10, 11, 32, 47, 55)
Friday	Rest day or weight training. (23, 31)
Saturday	1:00 at RPE 6.
Sunday	3:30-4 at RPE 6-8. Consider joining a group ride. (35)

LEVEL 3 – WEEK 8

Monday	Rest day or weight training. (23, 31)
Tuesday	1:15 at RPE 6-7. Include 6 sprints. (12, 34)
Wednesday	1:30 at RPE 6-7 with one-leg training. (9, 26, 31)
Thursday	1:15 at RPE 6-7. Include a 5-mile time trial test. (32)
Friday	Rest day or weight training. (23, 31)
Saturday	1:00 at RPE 6.
Sunday	3:30-4 at RPE 6-8. Consider joining a group ride. (35)

PART 4

SUPERCHARGED TRAINING

Introduction

If you've followed the advice in this book through a full year beginning last summer, you're in the best cycling shape of your life. You got fit during the season. You built a stronger base over the winter. Then you converted off-season strength and endurance into cycling-specific power during the 8-week spring transitional period.

Now it's summer and time to cash in on all your hard work. This may mean top performances in competition or fun and adventure riding centuries or tours.

During the season, it's natural to want something extra for a special event. Perhaps you'd like to sharpen your form for a hilly tour or the high-mileage demands of a cross-state ride. Maybe a century PR is your goal, or getting onto the podium in your club's road race championship.

"Something extra" is what this section is all about. I'll reveal dozens of special training and racing techniques used by outstanding riders to supercharge their performances. Some are secrets that coaches and pros would prefer to keep to themselves. Others are gleaned from physiology studies conducted by exercise scientists obsessed with finding out how the body performs. And some are just common sense—but go against traditional tenets of the sport that riders have clung to for years.

Some will help you peak for specific events. Others will guide your daily training. And several of these workouts are designed to fight the staleness that you might experience as the season wears on. They'll make you eager to get in the saddle at a time of year when other cyclists are losing interest in the bike.

HOW TO USE THIS SECTION

Don't indiscriminately begin to use these workouts! Picking a training technique that strikes your fancy and trying it on your next ride is a haphazard and potentially dangerous approach. Using this section as a "workout buffet" will probably stall your progress and could lead to overtraining and burnout. Instead, read each chapter carefully and decide if the workout suits your goals and current fitness. I've included guidelines to help you decide.

Many workouts in this section are designed to help you peak for specific events. They assume that you already have a solid cycling fitness base. If you don't, these techniques are still valuable. But use them with extra care.

CHAPTER 40

Manipulating Intensity

This concept in a nutshell: Go real hard when you go hard. Go real easy when you go easy.

Most of the training techniques in this book are hard work. Doing them correctly requires you to perform at painful levels of intensity. When you do stage race training (chapter 45), coach Dean Golich's "as hard as you can" intervals (chapter 47) or low-cadence, high-resistance workouts (chapter 48), you'll be working (some would say suffering) at levels most riders never reach except in competition—or when fleeing from a rabid mastiff.

That's what's required to nudge your fitness to new levels. As Golich says, "Training is hard work. But so is bike racing. If you want to be able to ride hard in competition, you have to ride hard in training."

Of course, training shouldn't be composed of nothing but miserable suffering. If you employ the techniques in this section during all of your training, you'll burn out quickly. So before you read the following chapters, get all fired up and flame out spectacularly in a couple of weeks, please read (and heed) the following wisdom I've gained from top coaches and riders of the last 25 years.

VARY THE INTENSITY

If there's one trait that distinguishes pros from recreational riders, it's how they pace their training. Professional riders can go fast because when they train hard (or race), they go like lightning. But when they train slowly, they go very, very slowly.

Conversely, most recreational riders train at a moderate pace—fast enough to feel like they're accomplishing something but not so hard that they're suffering unduly. You'll hear some coaches refer to this pace—about 80 percent of max heart rate—as "no-man's land." Like the shell-pocked wasteland between dug-in armies during World War I, you don't want to be there very often.

Why? Because no-man's land delivers a double whammy. It compromises recovery *and* improvement. At a moderately brisk pace of around 80 percent of max heart rate, you're not going slowly enough to recover. You need a pace around 65 percent of max heart rate to pump nutrient-rich blood to your leg muscles without stressing them further. Unfortunately, you're also not going fast enough to improve. That takes an intensity of about 90 percent of max.

Remember, when every ride is done at a medium pace, your results are bound to be mediocre.

FAST IS BETTER

There's an emerging consensus among researchers and coaches in favor of high-intensity training. In fact, some exercise scientists argue that about 25 percent of your total training time should be done at intensities slightly below, at, or slightly above your lactate threshold (LT). That's almost certainly extreme, but it illustrates the direction your training should take for maximum improvement.

Riding at high intensity saves training time, too. As American pro roadman Jonathan Vaughters says, "You can work intensely at 80 to 85 percent of max heart rate for an hour, or you can ride six hours at 70 percent of max and get the same benefit." If your training time is limited, you have little choice but to opt for intensity.

Lactate threshold is about 90 percent of max heart rate in well-trained riders. That's not a comfortable level. Think back to your last time trial or long, steep climb. You probably don't go that hard very often. Instead, you're either warming up at 65 percent of max or cruising at 80 percent. Sometimes, usually on hills, your heart rate may rise toward the 90 percent figure, but if you calculate the total percentage of riding time when it reaches that level, the number is likely to be closer to 5 percent than 25 percent.

Now think about spending a quarter of your training time at 90 percent. Intimidating!

What does it take to have the physical (and mental) reserves required to tolerate a program of intense training? Obviously, if you ride extremely hard a quarter of the time, you have to ride extremely easy the remainder of the time. The problem is that going slowly makes many riders feel guilty. And going fast is painful.

Nevertheless, if you're bent on improvement, you must schedule both hard training and "hard" resting into your program. This is especially important at the height of the season. When you go hard, go *really* hard. The techniques in this section will help you do it with maximum efficiency—and minimum pain.

Then when you go easy, ride at an effort and speed that anyone could do. In the words of coach Skip Hamilton, these rides should be "guilt-producingly slow." Vaughters cruises the bike paths of Denver on his easy days and says that "senior citizens on beach cruisers blow by me."

The result of carefully planned slow riding will be greater recovery between hard efforts and, because of that hard training, greater improvement.

IS NO-MAN'S LAND EVER APPROPRIATE?

Of course. As we've seen, early-season endurance training is often done, appropriately, at about 80 percent of max heart rate. There's an enjoyment factor, too. Some rides should be medium-paced because it's a vigorous-yet-comfortable intensity that's rewarding. It feels hard enough to be satisfying but not so hard that you're suffering. Riding your bike should be fun. There's no reason to avoid the intensity zone that pegs the fun meter rather than your heart monitor. Just don't give in to the temptation to dwell there ride after ride.

Also, some events—centuries, for instance—are usually ridden at a steady, moderate intensity. If you'll be riding 100 miles in no-man's land, it's appropriate to spend some training time there, too. It's up to you to listen to your body and determine the lower level of intensity that promotes recovery and the higher level that makes you faster.

CHAPTER 41

Warming Up for Top Performance

This concept in a nutshell: Get your body ready before you ask it to perform.

Why have a consistent warm-up routine? Why isn't it sufficient merely to spin easily for the first few minutes of a ride? A structured warm-up accomplishes several important things:

- **It raises body temperature**. Sweating means that your muscles are warm, loose and relaxed. There's some evidence that higher body temperature thins bodily fluids, lessening strain on joints and the heart.

- **It reduces initial levels of muscular stress**. If you've ever had to go hard on the bike without a warm-up—like when a group ride rages out of the parking lot—you know how your legs burn for the first few minutes. A good warm-up, on the other hand, alerts your systems that it's going to get harder soon.

- **It conserves glycogen**. Fast-from-the-gun workouts or races dip into your precious supplies of glycogen, your muscles' primary fuel. A slower start allows you to begin by burning a higher percentage of fat, conserving glycogen for later when you really need it.

- **It opens capillaries**. A warm-up dilates the capillaries that allow your blood to bathe muscle cells with oxygen and nutrients. More blood flow means more fuel and a better-performing engine.

- **It compensates for aging**. The older you are, the more you need a warm-up. When we were kids, we could go full speed right off the couch when a friend wanted to run pass routes in the back yard. That's not how it works as we age, and we're more apt to get injured, too. The quality of our training suffers if we don't prepare for hard work.

For all these reasons, the warm-up is a vital part of each ride.

> **TIP!** Get in the habit of using the same warm-up routine before every hard workout. There's a sample protocol on the next page. Many of this book's workouts require high intensity that approaches race effort. A full warm-up is crucial to help you perform well and avoid injury.

SHORTER MAY BE BETTER

For years, I used a fairly long warm-up routine before time trials and short road races. I patterned it after what I understood top riders do. I'd spin around for 20 minutes, ride a few hills hard, do some sprints and top it off with several minutes at TT pace. But sometimes this made me feel drained for the event itself. When the crunch came in a road race or I needed a strong final 10K in a time trial, there wasn't enough in my tank. I'd used too much energy in my warm-up.

Then I read that England's Chris Boardman, the world hour record holder, had switched from hour-long warm-ups to a focused routine of 15-20 minutes. I tried it and developed an abbreviated routine like the one described below. It worked great and left me plenty of energy for the race itself.

Most riders do long warm-ups for the wrong reason, such as calming pre-race nerves. Riders get to the event early and register, but then they're too antsy to relax in the car and review their race strategy. Instead, nervous energy pressures them into a long, "pro-style" warm-up. Too often, it's unfocused and burns precious reserves. When they get to the starting line, they feel flat rather than fiery.

A WARM-UP FOR TRAINING AND RACING

Here's a 20-minute warm-up routine that you can use for any event. Practice it during the first 20 minutes of each training ride that will include hard efforts or long distance. By beginning tough workouts with the same warm-up, your body will become accustomed to what's coming next.

Although this warm-up is based on the successful routines of top riders, it won't be ideal for everyone. Warming up is highly individual. You may need a 60-minute warm-up to perform at your peak, but most cyclists will do better with a significantly shorter session. Experiment to find the length that works for you.

WARM-UP TIME (minutes)	TECHNIQUE
0-4	Spin easily in a low gear. Begin at 75 rpm and gradually build to 90 rpm. Keep heart rate below 70% of max.
5-11	Gradually increase the gear and effort. Shift up every 2 minutes. Keep cadence at 90-100 rpm. In the last minute you should be breathing deeply, sweating lightly and your heart rate should be at 80% of max.
12-14	Do 3 controlled sprints. Using a moderate gear, stand, accelerate to 110 rpm, sit, and spin up to the point where your hips begin to rock. Then gradually slow until back to 90 rpm. This sequence should take about 20 seconds. Repeat 3 times with 40 seconds of easy spinning between sprints.
15-17	Do a 3-minute interval: Use a gear that you can turn at 90 rpm without pedaling all-out. Stand to accelerate, then sit and hold 90 rpm for 3 minutes. Power output should be equal to a training time trial of about 30 minutes. Your heart rate should rise to your lactate threshold in the last 15 seconds.
18-20	Spin easily in a low gear. At 20 minutes, your heart rate should be down to 120 or lower, with breathing stabilized and legs feeling lively.

CAUTION! Don't use this warm-up routine at the start of recovery rides. It requires too much effort. Instead, gradually increase cadence and gearing until your heart rate is about 70 percent of max. Don't go any harder than that.

Nowhere fast: Keep everything in control during pre-event warm-ups by using a stationary trainer.

STATIONARY WARM-UPS

At some events, particularly city criteriums, the surrounding roads can be so traffic-choked that warming up on them is dangerous or ineffective. The solution is to warm up on a trainer. This may even be required by the race promoter.

One year, for example, organizers of the Colorado time trial championship faced opposition from residents of the small town where the race was to be held. The locals could tolerate riders on the road chosen for the TT, but they objected to us warming up on town streets. So, we had to use trainers or risk losing the race venue. Most of us complained at first. How can we get a good warm-up on a trainer? But once we tried it, the benefits became obvious:

- There's no risk of a flat tire from road debris.

- You never leave your car, so help is right there if you have a problem.

- If the start time is changed for any reason, you're within hearing distance of the announcer.

- You can cope better with weather. If it's cool, there's no windchill on the trainer. If it's hot, you can set up in the shade, and cold drinks are as close as your ice chest. Raining? You can wear a poncho as you warm up or have a friend hold an umbrella over you. At least you'll stay dry until the race starts.

- You can wear headphones and listen to inspiring music, something that's dangerous (and may be illegal) when riding on the road.

- The warm-up routine outlined above can be done just as effectively on a trainer as on the road.

COOLING DOWN

The final few minutes of training are important, too. After a hard ride or race, don't immediately hop off your bike, panting and sweating. Instead, reverse the initial 5 minutes of the warm-up routine.

I live in a small town, so when I cross the city limit on the way home, I shift to the small ring, take a few deep breaths and spin through the residential streets. There's a small hill half a mile from my house, but I resist the temptation to do just one more hard bit over the top. In fact, I often choose a street that goes around the hill in order to cool down more effectively.

Some riders live atop climbs that make cooling down difficult. One example is my 1996 Race Across America teammate, Pete Penseyres, whose house crowns an 800-vertical-foot hill in southern California. He cools down by standing and "walking" up the hill with a slow cadence in a low gear, keeping his heart rate relatively low. When my business partner, Ed Pavelka, lived in southeastern Pennsylvania, his house was on top of a wall that he named "The Final Indignity." After scaling it, he'd stay in low gear and spin gently at 5 mph for the final 150 yards to his house.

CHAPTER 42

Power Training

T his concept in a nutshell: The recent development of reliable and lower-priced power meters allows us to measure and use training intensity in a whole new way.

For most of cycling's history, riders determined their intensity by feel. They went "easy" or "hard" or simply noted their gearing. A long aerobic ride was done in a 42x17-tooth gear and intervals were hammered out in 53x15. Although these were only approximations of intensity, they worked for generations of riders.

With the development of accurate and affordable heart rate monitoring in the mid 1980s, training entered the scientific age. Cyclists began downloading their workout heart rates into computers for analysis. Heart monitoring became a staple of aerobic exercise machines and cardiac rehab programs as well as a must for serious athletes.

The newest method of gauging intensity is power measurement. As of mid 2002, several products allow cyclists to put a number (watts) on power output. Two of these devices use strain gauges on the bike. The German-made SRM puts them in the bottom bracket. The PowerTap from Graber Products puts them in the rear hub.

Power can be determined by other means, too. In a bid to lower the cost, companies have eagerly innovated. The S710, from heart monitor company Polar, measures chain tension and chain speed to calculate power. The CicloSport HAC 4 doesn't measure power output directly but instead relies on a mathematical calculation. You input your combined body/bike weight and the computer adds a constant for rolling and wind resistance. It then computes wattage from the effort required to move your mass at certain speeds and rate of elevation gain.

I've trained with the PowerTap, Polar and CicloSport units. I'll review them at the end of this chapter. But first, let's look at why anyone would plunk down enough money to buy another bike just to know wattage output.

WHAT'S A WATT?

Because intensity is the best producer of fitness, measuring intensity is the key to efficient training. But why not simply gauge it by speed, or by how hard it feels like you're working, or by heart rate? Three key reasons:

1. The intensity needed to produce a certain speed varies depending on the wind, pavement quality and whether the road tilts up or down.

2. Measures of perceived exertion can be accurate but require practice and careful monitoring of how you feel.

3. Factors such as hydration status, air temperature and fatigue can cause heart rate to vary widely at a given power output.

Power monitoring, on the other hand, is accurate simply because a watt is always a watt regardless of outside factors. According to Allen Lim, a doctoral student at the University of Colorado who's doing definitive studies in the area, "Power training provides a direct and objective measurement. It's like giving a chef a thermometer. You can bake a pie without knowing how hot the oven is, but it takes a lot more attention and experience. Having a direct way to monitor the process (training or cooking) allows athletes to understand their training and race environment. You don't end up burning as many pies before you figure out the perfect recipe."

In fact, some coaches would argue that power monitoring is the Holy Grail of training because it tells you exactly how hard you're working, day after day. It's objective and foolproof, the sort of hard data that can transform training from art to science. According to SRM inventor Ulrich Schoberer, "The basic element of riding faster is to increase power output rather than heart rate or lactate. It is simply power. All other values are the second choice."

Even more important, exercise scientists can use power meters in races to pinpoint the demands of competition. How many watts did the winner of Paris-Roubaix generate on the cobbles of the Forest of Arenberg? How many times during the race did he have to achieve that wattage figure? How many watts does Lance Armstrong average when he's climbing l'Alpe d'Huez?

By knowing these figures, riders and coaches can set up training programs that duplicate the demands of racing. Recreational riders can use a power meter in centuries or local time trials to do the same thing. As Lim says, "We can finally see what athletes are doing in races and begin to manipulate their training so it's more specific."

APPLYING WATTAGE INFORMATION

Simply knowing how many watts you average as you blast up your local killer hill isn't enough. That number is simply a number unless you know what to do with it. According to Joe Friel, a Colorado endurance sports coach and author of *The Cyclist's Training Bible*, a good place to start is by determining your average power or "critical power" (CP) for various time periods. He recommends 12 seconds, 1 minute, 6 minutes, 30 minutes, 1 hour and 3 hours. Then you can determine exact training loads for interval workouts.

One way to visualize this is by comparing it to weight training. Let's say that a strength athlete can bench press 400 pounds one time with a maximum effort. So, 400 pounds is his one-rep max (abbreviated 1RM.) Once this has been determined, he can work out at a specific percentage of his 1RM, doing (for example) 5 sets of 8 repetitions at 80 percent of 1RM, or 320 pounds.

Similarly, once you know your CP for, say, 6 minutes, you can do intervals at a given percentage of that figure. If your CP for an all-out 6-minute effort is 400 watts, you might do 3-minute repeats at 80 percent (320 watts). As you get stronger, you can increase the wattage and the duration of the intervals. Power measuring means that the intensity of workouts can be precisely controlled.

THE RACE OF TRUTH

Power measuring is also great for time trials or non-drafting triathlons where it's just you against the clock (and the wind and the hills). These events require you to accurately dole out energy for the whole distance so you go as fast as possible and finish spent. Go too hard early and you'll slow abruptly before the finish and lose time. Start too slow and you'll finish with energy to spare, well above the best time you could have recorded.

Experienced time trialists apportion energy by feel. They sense exactly how hard they can ride to finish the race exhausted, their last dollop of energy burned in the final 200 meters. However, such knowledge of the body takes lots of time trialing.

Power metering makes success more objective. If you know the average power output you can sustain for the duration of the event, you can simply maintain that level, secure in the knowledge that it's your optimum pace. This works much better than trying to ride at a certain heart rate because of a phenomenon known as *cardiac drift*. Heart rate tends to rise as an event wears on, even though wattage stays constant.

Of course, time trialing isn't a steady-state effort unless the course is dead flat with no wind. Even then, you'll go harder when accelerating at the start and turnaround. On most courses, you have to go slightly over your limit on hills and out of turns, then recover a bit on easier sections. Many riders use a heart monitor to gauge their intensity in these conditions. But because heart rate lags behind effort, by the time you know you're going too hard on a hill, it's too late. According to SRM's Schoberer, "With heart rate, there's a delay in the response to effort, sometimes as much as two minutes. But with power, you can control your effort precisely." A power meter shows you immediately whether you're below, at or above the wattage that your experience says you can maintain.

COMPARE WATTAGE AND HEART RATE

All that said, knowing your heart rate is still important. One advantage of power measuring is the ability to see wattage and heart rate simultaneously. Even though heart rate is influenced by the environment and other factors, it's still a useful measure of what's going on in your body.

If you know the heart rate usually associated with a given wattage and duration, you can watch for variations and realize when you shouldn't be training hard. For instance, suppose you normally see a heart rate of about 170 while doing 3-minute repeats at 300 watts. Today, however, you're struggling to put out 250 watts at 170 bpm. That's a clear sign you're not fully recovered from previous training. Cancel the interval session and spin slowly home feeling smart, not guilty. Make sure you're rested, well hydrated and your muscle glycogen stores are replenished with high-carbohydrate foods before you try again.

IMPORTANCE OF PERCEIVED EXERTION

Nor does power monitoring mean that perceived exertion is passé. In fact, according to researcher Allen Lim, many pro riders use power meters to compare wattage to their subjective feelings of intensity. This is how Jonathan Vaughters, a big proponent of power measuring, does it.

Says Lim, "Make sure you listen to your intuition when you use a power meter. One of the major benefits is developing a better sense of feel when training and racing." Once you've "calibrated" your feelings of intensity to the objective measures made possible by a watts meter, you won't need to refer to the handlebar-mounted electronics as frequently.

Knowing wattage keeps you in line when going easy, too. Because intense training is so demanding, you need plenty of easy spinning to promote recovery. But despite the best intentions, it's common for effort to creep up during easy rides until the pace is too hard to allow recovery. Seeing the number of watts you're putting out prevents you from overriding perceived exertion and gradually increasing the effort. It also helps you avoid getting sucked along by a group that's too fast for the day's goals.

PERSONALIZING YOUR TRAINING

You're a unique bike rider with your own physical attributes and liabilities. No one else can decide how you should train. Power monitoring is a powerful tool to help you learn about yourself. Lim's advice is to "employ the scientific method to answer personal questions about training." These, he says, are the crucial ones:

– Do you produce more power at a higher or lower cadence when climbing?

- How do different pacing strategies in a time trial affect performance?

- What is the relationship between total work done and time spent in varying intensity zones?

- How does time in different intensity zones affect feelings of perceived effort, fatigue and performance?

- What are the specific power demands of key events, and how does competitive power output compare to your power output in training?

With a power meter, you can answer all of these questions, then tailor your training to your own talents and goals.

EFFICIENT USE OF TIME

Power monitoring is especially useful for time-challenged riders. If you have only one hour to train on a given day, it's important to use every minute to best advantage. A power meter makes it possible by telling you exactly how hard to work. No more inefficient guessing. Plus, a power meter is simply unbeatable for progressively increasing the workload over several weeks or months. I've talked with a number of riders who began using one and saw significant gains. They had reached a high level of power production in previous seasons but had plateaued.

Finally, a power meter converts any indoor trainer into an ergometer. Simply mount your bike and do a precise wattage workout at any time of day (or night) despite outside conditions.

THE DOWNSIDE

Despite all of these advantages, power monitoring isn't right for everyone. I won't fault you if any of these drawbacks are significant enough to stop you from getting into this new technology.

- **Cost.** At this writing in June, 2002, the cheapest power meter is the CicloSport HAC 4, which I've seen advertised for as low as $400 (with computer interface). Recreational riders and some racers may opt to spend the money on other equipment or for travel to events. It's likely that more-affordable units will be on the market soon, as power training gains popularity and competitive companies respond. Stay tuned for developments and lower prices.

- **Complexity.** Experienced riders may be content with simple perceived exertion as a gauge. Your RPE can be nearly as precise as a power meter for most training purposes, and it costs nothing.

- **Pressure.** Some riders object to yet another number that goads them into going at a certain pace. These riders may have tried heart monitoring and decided that they didn't like the constant judgment of their effort.

- **Clutter.** Some riders hate hanging things on their bikes, especially products like the Polar S710 with several wires that must be attached to the frame.

- **Information overkill.** Many recreational riders may not care about fine-tuned performance. For them, power monitoring is a waste of time and money.

PRODUCT REVIEW: POWER METERS

The German-designed **SRM** has been available to the rich and famous for more than a decade. (Greg LeMond used one in the last year of his career.) It's expensive at $2,500-$4,000 and hard to get in North America.

The strain gauges mounted in the bottom bracket require you to use SRM's crankarms. Pedaling power is measured directly—and extremely accurately, according to laboratory ergometers. I've talked with several pros who've used the SRM and all were enthusiastic about it. Unfortunately, price and availability put it out of reach for most of us.

Although I couldn't obtain an SRM, I did get hands-on experience with the 3 less-costly power meters currently available to North American riders. I trained with the original PowerTap for 3 years. After Graber Products bought the brand from Tune, the founding company, I rode Graber's redesigned unit for 4 months. The Polar S710 was announced nearly a year before units became available. I tested it for a month before this book was published. Finally, the CicloSport HAC 4 came on the market just before deadline. I was able to use it for 3 weeks.

Based on these admittedly too-short time frames for the last 2 units, but in the interest of providing some useful selection information, here are my impressions. All prices are an average of those in spring 2002 catalogs.

PowerTap

The $950 PowerTap measures wattage, speed, cadence, heart rate, time, distance and energy expended. The quoted price includes a rear hub, cyclecomputer, heart-monitor chest strap and download software. You need to have a rear wheel built around the hub or buy a wheel from Graber Products.

The PowerTap is easy to set up. I simply removed the Shimano 9-speed cassette from my standard rear wheel and slipped it on the PowerTap wheel. The sensor mounted quickly on the left chainstay about 6 inches from the hub. Although transmission from the hub to the sensor is wireless, a wire leads from the sensor to the handlebar-mounted computer. To make the wire less obtrusive, I wrapped it around the rear brake cable, routed it along the top tube, then wrapped it around the front brake cable. A completely wireless system would be cleaner, but there's too much distance from the rear hub to the handlebar. I didn't notice any interference from heart monitors worn by nearby riders.

> **TIP!** If you use zip ties to secure the PowerTap's cable, don't overtighten them. Doing so can cut off data transmission to the handlebar computer. To be safe, use electrical tape instead.

The PowerTap display shows wattage and speed simultaneously, along with your choice of time, distance, heart rate, torque, cadence or energy expenditure. It's easy to toggle among these readings as well as between average and max speed and wattage. Crucial to the design is an interval function. By holding down one control button for 2 seconds, the unit will record up to 9 intervals so you can play back max and average power, speed, cadence and heart rate for each effort.

The download option allows you to create graphs of rides and compare them over time. There's a power-to-heart-rate ratio to track your fitness, and a power-to-weight feature. You can view a whole ride on the graph, look at certain sections or examine individual intervals.

That's all good, but I also found these drawbacks:

- The PowerTap's rear hub is hefty. It adds about 8 ounces to your bike. At least the beef is at the center of the wheel where it has the least impact on rotating weight and speed.

- If you want to record your power output during a race, you have no choice but to use the wheel with the PowerTap hub, even if it's built around a heavier training rim. However, you can mount regular race wheels on your bike and still use the PowerTap handlebar monitor for speed and heart rate. Simply put a magnet on your rear spokes and switch to a special mode.

- Early PowerTap hubs had poor seals that let water in, ruining the unit. Graber Products redesigned the seals. I rode the new version in showers (but not drenching rain) and had no problems. Riders in wetter conditions report that the new seals seem to be effective.

Polar S710

This $640 product uses chain tension and chain speed to calculate power. Chain speed is measured with a magnetic sensor on the rear derailleur that counts links as they pass. Chain tension is measured with a sensor on the chainstay. The sensor doesn't touch the chain but feels vibration. According to Polar, this is a highly accurate method used in precision scales.

The S710 is easy to put on a bike in one sense: You don't have to replace existing components such as the crankarms with SRM or the rear wheel with PowerTap. The system zip-ties to the frame. Because 2 non-contact sensors and digital signal processing is used to measure power, there are no moving parts to wear out. Polar argues that competing systems employ delicate strain gauges mounted with epoxy that can degrade over time.

You must enter 3 values during installation: chain weight, chain length, and distance from crank axle to rear wheel axle. Default settings are included. The system is consistent if you use them, but better accuracy is achieved by entering numbers specific to your bike—assuming you are precise with weights and measurements.

The Polar has several unique features, including power output balance between right and left legs during pedaling. Results are viewable in real-time and later in the download. You also can see the roundness of your stroke. The Polar (and the CicloSport HAC 4) has an altimeter, too. With this, you can calculate meters-per-minute climbed, a key to the performance evaluation described in chapter 43.

Drawbacks? The S710 has a few:

- The instructional manual is complicated. It took hours to digest it and install the system.

- The Polar has so many options that sorting out which to use and which are extraneous is a major task. Of course, if you like data deluge you'll be very pleased.

- Precision is paramount. If you enter a chain weight that's incorrect by 5 percent, your wattage will be wrong by the same percentage.

- Wattage readings can vary by 50-70 watts for the same intensity, depending on whether you're in the big or small ring. The chain has to be the correct distance from the sensor and the "window" is rather small. Polar provides a shim kit to help you get it right.

- The S710 has more wires than a regional electric power station. They clutter the bike so it's hard to clean the frame. The right chainstay sensor has 3 wires. The most problematic one runs to the rear derailleur and requires that you replace a pulley bolt. This wire is wrapped around the derailleur cable. You have to leave enough slack or the derailleur won't shift properly. Getting it right requires considerable trial and error.

CicloSport HAC 4

The $400 HAC 4 doesn't measure wattage directly but estimates it from a mathematical calculation. You input the combined weight of your body, clothing and bike. Then the computer estimates wattage based on the effort required to move that mass at the speed you're traveling and the elevation you're gaining. This calculation is similar to Jonathan Vaughters' method of determining wattage and VO_2 max from meters-per-minute climbed (next chapter). That has become a hot performance parameter. Data can be downloaded into your PC so you can analyze your workout in a computer training log that comes with the unit.

The HAC 4 puts significantly less clutter on the bike than the other units. It has only a spoke magnet and a fork-blade sensor that relays information to a handlebar-mounted heart monitor watch. There are no wires on the bike.

On the negative side:

– The wattage figure provided by the HAC 4 is only an estimate. The company argues that it's a consistent estimate and provides reliable comparative figures from one workout to the next. However, there's no pretense that the numbers can be usefully compared to those you'd get in a lab test.

– Power output figures were fairly close to those from the PowerTap when I was climbing a steep hill. But numbers on the flat were quite low and changed little when I accelerated.

RECOMMENDATIONS

If you want to monitor your power, which of these 4 devices should you get?

• **Buy the SRM** if you have a flush bank account, you want state-of-the-art power monitoring and you're willing to mount a new pair of crankarms.

• **Buy the PowerTap** if you'd like to spend considerably less than you would for an SRM but still want direct power measurement, relatively simple setup, data analysis and can accept using a heavier rear wheel.

• **Buy the Polar S710** if you are comfortable with Polar products and instructional manuals, enjoy figuring out a fairly complicated setup procedure, and want to analyze each leg's power production and pedaling smoothness.

• **Buy the CicloSport HAC 4** if you're on a tighter budget, want the altimeter function and are satisfied with estimated rather than accurate power figures.

CHAPTER 43

Simplified Testing For Wattage and VO₂ Max

This concept in a nutshell: You don't need an expensive lab test to determine 3 important performance numbers—power at lactate threshold, maximal oxygen uptake (VO₂ max) and meters-per-minute of climbing.

As we've seen, it's important to know how much power you can produce. But power meters are expensive. It would also be great to know your VO₂ max. But laboratory tests cost around $500. Fortunately, there's a simple test you can do on your own training roads to get this information. It requires only a suitable hill, your bike, a scale, a stopwatch and an altimeter or topographic map. Oh—and an all-out effort, too!

I learned this technique from pro roadman Jonathan Vaughters at his April 2002 training camp in Denver. Based on sound physiological principles, it produces numbers quite close to those you'd get if you were lab-tested. Here's how it works:

By the numbers: Vaughters vouches for self-testing.

1. Find a tough hill that takes at least 10 minutes to climb. A steep (6-8 percent) and steady grade is necessary to negate the effects of wind resistance. Hills that take less time to ascend mean you'll rely too heavily on your anaerobic energy production system, thus skewing the results.

2. Determine the climb's elevation gain in meters. Use an altimeter such as those found on the Polar S710, the CicloSport HAC 4 or cyclecomputers such as the Cateye AT100 or Specialized Speedzone Pro. You could also figure your elevation gain from contour lines on a topographic map, but it won't be as precise and test results won't be as accurate. Try to use an altimeter.

3. Weigh yourself and your bike while you're wearing riding clothes. Include your water bottles, frame pump and seat bag if you'll have them on during the test. Once you've determined the total weight you'll be propelling up the hill, convert pounds to kilograms by dividing by 2.2.

4. Warm up well, then time yourself while riding the climb as hard as you can. Begin the test from a standing start like you would in a time trial. Climb with any technique you choose— seated, standing or alternating in and out of the saddle. The idea is to get to the top as fast as possible.

Recovered? Now you're ready to assess your performance in 3 key categories.

METERS-PER-MINUTE CLIMBED

According to Vaughters, this measure is the latest rage among pro riders. "Lance Armstrong is obsessed by it," he says. Why? Because climbing is contingent on your power-to-weight ratio. Determining meters-per-minute climbed gives you an objective rating of your uphill ability without the need for other calculations.

To do it, simply divide the height of the climb by the number of minutes it took you to get to the top. For instance, if you climbed 186 vertical meters in 10 minutes, your meters-per-minute figure is 18.6. What does this number mean? According to Vaughters:

19 meters per minute	Survive the Tour de France
22-25 meters per minute	Place top 30 in the Tour
30-32 meters per minute	Win climb of l'Alpe d'Huez

Data for recreational racers isn't available, but here's an educated guess: Category 1-2 riders will range from 20 to 25 meters per minute. Masters will do 17-22, depending on age. If these numbers seem high compared to Vaughters' values, remember that in U.S. racing, climbs are usually short by European professional standards. The shorter the hill, the easier it is to maintain a high rate of climbing speed. And if a domestic race does have a long climb, it's usually done just once in contrast to the Tour, where the l'Alpe d'Huez ascent is typically the third or fourth mountain of the day.

AVERAGE WATTS

To calculate your average watts for the climb:

1. Multiply the vertical meters in the climb by the total weight of bike and rider in kilograms.

2. Divide the result by the time of the climb in seconds.

3. Multiply that answer by 10 and add 60 (a constant for rolling resistance, chain friction, etc.)

For example, if you climbed 186 meters in 10 minutes and your total body/bike weight is 80 kg, your average wattage is 308.

MAXIMAL OXYGEN UPTAKE (VO$_2$ MAX)

To calculate your VO$_2$ max:

1. Divide your average watts from the above calculation by an efficiency factor of 72 to get your total oxygen consumption in liters per minute.

2. Multiply the result by 1,000 to get milliliters of oxygen consumed.

3. Divide milliliters of oxygen by your body weight in kilograms to get VO$_2$ max expressed in the standard ml/kg/min.

For example, if your average watts is 308 as in the example, and your body weight is 70 kg, your VO_2 max is 61.1 ml/kg/min.

In Vaughters' view, speaking from his experience in European cycling, a VO_2 max of over 70 is outstanding and anything above 60 is excellent. These figures are for his home testing grounds west of Denver at elevations around 7,000 feet. At sea level, VO_2 max results are about 8 percent higher. So, you flatlanders need values of about 76 and 65, respectively, to earn his ratings.

CHAPTER 44

High-Cadence Pedaling

This concept in a nutshell: Pedaling cadence is individual. Don't copy high-cadence riders like Lance Armstrong unless you determine that it's your most efficient style.

The Lance Armstrong story is compelling for many reasons—his challenging youth as a child of a single mother, his triumph over cancer, his mastery of race tactics after winning early events on bullish strength alone. Indeed, it's remarkable that he even found the sport of cycling in the football hotbed of Plano, Texas.

But Armstrong's most important technical legacy to cycling may well be his high-cadence pedaling. While big gears and a moderate cadence have marked modern pedaling technique, Lance's preferred rpm of 100+ in time trials and 90-100 on steep climbs represents a return to the classic years of the sport. Then, a 52x13-tooth gear was considered huge, and riders broke the hour for 25-mile time trials on a fixed gear of 70 inches (equal to 39x15 on your bike), pedaling at 120 rpm.

Seeing Lance's supple stroke on steep climbs like l'Alpe d'Huez is like being in a time machine and witnessing famous pedalers of the 1950s and '60s—Jacques Anquetil or Federico Bahamontes—riders who never looked like they were feeling the pedals as they slid through the wind or flew up steep slopes.

As a result of Lance's success, many recreational riders and racers have spent inordinate amounts of training time trying to pedal faster. The thinking goes: If Lance does it, I should do it, too. But not so quick. Like most cycling techniques, rapid pedaling is appropriate for some riders but not for all riders. Just because it works for Lance doesn't mean it will work for you.

EXAMPLE! In 2002, I had the opportunity to ride with the Saturn pro team at its preseason training camp in California. On climbs, I was amazed at the variation in cadence. Some riders sat and spun at 100 rpm while others plodded up the slope in the big ring and a cadence closer to 60 rpm.

You'd think that in a small and elite group of riders, natural selection would guarantee that everyone would pedal at about the same cadence if one cadence were the most efficient. But that certainly wasn't the case.

LIM'S LAW

For perspective on this issue, I talked with Allen Lim, the doctoral candidate at the University of Colorado who has been studying power output in cyclists (see chapter 42). As a result of his studies, he has formulated what might be termed Lim's Law:

"A fast spin isn't a technique for producing power. It's a result of having power."

In other words, Lance doesn't spin fast in order to increase his wattage at a given heart rate. Instead, he spins fast because he has so much power that he can afford to ride at a faster cadence, thus sparing his leg muscles and transferring the strain to his cardiovascular system. It's an important distinction.

The heart muscle doesn't fatigue like leg muscles do. Spinning fast on early climbs in a long race means that Lance has plenty of leg power left when it's needed near the end.

Here's an analogy. Suppose you're riding with a slower companion. You don't want to ride away from him on climbs, so what do you do? You gear down and spin while he chugs up the hill in his usual climbing cadence of 70-75 rpm. "Wow," he thinks. "This guy [you] is much stronger and it must be because his cadence is faster than mine. I should work on increasing my cadence, too." But in order to spin as fast as you, he has to use a lower gear. He still climbs slowly even though he's pedaling faster. If the situation were reversed and you were the one riding with a stronger companion, you'd be laboring while he spun blithely along by your side.

So, Lance pedals fast because he has more power than his competitors. To restate Lim's Law, fast pedaling isn't a training technique to help you gain power, it's a byproduct of being powerful.

Jonathan Vaughters agrees. As a former teammate of Armstrong's and now a Tour de France rider himself, he has watched the Texan's pedal stroke up close and personal. Says Vaughters, "Lance doesn't pedal any faster than other riders when he's in the pack. He only pedals a very high rpm when he's going hard. He does it because he produces more power than anyone else."

Fine. So how do you determine what cadence is best for you?

TESTA'S CLIMBING TEST

Max Testa, M.D., is a former pro team physician who directs a sports medicine clinic in Davis, California, owned by Eric Heiden of speedskating and cycling fame. According to Testa, the key to discovering your most-efficient cadence is to pay attention to what happens when you're about to blow up on a climb.

"What fails when you're trying to keep up on a hill?" he asks. "Do you shift to a lower gear and spin fast because if you go to a bigger gear and grind your legs die? In that case, you need strength. But if, when you use a smaller gear and spin, your breathing goes out of control, you need more cardiovascular conditioning."

Try Testa's test when you're doing hill repeats. On the second or third time up the climb, when you're warmed up but not yet tired, push as hard as possible. Near the top, at the point when you begin to lose power and your pedal stroke gets ragged, shift to a harder gear and try to maintain the same speed. Pay attention to what happens.

Recover. Then on the next climb, when the going gets tough, shift to an easier gear and try to spin. Compare your sensations and your speed. Done several times, this experiment should tell you whether you're more efficient as a spinner or a grinder. It should also reveal if you need to work on leg strength and power or cardiovascular conditioning in order to become a better climber.

EXPERT EVALUATION

When Testa put me on an ergometer at Colorado's Boulder Center for Sports Medicine, I could feel graphically what cadence my body preferred. I began pedaling at a low wattage and 90 rpm. Every minute, Testa increased resistance by 25 watts while I kept my cadence steady. Soon I was laboring, and a blood draw revealed that I had reached my lactate threshold.

But Testa continued to increase resistance. In order to maintain the cadence, I moved to the rear of the saddle and started muscling the gear. Soon I ran out of steam, my cadence slowed and the test was finally over. My reaction to this extreme effort revealed a lot.

"When you went above your lactate threshold," Testa told me, "you moved your effort from your cardiovascular system to your muscles. Some riders, with outstanding cardiovascular conditioning, would move forward on the tip of the saddle and spin as they neared their maximum. But because you have good leg strength and power, you moved to the rear and let your muscles take over."

The doctor's prescription? I should (1) work on my cardiovascular system with high-cadence intervals; (2) improve my pedaling efficiency with fixed-gear riding; (3) raise my lactate threshold with 12-minute time-trial repeats at a fast cadence and an intensity about 10 beats below my LT.

Apply this example to your own reaction under stress. Even better, do a similar test with an experienced coach and get a personal training recommendation.

HOW TO USE WATTS

If you have a watts-measuring device and a heart monitor, ride one of your favorite climbs using a high gear and low cadence. Note your wattage, heart rate and feeling of perceived exertion. Recover, then ride the climb again. Keep wattage the same but decrease the gear and raise cadence. Again, note your heart rate and feeling.

You'll probably need several such experiments over a couple of days or a week to notice a pattern. But one will eventually emerge. You'll see that lower heart rates are associated with a particular cadence at a given wattage. You'll probably feel better when you find your cadence "sweet spot," too—more in tune with your body as you're climbing.

MUSCLE FIBER TYPE

One more important point: Your preferred cadence may be related to muscle fiber type. There's some evidence that riders with predominantly fast-twitch fibers—sprinters, for instance—do better with a faster cadence. Endurance riders with a preponderance of slow-twitch fibers ride more efficiently at a lower cadence in a larger gear.

> **RESEARCH!** In a study conducted by scientists at the University of Wisconsin and the University of Wyoming, 8 experienced cyclists rode at an intensity of 85 percent of VO_2 max (about 90 percent of max heart rate) for 30 minutes in 2 different trials. First, they rode at 50 rpm in a high gear. Next, they lowered the gearing and increased rpm to 100.
>
> The riders' oxygen consumption rates, heart rates, power production and blood lactate levels were similar in both scenarios. Slow-twitch muscle cells lost comparable amounts of their glycogen at 50 and 100 rpm, but fast-twitch cells lost almost 50 per cent of their glycogen at 50 rpm and only 33 per cent at 100 rpm, even though the exercise bouts lasted 30 minutes in each case.

Rapid loss of carbohydrate in fast-twitch cells during slow, high-force pedaling demonstrates why slow pedaling is less efficient. Low-rpm pedaling depletes glycogen from fast-twitch muscle cells because it's associated with high gears and elevated muscle forces. On the other hand, fast cadences coincide with low gears and less-forceful muscle contractions.

Because fast-twitch fibers are more powerful than their slow counterparts, they activate at low cadences when lots of muscular force is needed to propel the bike. Conversely, more rapid pedaling rates of 80-100 rpm are not too fast for slow-twitch fibers to handle. They can contract 80-100 times per minute, easily within the range of force required to pedal in low gear.

The bottom line: Like so many other aspects of cycling, pedaling cadence is highly individual—perhaps even more than other personal choices in the sport like whether you prefer to climb seated or standing. Your job is to find out what works best for your body, then hone that technique.

CHAPTER 45

'Stage Race' Training

T his concept in a nutshell: Stage races, tours or consecutive days of hard training can lead to peak fitness.

Pros ride flat out every day for 3 weeks in the major European tours. Yet instead of becoming chronically fatigued and overtrained, these events often take them to peaks in performance. In fact, the Tour of Spain in September is considered the best preparation for the world road championship in October.

The same is true for recreational riders on a challenging week-long tour such as Colorado's Ride the Rockies. Although the intensity is less than in racing, many riders have to dig deep to finish each day. Then, after the tour, they find themselves in their best form of the summer.

This seems like a paradox because modern training theory is based on the "hard/easy" approach—do intense training today, go easy or rest tomorrow in order to recover. Why don't stage racing pros and hard-riding rec riders collapse in a quivering mass of protoplasm? The answer is simple: The body is highly adaptable. If you ask it to perform, it will. Of course, you can't ask very often. And you'd better ask politely. But done correctly, a program featuring consecutive days of hard training is a potent weapon in a rider's arsenal.

Let's look at how pros use stage races to increase fitness, then at how the rest of us can employ the same principles.

THE PRO APPROACH

A professional's method of riding and recovering from stage races has been honed over a hundred years of the sport's existence. Now, science has been added to tradition. The result is a standardized protocol.

First, pros wait for their bodies to mature. It's rare for riders younger than their mid 20s to complete 3-week stage races. If they enter, they usually race only the initial, flatter stages in their first couple of attempts. This was the approach of 2 recent Tour de France competitors who went on to become multi-time winners, Miguel Indurain and Lance Armstrong.

Second, pros prepare properly. No rider who hopes to do well in the Tour starts the race with only training rides and one-day events under his wheels. Instead, he'll progress from early-season 3-day events to 1- and 2- and maybe even 3-week tours. The body can handle these longer events but only if it's given advance notice of the demands and has time to adapt.

Third, pros save energy when possible. Every stage doesn't have to be raced all-out. It's possible to hide in the shelter of the pack and rest. Riders who have nothing to gain on general classification may sit up on the last climb of the day, losing time but saving energy for subsequent stages, perhaps to help their team leader. On mountain stages, poor climbers look for the *autobus*, the group that contains the sprinters and others who struggle on long ascents. These riders have an uncanny ability to go just fast enough to beat the time cutoff and remain in the race. They get maximum rest while waiting for terrain better suited to their talents.

And pros eat and drink a lot. A stage-racing truism is that when you eat today, you're actually eating for tomorrow. If you fall behind on calories or hydration, the deficit may not hit until a day or 2 down the road. Then you'll bonk hard. Because of this, experienced stage racers eat a substantial breakfast consisting of carbohydrate such as bread and pasta, as well as eggs or lean meat for protein.

Studies of Tour de France riders show that they consume a diet of 55-60 percent carbohydrate, a lower percentage than is often recommended for endurance athletes. But because they're eating so many calories (6,000-8,000 per day on average) they still get enough carbo to restore their glycogen levels. They also have room for the protein that helps repair tissue damaged by the stresses of racing.

In addition, stage racers hydrate with water and sports drinks both on and off the bike. They're careful not to miss feed zones during the stages, and they eat as much as they can choke down during the action. Finally, they begin to eat and consume carbo-replacement drinks as soon as the stage is over.

Pros take care of themselves in adverse weather. Stage races, like recreational tours, go on no matter what the conditions. Cold and wet can sap energy, so rain jackets are a must. When it's hot, they open the full-length zippers in their jerseys, drink continually and conserve as much energy as possible early in stages.

On rest days, pros still ride, usually from 1 to 3 hours at a steady pace. Often they'll reconnoiter the next day's stage if it's a time trial. And they may throw in a few hard, short efforts to remind their legs that the race isn't over.

After completing a stage race, pros usually take a couple of days off the bike, then spin gently for 2 or 3 additional days. By the next weekend, they're racing again and into their usual training routine. Assuming they finished the stage race strongly and without injury, they'll reach a new peak of power in about 10 days.

GOLICH'S BLOCK TRAINING

How can you use these pro insights to improve? Colorado-based cycling coach Dean Golich, who works with Carmichael Training Systems, suggests that his riders incorporate the day-after-day elements of stage races into their normal training.

Golich calls it "block training." Instead of alternating hard and easy days, Golich's riders sometimes train ferociously hard (see chapter 47) for 2-4 consecutive days, then rest for 2 or 3 days by spinning at an easy pace. When they feel recovered, they put in another block of tough training days.

At first glance, this approach seems to be a recipe for overtraining and burnout. But it works. Golich's clients have included U.S. time trial champion Mari Holden and U.S. hour record holder Norman Alvis.

"Pro racers go all-out for three weeks in a row in the Tour de France," Golich argues, "and if they rest properly after the Tour, they're flying." He also points to research that supports block training. In a study done at the University of Wyoming, 8 top cyclists were subjected to 3 weeks of hard training. Each week included 8 interval sessions at maximum effort, a sprint workout and a 5-minute, all-out test. Cycling performance improved significantly during training and increased even more after 2 weeks of recovery.

"Sure, this is hard training," Golich says. "Most people don't train this way. But then again, cycling is a hard sport."

Golich's program isn't just for elite racers. In fact, it makes plenty of sense for recreational riders who have limited time to train. They can get all the intensity they need during blocks of time when they have extra hours for the bike. Then on those days when work or family responsibilities fill up their schedule, they can recover by resting or doing short, easy spins.

Suppose, for example, that you can ride long and hard on Saturday and Sunday. Add one more hard workout on Friday evening after work, perhaps on an indoor trainer, and by Sunday night you'll have done a block of 3 hard workouts. During the week, fit in 2 short rides at an easy pace. This also works great if you're on a 4-day workweek. Train hard on your 3-day "weekend," then rest or take easy spins on the 4 days when you work long hours.

VAUGHTERS' BLOCK TRAINING

Jonathan Vaughters advocates block training, too. Essentially, he does 3 days hard, takes a rest day, then does another 3-day hard block. Each block consists of increasing volume and decreasing intensity. Here's how it works:

- **Day 1** is a ride of about 3 hours, including intervals of hard pedaling for 10 seconds followed by easy pedaling for 20 seconds. He repeats this pattern for 15-20 minutes. (See page 244.)

- **Day 2** is a 4-hour ride with 2 repeats of 20 minutes at time trial intensity, pedaling at about 100 rpm.

- **Day 3** is longer yet—5-6 hours—at a moderate and steady pace with some climbing.

- On the **rest day**, Vaughters spins gently for 1-2 hours at no more than 60 percent of his max heart rate.

This is pro training. Most recreational riders need far more rest than Vaughters does. Masters-age riders certainly do. If you try this, cut back mileage and intensity and increase rest or you'll soon fall victim to overtraining.

TOURING TO BOOST FITNESS

If pros can use 3-week stage races to elevate fitness, recreational riders can employ week-long cross-state rides, tours or even weekend getaways to get similar benefits.

In 1993, Ed Pavelka and I rode Lon Haldeman's PAC Tour—3,400 miles from Seattle to the Virginia shore in 24 days. That's an average of 140 miles per day with no rest days, and a total of 100,000 feet in vertical gain. It was more than 1,000 miles longer than the Tour de France, which has 1 or 2 rest days. And we rode athletically, averaging 19.5 mph for the U.S., including an easy warm-up the first 25 miles each day and some slower pacelines when feeling sociable or battling headwinds.

Before this, my longest career ride had been 140 miles. Now, I was going to average that distance every day for 3-plus weeks. I figured that I might make it to Yorktown but then I'd surrender to overwhelming fatigue. I'd probably need to spend the winter knitting or playing chess in order to recover.

Instead, 2 weeks after this long, hard tour, Ed and I felt big benefits. He used his peak fitness to break New York's cross-state record, time trialing the 277 miles from Buffalo to Albany in 14 hours.

Weekend wandering: Touring is training, too.

I felt fine after a couple of weeks of easy riding. That was a surprise, and the long-term benefits were even more shocking. The fitness that I gained changed me as a cyclist. Long rides weren't as hard. My stamina increased. Most important, my conception of what was possible on the bike widened.

Those were all good things because in 1996, Ed, Skip Hamilton, Pete Penseyres and I set a senior (age 50-plus) world record for the 2,904-mile Team Race Across America. We rode from Irvine, California, to Savannah, Georgia, in 5 days and 11 hours. It was nonstop, around the clock, 30-minute shifts flat out in rotation. For each of us, it equaled about 65 30-minute intervals at or above our lactate thresholds.

Most riders don't train this way! When is the last time you did 65 12-mile time trials in 5 ½ days? It was extremely demanding and an incredible experience. Each of us had great morale because we were doing well and didn't want to let our teammates down. But I confess that in the middle of the night in the humidity and hills of Tennessee, I realized just how tired I was.

I expected to be fried for months after RAAM, both physically and emotionally. Yet 3 weeks after finishing in Savannah, I set my personal record for the 40K time trial. I was almost 51 and had been racing that event for more than 20 years.

You probably won't have the opportunity to ride Team RAAM. But I'll bet there's a weeklong ride you'd love to do, or maybe a cycling camp where there's coaching as well as plenty of riding. Maybe you'd like to set off for a week with a friend on a credit-card tour, carrying a minimal load by staying in motels and eating in restaurants. Or, you're shooting for the adventure of a lifetime by riding a PAC Tour or similar odyssey.

GAME PLAN

To use recreational tours to sharpen your fitness, apply the lessons I detailed above in "The Pro Approach," plus these tips:

- **Prepare right**. The key to riding long distances well on consecutive days is to do some back-to-back long rides in training. Go long on both weekend days in the 4-6 weeks leading up to the tour. It's more important to do these consecutive long rides than to log high-mileage weeks in which you ride about the same amount each day. The key is to do 2 big rides on 2 days, then back off during the week. (See "Weekend Getaways" below.)

- **Check equipment**. Use your long training rides to dial in everything. The lightweight saddle that's comfortable for a 30-mile hammer session may be excruciating when you sit on it at lower riding intensities for 6 hours. The liner in your shorts might be fine for daily training, but on long tours its shape, thickness or stitching could rub you the wrong way. Work out these issues before the big ride starts.

- **Get organized**. On tour, organize your gear before going to sleep each night. Lay out your riding clothes for the next morning. Pack your rain gear, sunscreen, food for jersey pockets, ID and money. Then you can get on the road without delay when each day dawns.

- **Establish a post-ride routine**. Some riders like to do crunches and pushups right after reaching the day's destination. These simple exercises counteract the rigor mortis that sets in during hours of leaning on the handlebar. Next, eat about 500 calories of carbohydrate with a little protein to benefit from the glycogen window. (One rider I've toured with likes to hit the local Subway for a 6-inch turkey sandwich, chips and a big soft drink.) Then, wash out your riding clothes so they'll have maximum time to dry overnight.

> **TIP!** When staying in motels, wash your cycling shorts and jersey in the room sink, using a few drops of the complimentary shampoo. Squeeze out the suds and rinse under the gushing flow of the bathtub faucet. Wring the clothes by hand, then roll them in a towel. Put a foot on one end and wind the other, twisting the towel tightly with both hands. This squeezes out most of the water, helping the clothes dry by the next morning.

- **Set next-day goals**. Each evening, decide what you want to accomplish during the next day's ride. Will you try to stay with a specific group? Ride hard for the hour before lunch, then easy the rest of the day? Or simply use climbs for work and tailwinds for rest? Have a game plan and you'll get more training benefits from the tour.

- **Eat and drink**. Take a tip from pro road racers and eat your way through the tour. When you're off the bike, ensure sufficient hydration by keeping a water bottle with you. If you're not getting up at least once or twice each night to urinate, you're not drinking enough.

- **Take on-bike recovery days**. When Ed Pavelka and I coach at the annual PAC Tour Endurance Camp in southern Arizona, we have at least one "designated weenie day" and spin gently. It's necessary when piling 620 miles into an early-season week. In 2002, for example, our DWD was the day from Douglas to Sierra Vista by way of Bisbee. We stopped at a coffee shop in the old mining town to enjoy muffins and cups of the blend of the day. Then we granny-geared over Mule Pass (after the food there was no other choice) and cruised to the lunch stop in Tombstone, where we also took a leisurely walk around the Old West replica town center. Only 20 miles remained to the destination motel. It took us nearly 90 minutes to cover them. After hammering for 5 days, it sure felt good to weenie.

WEEKEND GETAWAYS

You don't have to take a weeklong vacation to do a fitness-boosting tour. In fact, stage race training is as close as your front door. Simply ride hard on Friday evening after work, then do a mini-tour over the weekend, staying at a motel or B&B on Saturday night. Advantages include:

- **Adventure**. You'll see roads and towns out of range of your normal rides. Are there long climbs 50 miles away you'd like to try? How about that winding, riverside road that you've heard about? Anything within a radius of 75-100 miles is accessible with an overnight stay.

- **Variety**. Many riders grow tired of the same old roads for training and find it harder to get out there. A weekend tour mentally refreshes you with new sights and challenges.

- **Motivation**. It's easier to ride long when there's someplace you need to go. Rain or headwinds won't stop you when you must get to the motel or back home by dark.

We often associate touring with large loads and unwieldy bike handling. But for an overnight motel ride in summer, here's all you need to carry:

- A multitool and 2 spare tubes

- Arm and leg warmers and a rain jacket

- Off-bike clothes (shorts, T-shirt, sneakers or sandals)

- A stripped-down toiletry kit (men, no need to shave)

- A credit card and ATM card

You don't need a second set of cycling clothes. Wash out your duds in the motel sink as soon as you arrive (use the towel-wringing tip on page 216) and they'll be ready for Sunday's return trip. The rest of the above stuff can fit into an extra-large seat bag, so you won't need a rack and panniers. Or, you can opt for a lightweight rear rack (frame- or seatpost-mounted) and rack trunk. Your bike will handle—and climb—in nearly normal fashion.

Camping is less expensive and perhaps more fun, but most riders with fitness as a goal shudder at the thought of laboring on a bike laden with overnight gear. The solution is to adopt the approach used by "light-packing" backpackers:

- Carry a bivouac sack or one-person tent, a lightweight sleeping bag and pad.

- To avoid the weight and bulk of a stove and cooking supplies, eat in restaurants or carry cold food.

- Pack these supplies using a front rack, small panniers and a large seat bag or trunk. With careful choices, you can keep the total load under 20 pounds.

CHAPTER 46

Speedwork for Faster Long Rides

This concept in a nutshell: To ride long distances faster, train with short-distance speedwork.

Conventional wisdom says that if you include one endurance training ride each week, your time for long events such as centuries will come down. Unfortunately, improving your long-distance pace isn't that easy. The best way is by going beyond the lactate threshold in training, and this is painful. It makes you breathe hard and perspire.

Research and experience show us that training fast for short distances improves cruising speed for long distances. It helps you ride as much as 2 mph faster for several hours but without an increase in perceived exertion. If you raise your average speed from, say, 17 mph to 19 mph for 100 miles, you'll cover the distance nearly 40 minutes faster.

There are other important advantages, too. Speedwork can be done in a much shorter amount of time than endurance slogs, glad tidings for time-challenged recreational riders. And fast workouts are fun. They don't have to be head-down pain fests if you know how to do them right.

WHAT RESEARCH TELLS US

A 20-year-old study from the University of California at Berkeley gives us a clue about how speedwork increases endurance performance. Researchers put 10 rats on a 4-week fast training program. The rats worked out just 5 minutes every day for 4 weeks. On the treadmill, they warmed up for 3 minutes, ran hard on a 15 percent grade for 50 seconds, recovered for 10 seconds, repeated the 50-second hard effort and cooled down for 10 seconds. (How's that for a time-efficient workout?)

Results were impressive—the rats increased their VO_2 max by 15 percent, and the maximum speed they attained in the 50-second repeats increased 25 percent. At first researchers were puzzled when they found that although VO_2 max and speed had risen so impressively, the concentrations of aerobic enzymes in muscles didn't rise. How could rats use more oxygen when levels of oxygen-using enzymes stayed the same? Apparently, the rats had enough enzymes before their sprint work but didn't have the neuromuscular coordination to sustain fast running. The rapid repeats gave them the muscular and nervous system abilities to do so. For rats, as for humans, the faster their maximum speed, the greater their aerobic potential.

Now, you may smell a rat in this research. How can we be sure that rat running translates to human bike riding? The scientists know that muscles and cardiovascular systems in rats and in humans work nearly the same way. The rats' VO_2 max translated to about 70 ml/kg/min in people— approaching the level of elite human cyclists and runners.

FROM RATS TO RAAM

In case you're not convinced, let's look at a classic human example.

In 1984, nuclear engineer Pete Penseyres was training for the solo Race Across America. He worked full-time and had a family, so his training time was limited. How could he prepare for a 3,000-mile event when he was working a 40-hour week?

Penseyres solved the problem by incorporating workouts into his daily bike commute to work. He lived 30 miles away and often took a longer route home to total 100 miles per day. Most of this was slow, steady riding in the belief that training volume was the key to success in RAAM.

Leaving work on Friday afternoons, Penseyres would ride for 24 hours or about 400 miles to simulate RAAM demands. These rides, too, were done at a steady pace of 15-17 mph. This training paid off when Pete won the '84 RAAM in 9 days and 13 hours. The next year he didn't race but instead helped his brother, Jim, a Vietnam vet who became the first amputee to finish the grueling event.

The winner in '85 was Jonathan Boyer, who several years earlier had become the first North American to compete in the Tour de France. Boyer bettered Pete's winning time from the previous year and was expected back in '86 to defend his title. It looked like the stage was set for Pete's return and a classic confrontation between an endurance specialist and a Euro racer.

Penseyres knew that to beat Boyer, he had to be as fast as Boyer. So, he changed his training. Instead of long, steady slogs every day, he incorporated 5 speed workouts per week. Two were team time trials of about 15 minutes each. When pulling at the front, Pete went well over his lactate threshold with a heart rate around 170. Riding at the back provided some rest but not much—his heart rate dropped only into the 150s. On 3 other days, he did a training race against younger and more-rested riders. (Pete was 43.) They made it tough for him because they knew what he was training for. He made it tough on himself by riding his 35-pound commuter bike complete with a rack, lights and battery.

The result? Although Boyer didn't show for the race, Penseyres knocked more than a day off his own '84 performance and beat Boyer's '85 time by some 16 hours. In fact, Pete finished the 3,107 miles in 8 days, 9 hours to set an average speed record of 15.4 mph that still stands.

According to Penseyres, the speedwork "did what I intended it to do. It raised my cruising speed by about 10 percent, by at least 1 mph. For the same perceived effort, for the same heart rate, I was going faster. My lactate threshold was higher, so I was comfortable at a faster speed."

EASY SPEED

Impressive results! So how can you incorporate speedwork into your routine? You could always do traditional interval training as described in the next chapter. But many riders dislike the regimentation of intervals. Even Penseyres, who has become a multi-time national champion masters road racer in his post-RAAM career, has a hard time forcing himself to do structured solo intervals. Fortunately, there are several simple ways to get the advantages of speedwork without the drudgery of "3 minutes on, 3 minutes off."

- **Wind ups**. On your easy riding days, do several brisk "wind ups." Shift to a moderate gear, get off the saddle and sprint at about 90 percent effort for 8-10 seconds until you're about to spin out. Then sit down and spin a bit faster for another 10 seconds. Concentrate on good form, a round pedal stroke and keeping "quiet hips" on the saddle. This isn't an all-out effort. Instead, focus on pedaling form. These sprints will help your neuromuscular system adapt to going faster more efficiently.

- **Fartlek**. This Swedish word translates to "speed play," another substitute for structured intervals. It's all about going faster in an unplanned way, scattering random harder efforts through a ride. Sprint when the spirit moves you—away from stop signs or when you crest small hills. A good way to initiate harder efforts is to choose a "trigger" before the ride. For instance, you may decide to sprint whenever you see a certain kind of bird in the roadside bushes or a yellow mailbox. (Don't pick something too plentiful!) Longer, time trial-like efforts can be triggered when you roll down a hill and hold a fast pace for a mile on the flats, or when you turn and catch a tailwind. Keep these efforts fun, unstructured and free flowing. You'll get outstanding speedwork without feeling forced to work hard.

- **Training time trials**. Many cycling clubs have time trials once a week or month. Usually 10 miles long, they're a great way to get a dose of speedwork with the excitement of competition to boost your enthusiasm and adrenaline. As a bonus, you can use times to chart your improvement over the season.

- **Club crits**. Some clubs have evening criteriums, too. The advantage of a crit is that you have to sprint out of every corner, getting spikes of intense work instead of the steady-state effort of time trialing. You'll also hone bike-handling skills that are useful in the pacelines of century rides.

- **Group rides**. A club ride is a great way to get some speedwork. Choose a group that's as fast as you or just a bit faster. Typically, these rides feature sprints for road signs, hard jams over hills and lengthy chases when someone goes off the front. They're the next best thing to road racing to help you develop a turn of speed.

- **Short pacelines**. When you train with a couple of buddies, talk them into going hard for 5-10 miles in the middle of the ride. Trade off the lead, taking hard pulls of 1-2 minutes. You'll get a great team time trial workout with enough rest while you're drafting to let you go anaerobic each time you hit the front. As a bonus, this is an effective way to battle the wind on a gusty day.

- **Hills**. Riding in hilly terrain is perhaps the best way to get a naturally intense workout. You can't cheat gravity by sitting in or faking your effort. To get to the top you have to work hard. Ride hilly routes a couple of times a week and your fitness will improve rapidly. So will your climbing ability.

CHAPTER 47

How Hard? As Hard as You Can!

This concept in a nutshell: Forget heart monitors and power meters. Just go flat out when riding intervals up to 5 minutes long.

Coach Dean Golich is not only infamous for his block training (see chapter 45), he also preaches a heretical approach to doing intervals. He counsels his riders to ignore the usual methods of gauging intensity, such as heart monitors and watts measuring devices. He eschews elaborate training zones based on percentages of max heart rate or lactate threshold. Instead, Golich wants you to ride every interval as hard as you can. He doesn't want you to go at a steady high pace, calculating how hard to push so you can last the distance. No such luck. He wants you to start each interval with a sprint and hang on for all you're worth.

"Don't pace yourself," says Golich. "Start each interval flat out. You'll be struggling at the end, but that's okay. That's when you get the adaptation."

WHY DO THIS TO YOURSELF?

Golich likes to invoke the "30 miles per hour rule," which states that if you never go 30 mph, you'll never go 30 mph. Put another way, if you don't train at race intensities, you won't be able to go fast enough to race.

Don't expect to do well at your goal pace, whether it's 20, 25 or 30 mph, if you consistently train at lower speeds. If your goal is 25 mph in a time trial, start your interval with a hard charge off the line, then do your best to hold that pace. As you get tired, your speed will decrease but your effort won't. "If you do intervals this way, next week or next month you'll be able to hold the speed longer," says Golich. "You'll feel fatigue but it will be temporary. It isn't overtraining, so tough it out."

Gearing is crucial to this type of interval training. If you start the effort in a relatively large gear at a reasonable cadence, say 90 rpm, and you don't shift down, your cadence will get slower and slower as you fatigue.

Most cyclists aren't accustomed to progressively shifting lower during an interval's work phase. They equate it with giving in. But for Golich's intervals, effort is the most important thing, then high cadence. Gearing is a distant third—it's only a tool to help you work as hard as you can. There's no shame in shifting down. In fact, it's necessary to keep effort flat out and your knees healthy.

This intensity won't lead to chronic fatigue, Golich promises, as long as you rest properly after hard workouts.

NO HEART MONITOR

Some riders may hesitate to do Golich's intervals because they're afraid of going too far over their lactate thresholds. They're tied to heart rate training zones. Hard intervals, without feedback from a monitor, make them nervous.

"You don't need a heart monitor for hard training," Golich contends, "because there's little correlation between heart rate and power output. When cyclists look at their heart rates during hard efforts and see low numbers, they're supposed to stop the interval session and go home. But when I examine SRM Powermeter data [watts], often riders are putting out more power than a day or two earlier when their heart rates were higher. Heart rate isn't a reliable indicator of power."

THREE TRAINING ZONES

Golich recognizes only 3 training zones—easy, medium and hard—determined subjectively. An easy pace is for recovery days. It's really easy—no pressure on the pedals—great for riding with a slower friend or spouse. A medium pace is defined as the effort you can sustain for an hour. Golich often prescribes longer, 15-minute intervals at medium effort as a way to increase time trialing ability.

SHOULD YOU TRY IT?

Any program this hard has dangers. Don't attempt "hard as you can" intervals without heeding the following warnings:

- **Get medical clearance** before attempting this or any other form of intense athletic training.

- **Have a solid base.** You need aerobic conditioning for at least 8 weeks based on progressively longer and harder rides. My programs in parts 2 and 3 of this book are ideal for preparing you for the rigors of Golich's intervals.

- **Keep your cadence up.** Save your knees by pedaling at 90-100 rpm throughout each effort. Shift to an easier gear as the interval progresses to keep both effort and cadence high.

- **Limit the workouts.** Train this way only once per week for no more than 4 weeks. Then use a training time trial or other test to gauge improvement. Don't resume these intervals—or increase their frequency—until you're sure your body is coping well.

- **Stop in time.** Don't do these intervals within one week of an event you hope to do well in. Plan an appropriate taper (chapter 54).

- **Monitor your recovery.** If you experience symptoms of overtraining such as deep fatigue, insomnia, apathy or loss of appetite, stop hard training and do steady-pace recovery rides until you feel fresh again. See chapter 8 for the lowdown on overtraining.

CHAPTER 48

'Spinning' for Strength and Power

This concept in a nutshell: Use a "spinning" bike indoors to build strength.

One of the best techniques for building leg strength is low-cadence, high-resistance pedaling. Cranking along at about 50 rpm with significant resistance builds strength in much the same way as high-rep leg exercises in the weight room.

Although this technique is usually associated with off-season training, it's actually appropriate at any time of year. The Italian pro, Francesco Moser, popularized it when he was training for the world hour record in the early 1980s. He rode long climbs in a 53x12-tooth gear to build the strength necessary to turn a relatively big ratio at over 100 rpm for the 60-minute ordeal.

Low-rpm strength by itself doesn't mean you can ride fast. For speed, you need power. Strength comes first, and then it's a simple matter of adding high-rpm workouts for power.

Also, strength workouts are crucial for riders over 50 who want to retain muscle mass. Squats and leg presses in the weight room do the trick—but it's more cycling-specific to do "squats on the bike" in a big gear.

This training can be hard to do outdoors, though. It isn't easy to find a suitable road with the proper gradient, free from stoplights, traffic and cross streets. And if it's chilly outside, knee problems can be exacerbated by the cold. That's why it makes sense to do high-resistance workouts inside. The problem is that standard trainers may not supply enough resistance, or your rear tire may slip on the roller under hard effort. The solution is as near as your local gym if it offers indoor cycling classes using "spinning" bikes—stationary bikes with hefty flywheels, a non-freewheeling fixed gear and enough resistance to suit even Moser.

HOME MACHINE

You could also invest in a spinning bike for your home. During the winter of 2001-2, I used a LeMond RevMaster, designed with input from Greg. It was a great advantage for high-resistance workouts.

The RevMaster is adjustable for my road bike position, and its stability lets me crank as hard as I want or stand and sprint without concern that it might topple over. Its biggest advantage over a trainer is that pedaling resistance can vary from none to so much that I literally can't move the 40-pound flywheel. It's easy to do Moser-like 50-rpm drills. Turning the crank feels fluid like on the road, even at high resistance.

A high-quality machine like this will set you back around $1,000, but you'll save health club fees and be able to work out when and how you want at home. If you're dedicated to cycling and see yourself training for years to come, a spinner is a sound investment. Just think of it as buying another bike—one that other family members can ride, too.

THREE DRAWBACKS

No cycling solution is without faults, and spinning bikes usually have 3.

1. There's apt to be a wide, padded saddle. I didn't like the one that came on the RevMaster, though it worked okay. It's as easy as on a regular bike to install a different saddle.

2. Spinning bikes usually come with a handlebar that resembles the "cow horn" aero bars used by time trialists in the late '80s. This shape is not ideal for general training, and it doesn't let you dial in your precise road position. To solve this, the RevMaster has an adapter for installing drop bars. It works great and makes the unit much more road-specific.

3. There's no way to tell exactly how much resistance you're using. Resistance is controlled by turning a knob that moves a brake pad against the flywheel. Although you can count knob rotations, without a consistent starting point you get an estimate at best. In reality, though, I find that this doesn't matter much. I use a heart monitor while pedaling the RevMaster and simply check my pulse against my perceived exertion just like riding on the road. It works fine, although a spinner that tells resistance in watts would be a useful improvement.

THE WORKOUT

Okay, I've talked you into going to the club (or your basement) once or twice weekly to build leg strength. Here's how to do this workout.

> **CAUTION!** Don't train this way if you have a history of knee problems. Make sure your saddle is the correct height. If you feel knee pain, stop the workout.

1. **Warm up well**. You're going to combine high resistance with low cadence, so get your knees ready for the task. Do the warm-up procedure in chapter 41 or something similar.

2. **Start with low resistance and short efforts**. Don't proceed from the warm-up directly to big-gear grinds. Instead, begin with brief seated sprints at 90 percent effort with a resistance you can spin. Do 3-5 of these, increasing resistance a half turn of the knob each time. Lengthen sprints from 10 seconds to 30 seconds.

3. **Include one-leg training**. Unclip a foot and rest it on a chair or stool. Pedal with the other leg, trying to stay smooth. Alternate legs every couple of minutes. At first, your stroke will quickly deteriorate as you tire. But soon you'll feel smoother and more powerful. This workout is easier on a spinning bike than on a trainer (or on the road) because the heavy flywheel and fixed gear provide momentum. As a result, you can use more resistance and get more strength-building benefits. See chapter 26.

4. **Muscle the pedals**. The real meat of this workout is 1-3 intervals of 3-5 minutes each. Choose a resistance that you can barely turn at 50 rpm. (Cadence is crucial, so count each time your right foot hits bottom for 15 seconds and multiply by 4 to get revolutions per minute.) This isn't a cardiovascular workout! Don't let your heart rate get closer than about 10 beats below your lactate threshold. You definitely shouldn't be panting and gasping. It's a muscle workout, not training to improve anaerobic power.

CHAPTER 49

Cardio-Resistance Workouts

This concept in a nutshell: Combine intervals on an indoor trainer with upper-body weight training for a workout that boosts both strength and lactate threshold.

I get dozens of questions for my "Ask Coach Fred" column in the weekly *RoadBikeRider.com Newsletter*. Many are about finding enough time to train. Particularly, riders have trouble fitting in workouts on the bike along with the upper-body resistance training they know they should do several times a week.

Resistance training is important for reasons other than helping us ride faster. It retains muscle mass that would otherwise be lost to the aging process. A good weight-training regime is important for bone health, too.

But, readers lament, how can we find time to lift, ride, go to the grocery store and mow the lawn? Time on the bike for serious training, not to mention social rides and fun solo cruises, is woefully short for most cyclists.

One promising answer lies in research done by Gary Sforzo of the Graduate Program in Exercise and Sports Science at Ithaca College in upstate New York. His study shows that a high-intensity combination of weights and indoor cycling can increase muscular strength by nearly 25 percent *and* significantly improve VO_2 max. Additional research by other sports scientists confirms Sforzo's finding and shows a significant increase in power at lactate threshold—probably the single most important factor in cycling ability.

The workout is done by alternating the exercises of a standard upper-body weight-training routine with hard intervals on the trainer.

Okay, I know what you're thinking: Get on the trainer in the summer? That misery is usually reserved for winter days when riding outside is impossible. But there are good reasons for hitting the nowhere road even when the weather is beautiful. Let's look at Sforzo's program and then see why you should consider implementing it, even at the height of the outdoor season.

TRAINING SESSION

1. Warm-up for 20 minutes on the indoor trainer with the routine detailed in chapter 41.

2. Get off the bike and do light calisthenics to loosen your upper body. Include abdominal work—several sets of crunches or other exercises you prefer.

3. Do 5 upper-body exercises. At home with minimal equipment, you might do pushups, pullups, upright rows, bent rows and triceps extensions (the last 3 exercises with dumbbells). If you go to a gym, bench presses, lat pulldowns, dips, seated rows and triceps extensions are popular choices. (Note: At a gym, reserve an exercise bike for 45 minutes so you can implement the next part of the program.)

In standard weight-training protocol, you do one set of an exercise, then rest for several minutes while your muscles reload before you do the next set. But in this program, you don't lounge around resting between sets. Instead, you immediately hop on the trainer and crank for 2-3 minutes.

4. Choose a gear or a resistance that allows you to maintain a cadence of about 90 rpm. Your heart rate should rise to about 85 percent of maximum during the last minute. Your rating of perceived exertion should be about 8 on a scale of 10. The idea is to work hard but not be so blown that you can't immediately do another set of upper-body strength work in good form.

5. Continue to alternate one set of each resistance exercise with a 2-3-minute interval on the trainer. At the end of the workout, you'll have done 3 sets of the 5 exercises (15 total sets) with each set separated by a cycling interval (15 total intervals). You'll be tired!

> **CAUTION!** This is effective training, but it's hard. "All the subjects in the study thought it was a great workout and worth the effort," says researcher Sforzo. But you need a physician's approval before you undertake this or any other intense training, and you also need to be aware of the signs of burnout and overtraining, such as deep fatigue, insomnia, apathy or loss of appetite.

Limit this workout to twice a week at most. Once weekly will be sufficient for most riders. Improvement should come quickly. After all, how often do you perform 15 intervals totaling 30-45 minutes of hard effort? This is a "high cost" workout in the sense that it demands a great deal of recuperation ability. If you combine it with a hard ride or race on the weekend and a couple of fast or hilly weekday rides, you'll be fried in no time.

So, go easy in the beginning. The first time you try this workout, do only one set of each exercise alternated with a cycling interval. That's a total of 5 sets of weight exercises and 10-15 minutes of hard pedaling. The next couple of times, increase to 2 sets of each exercise and 10 trainer intervals. If you're still having fun, you can consider moving up to the full 3 sets and 15 intervals.

RAPID RESULTS

For time-challenged cyclists, this is an effective workout to do once a week during the season, especially when weather or other obstacles preclude riding outside. For instance, if it's raining on your scheduled interval day, do a cardio-resistance workout instead. If a meeting at work runs late and scotches your hill workout, do this training in the evening at home. You should see improvement in as little as 4 weeks—increased strength, more power on hills and better time trialing speed. In addition, improved power at lactate threshold will raise your cruising speed during long rides.

One final point: You don't have to use heavy weights to get benefits from this workout. You're aiming for strength, not big muscles, and strength doesn't necessarily show. As Jonathan Vaughters notes, "Most pros don't have strong-looking physiques. We look like Yoda off the bike."

CHAPTER 50

Painless LT Training

This concept in a nutshell: "Play" at high-intensity training to avoid the drudgery of intervals.

I've made the case in this book that lactate threshold (LT) is a magic number. Generally defined as the heart rate (or wattage) you can maintain for an all-out effort of 30-60 minutes, LT is key to performance on a bike. The power you can generate when going as fast as you can in a time trial or on a long climb dictates your cycling ability.

The other physiological measurement that's often invoked is maximum oxygen uptake (VO_2 max). However, this is not very trainable because genetics imposes a "ceiling" on every person's ability

Fast fun: Zesty training partners can hurt you in a good way.

to improve. Also, the limiting factor in cycling ability isn't the amount of oxygen your tissues can process. Rather, it's the amount of power you can generate at a given percent of oxygen consumption.

Some great cyclists have had relatively low VO_2 max numbers. But their ability to generate significant power allowed them to compete very successfully against riders whose oxygen uptake was higher but whose efficiency was less. LT, on the other hand, is highly trainable. Using the proper workouts, you can improve the percent of maximum heart rate you can sustain, and improve the amount of power you generate at a given heart rate. You can also boost your body's ability to process lactate. This lets you venture over the threshold where lactate is accumulated, but rid it from your tissues quickly. These improvements mean big gains in useable speed and power.

Fine—so how can you boost your lactate threshold and reap these wonderful benefits?

TURN WORK INTO FUN

The answer, as you know by now, is hard work. As mentioned in chapter 40, there's an emerging consensus that endurance athletes should spend large amounts of training time—some say as much as 25 percent of total on-bike time—at heart rates (or power production rates) ranging from 10 percent below LT to slightly above. That's a lot of time to dwell in painful territory. And it's made even tougher by the mental demands of pushing yourself to such an extent. Imagine spending 1 hour in every 4 riding as hard or harder as you do in a time trial you really want to win. Ouch!

Fortunately, there's an easier way to reach LT levels in training. It changes pain and suffering into something closer to fun. All you need is to find ways to go hard without goading yourself to go hard. Sound like a contradiction? Not really.

Let's take running as an example. Suppose your coach orders you to run 6 miles with 40 short sprints scattered throughout. These sprints must be nearly all-out. You'll go anaerobic and then recover only enough to sprint again. This workout doesn't sound like fun. You may be able to handle it occasionally—but 2 or 3 times a week for the whole season, or your whole career? Forget it.

Now let's suppose that instead of doing the grueling workout, you were told to play a game of full-court basketball. The effort would be similar to the loathsome running workout. Studies show that NBA players run about 6 miles during a game and accelerate dozens of times while maintaining heart rates at or above their lactate thresholds. But guess what? Basketball is fun. You'd have such a great time that you'd barely think about how hard you were working. The game would fly by.

In the same way, you can design workouts on the bike that elevate your heart rate to LT and above without the physical and mental ordeal of structured intervals. Here are some ways to get this "basketball effect" on the bike.

GAIN WITH LESS PAIN

Fast groups. Make an effort to hook up with riders who are as fast or slightly faster than you. Train with them once or twice a week. The effort required to stick with the group on climbs and hang in during chases and sprints will equal a tough structured workout. But the mental effort is less demanding because your mind is occupied with group dynamics and bike handling. You'll know you're working hard, but you'll have little time to dwell on it.

The group doesn't have to be large. In fact, just one training partner can be enough as long as you have the same agenda. A spirited 2-man time trial along with competition when hills or designated sprint lines approach mean you'll each get a great workout. In fact, it may be harder than in a big group because your partner will see to it that you don't hide in the back—especially when plugging away into a headwind!

Training races. Some bike clubs have a week-night racing series, usually criteriums. Fun, but they won't teach you climbing tactics or how to ride in an echelon on a long, windy road. So, talk your clubmates into making part of the weekend ride a "race." Warm up by riding for an hour until you arrive at a country road loop that's about 15-20 miles around. If it has stop signs or lights, make a rule that everyone has to obey them. You could also use a shorter circuit that has no traffic controls, but riding around in circles isn't as much fun as using a longer loop.

Re-group at the start of the race loop and begin. All tactics are fair—the idea is to see who can get away or win the sprint at the end just like in a regular race. Training like this expands your ability to "read" a race. It's great for your fitness, and the miles will go by fast because you're having fun and competing.

Club time trials. Some riders hate time trials. In a road race, they can draft in the pack. The pace is easy part of the time. But in a time trial there's nowhere to hide. The secret to success is to ride flat out for the distance. If you rest, you lose.

Time trials put you right at your lactate threshold. Or, in the case of TTs lasting less than an hour, slightly over lactate threshold. That's prime training intensity. So, it pays to psych up and get out there for club time trials. They're good for you! Use the adrenaline of competition to ease the pain of intense effort. You may even find that you have a talent for the concentration required for top performances against the clock.

Hills. Climbing is automatic intensity. If you have a hilly route, ride it twice a week. Bear down on the upgrades. Ride some in a large gear at a fairly slow cadence. On others, shift lower and spin faster. Sprint the short ones and apportion your energy up the longer one. Stand for the first climb, remain seated for the second, alternate on the third.

Hills are hard work. But when climbing is your goal for the day, ride as many as you can. This natural pain is easier to tolerate than intervals mandated by a watch. Besides the valuable time spent at your lactate threshold and beyond, riding hills builds leg strength and develops your climbing technique. You'll finish these workouts feeling the satisfaction that comes with getting the most out of your training time.

SERENDIPITY

The best way to include painless intensity in your training is simply to take advantage of every opportunity for riding hard. Be alert for impromptu situations when your legs beg to go fast—then let them go. Examples:

- **Race a thunderstorm**. Have you ever been 5 miles from home when an innocent-looking cloud threatened to open up? Or gotten caught in open country with lightning flashing on the horizon? You know what to do—jam like crazy to get home before the storm catches you. Use such "tactical retreats" as great training. This doesn't mean to purposefully start your ride when a thunderstorm looms! But take advantage when you hear the rumble. It just might save you a serious bike-cleaning session, too.

- **Chase a rider**. When you see another rider ahead, it's natural to pick up the pace. You wonder, "What's this guy have under the hood?" Give in to your competitive instincts and give chase. If you catch your target, don't blow by without at least saying hi. After all, he probably didn't even know he was being chased. Keep an eye on your back porch, too. If you notice a rider behind, you might be the prey. Nonchalantly pick up the pace and see how long you can hold him off. Whether you're the pursuer or pursuee, this game can give you a shot of adrenaline and several minutes of beneficial time-trial-like intensity.

- **Motorpace a passing vehicle**. Motorpacing (following closely in the draft of a car or motorcycle) is a risky and advanced training technique that I don't recommend. There are too many opportunities for error and serious crashes. But occasionally you'll get passed by a slow-moving piece of farm equipment or a heavily loaded truck. Being very careful, you can accelerate, linger briefly in the vehicle's draft to get up to speed, then move back to the edge of the road. Keep the fast pace as long as possible while the harvester pulls away. Don't forget that the driver doesn't know you're behind and could suddenly slow or turn.

- **Win with a tailwind**. Headwinds create an opportunity for intense riding, but battling a gale in your face is rarely much fun. On windy days, choose a circuit about 4 miles around so you won't have to fight the headwind for long periods and you can treat the tailwind as a form of motorpacing. Rev up your big gear, go as fast as possible and work on leg speed.

- **Sprint away from dogs**. If you have aggressive bowsers on your training routes, use them instead of avoiding them. Turn them into training partners. When approaching a mutt's yard, prepare to sprint by selecting an appropriate gear, gripping the bar drops and steeling yourself. Pick up the pace. When Fido comes boiling out from the porch, get off the saddle, accelerate hard and sustain the sprint until you're safely out of his territory. Again, use caution. If the dog sees you early, you might need to work on your bike handling, too, in order to keep him away from your front wheel. Always glance back for overtaking traffic. If the dog is on an uphill, you won't be able to outsprint him. His name might as well be Cipollini. You'll need to use standard dog-thwarting techniques, such as sternly yelling "No!" or "Bad dog!" to give him pause. Once he's behind or keeping his distance, pour on the coals. Most dogs are making a game of it, too, and aren't really intent on having you for a snack.

- **Pound off a hill**. Descents never last long enough. Just when you get your speed going, the road flattens. But don't shift to the small ring and spin. Instead, stay in top gear and keep your cadence over 90 rpm as long as possible. You can ride at high intensity for several minutes with a descent-induced boost at the beginning.

Pay attention and you'll find other opportunities to enliven training rides with intense sections that make hard work seem more like play.

CHAPTER 51

Using Centuries to Boost Fitness

This concept in a nutshell: Make road cycling's classic event, the century ride, a key part of your training plan.

Most riders view century rides as goals in themselves, events to be ridden almost like a race. They train *for* centuries rather than viewing these 100-milers as a way to prepare for other objectives.

A century can be both—a great goal and a superb training device. It's a long ride, for one thing. And a century can be as competitive as you want to make it, either against the other guys at the front or against yourself as you push for a time under 5 hours or your PR. In fact, I think centuries are one of the best training tools in a rider's arsenal.

EXAMPLE! Germany's Erik Zabel has won the Tour de France's green jersey (honoring the best all-around rider) a record 6 times. Obviously, he's a rider who does everything well. He's among the world's top sprinters, he can time trial when he has to, and he gets over the climbs although not with the specialists.

You'd think Zabel might have a complicated training formula, but he doesn't. He's done the same off-season program for 10 years, consisting primarily of base miles at a moderate intensity with sprints when he feels like it. In fact, Zabel is famous for putting in a huge early-season foundation—around 6,000 miles most years before the racing schedule even starts.

So how does Zabel go so fast when he races if he doesn't go fast in training? Isn't a training program of slow miles exactly the opposite of the approach I've put forth?

The answer is simple. Sure, Zabel rides lots of slow miles in training. But he never stops racing. He does 6-day track races in winter, and he rides February's early-season events. He doesn't need to ride hard while training because he gets all the intensity he needs while racing.

In the same way, you can use century rides as "races" to boost your fitness and help you achieve cycling goals later in the season. Here's how.

BEFORE THE RIDE

- **Build your base**. Don't do a century without adequate base miles. (Remember Zabel's huge foundation.) It's okay to ride your first century on training rides of 60 or 70 miles—most first-timers just want to complete the distance. But if you want to get a PR or use the century to best advantage, it pays to give it the respect it deserves. This means at least 8 weeks of gradually increasing long rides on weekends. Ideally, you'll work up to rides of 75-90 miles with speedwork during the week.

- **Taper**. Treat the century just like an important race. Use the tapering procedures I discuss in chapter 54 for at least a week before the event. You won't get maximum benefit from the ride if you aren't rested and raring to go.

- **Eat and drink**. Perhaps the biggest mistake a rider can make is trying to lose weight in the few weeks before a big event. "If I were just five pounds lighter, I'd be able to climb with the front group," a rider thinks and promptly begins to limit food portions. Inadequate calorie intake is the primary cause of fatigue and poor performance. In fact, some experts say that overtraining is almost always caused by not eating enough carbohydrate to restock the muscles with glycogen after hard rides. The basic rule: Eat a lot to ride a lot. The same goes for hydration. Down plenty of sports drink and water in the days before the event. Keep a bottle on your desk at work. You should be urinating 4 or 5 times a day and getting up at least once each night to empty your bladder. If not, you're probably going into the century dehydrated. A loss of even one percent of your fluid weight can erode performance.

PLAN YOUR STRATEGY

Formulate a plan for the century well in advance. The least-effective way to do the ride is by winging it, figuring that you'll adapt to situations as they occur. You won't get maximum benefit that way. To make your plan, ask yourself these key questions:

1. Should I ride solo or in a group?

If you're training for ultra-distance cycling, non-drafting triathlons or time trials, it may make sense to ride the century by yourself, avoiding help from other riders. But for most other goals, it's better to join in. And, after all, you can ride 100 miles solo anytime without paying an entry fee.

2. How do I select a group?

You can ride a century with your clubmates. In fact, some race teams form their own packs, discouraging anyone not wearing team colors from joining in the paceline. Advantage: You know the guys, so it's safer. But most riders simply jump onto pacelines that seem to be going the right speed. If the group is actually going too slow, you can ride off the front, solo a while, and wait for a faster train to come rolling by. Jumping on and joining in makes the situation more race-like.

The drawback is when you have no idea of the group's riding skills. Some people may be strong enough to stick with the paceline but lack knowledge and experience, which can lead to mistakes with painful consequences. Identify these riders and avoid them. This is particularly important in crosswinds when echelons form. Wheels will overlap, so one mistake can cause contact that takes several riders down.

3. Will I use aid stations or ride non-stop?

Stopping at aid stations means you don't have to carry as much fluid and only an emergency supply of food. Pause briefly and stock up as needed. Plus, this breaks your effort into several chunks. You can ride hard to a stop, rest a bit while filling your bottles, munching some cookies and visiting the portable toilet, then resume your pace to the next stop. On the negative side, stopping nearly always means the end of a fast-moving group. Not everyone stops or stops for the same amount of time. And no matter how fast you hurry, it'll take a few minutes for your legs to loosen once you're rolling again.

The alternative is to ride the century non-stop. If you have the ability to finish in the 5-hour range, you can carry enough to eat without arranging for someone to meet you and provide hand-ups. Four energy bars and a couple of energy gel packets should be plenty. It's tougher to carry enough fluid. In warm-weather centuries, you should start with 2 large water bottles (about 28 ounces each) on the bike. Plus, wear a backpack-style hydration system that holds at least 70 ounces.

All of this makes for a lot of weight, but it does get lighter as the ride wears on. If you run out of fluid or food, you can always abandon your plan and stop briefly at the final aid station. Otherwise, you'll bonk, finish exhausted and degrade your fitness rather than improve it.

One more point: If you're hydrating sufficiently, you can't ride a century without urinating. Male riders can learn to do it from the bike. It's relatively easy once you get over the ingrained psychological barrier. But it's not something you should do with other people in view, and it can be mighty unsanitary. For these reasons, many guys prefer to make a quick stop along the roadside or at an aid station. Females have no choice but to stop. Seana Hogan, a multi-time winner of the women's Race Across America, could compete with the men—until she had to stop to urinate while the guys didn't. Over the course of a 3,000-mile transcontinental race, substantial time can be saved by answering the call of nature on the roll.

4. How will I apportion my effort?

The classic way to ride a fast century is to go at a brisk pace for the first third, go hard in the middle third, and go for broke in the push to the line. But century courses may not play so neatly into this strategy. For example, the big climb may come early, requiring you to work hard only 90 minutes into the ride. Or you may latch onto a fast paceline from the start. In order to hang in and make good time, you must push harder than planned.

Every century is different, so it's important to identify your goals. Do you want to try for a PR? Then classic pacing is probably best. Do you want to increase your fitness for mass-start racing? Then the fast/slow pattern of pacelines works well. Do you want the benefits of hill work? Then push the climbs so you're hovering on the edge of your lactate threshold, then recover on the descents.

By the way, a fast time doesn't necessarily mean you worked as hard as possible. If you go extremely hard on hills or in pacelines, then roll along at an easier pace between climbs or until another paceline comes along, you may finish slower, but much more tired, than if you keep a steady, moderate effort. You'll get a better training effect out of the inconsistent pace.

5. How will I recover?

Working hard in a century is only part of the recipe. Rest and recovery after the event is at least as important for improving. Check chapter 54 for recovery suggestions.

CHAPTER 52

Hill Circuits for Better Climbing

This concept in a nutshell: Designate a hilly course and use it only for climbing workouts.

There's no doubt that hard climbing is one of the best ways to get fit. Gravity forces you to work hard. And this hard work is easier mentally than flat-road intervals of similar intensity. Hills give you a goal you can see—the top.

Because hills make for tough riding, most cyclists avoid them or at least limit them when they choose the day's training route. Unless you're a rabid climber, you probably opt for a flat or rolling course. Nothing wrong with that—except you're missing out on the considerable extra fitness you get from climbing.

A great solution is to identify the hilliest circuit in your area and designate it for climbing workouts. I'm not sure why, but having a route that's labeled "For Climbing Days Only" makes it less onerous to ride.

Dirty work: Sometimes the best training hills are unpaved, no problem on a road bike with stout wheels.

CHOOSE A COURSE

The ideal hill circuit is 3-5 miles long with one hill that takes 5-10 minutes to climb and at least one "sprinter's hill" of 100-300 yards. No such loop in your area? You can also use a stretch of road that has appropriate hills. Simply ride the hills in one direction, hang a U, and return. Out-and-back courses make training seem more regimented, but they work.

In some areas, suitable roads may be too heavily trafficked for safe training. In this case, look for dirt roads, which may also provide steeper climbs. Rig a mountain bike with drop bars to duplicate your road bike position, or use a cyclocross bike or your winter training bike. No hills at all? In the worst-case scenario, look for a bridge or highway overpass that you can repeatedly ride in both directions. Gruesome, but better than nothing.

HILL TRAINING TIPS

Save your hill circuit for days when you want to climb hard. Don't ride it casually. If you associate it with hard work, you'll be primed to make a strong effort when it's time to ride there. It's a little like Pavlov's dog, but instead of salivating on cue, you'll be slobbering as your hammer over the hardest hill.

- **Ride the circuit both ways**. Variety isn't this workout's primary attraction. You want to develop a blue-collar routine of work on cue. But riding the circuit both clockwise and counterclockwise gives you different gradients because most hills are steeper or longer on one side than the other. If you have an out-and-back course, you'll automatically see both sides of each climb.

- **Get a training partner or 2 to ride with you**. Solo slogging up climbs very quickly becomes a mental challenge. It can drain your enthusiasm. When that happens, your workouts get slower and less effective. So, find some like-minded masochists to share your hill circuit. Competition will heat up the pace, stop you from dwelling on every second of your effort and boost your rate of improvement.

- **Use different climbing techniques**. Do the ascents in a variety of ways—big gears, small gears, seated on the tip of the saddle or at the rear, standing or sitting, with a still upper body or pulling rhythmically on the handlebar with each pedal stroke. Over time, you'll find the techniques that work best for you in different situations.

- **Don't overgear**. Unless you're doing specific, big-gear/low-cadence intervals, don't let your cadence drop below 80 rpm on these climbs. If your loop has very steep hills, you may need a lower gear than you usually employ. In this case, buy a training wheel and cassette with the bigger cogs. Change to your "climbing wheel" before each hill workout.

- **Practice standing**. Heavier riders usually climb seated. When legs don't have to support bodyweight, more energy can go into getting up the hill. But regardless of how much heft you're hauling, it pays to stand some of the time for variety, getting over steeper pitches and to give your butt a rest.

> **TIP!** Here's a standing technique from pro super-climber Jonathan Vaughters, who set the record for the ascent of France's infamous Mont Ventoux:
>
> "When the pedal nears the forward horizontal position, your knee should be almost locked. Then, let your body weight fall so the leg muscles aren't involved as much. Stand tall on the bike. Let your hips move up and down slightly as you shift weight from one leg to the other. This is a subtle change from most people's standing climbing techniques, but it can make a huge difference."

- **Ride the circuit only when you're fresh**. You won't get anything positive out of the training if you force yourself to hammer when your legs are dead.

- **Hydrate and eat**. Make sure you carry enough food and fluids to see you through the workout. If you ride for 45 minutes to get to your circuit, then spend another hour in the hills, you still have to ride back. If you emptied your bottles and didn't bring a snack to eat after the final climb, you'll be bonked before you get home. Studies show that you need about 300 calories per hour to ride long and hard. That's equal to an energy bar and bottle of sports drink every 60 minutes. Of course, you probably shouldn't eat anything solid within 2 hours of this hard training. Switch to your energy drink as you ride out to your circuit.

- **Don't keep a record of average time or speed**. They're all but meaningless for this training. When you push hills hard, you have to ride the descents and flats easily to recover. Better to time yourself on the uphills to track improvement while ignoring your total-ride numbers. Beware, though, that speed on climbs can be misleading on a windy day. It can vary considerably for the same power output.

If you want the best means of tracking improvement, use a watts meter and check average wattage after each climb. (See chapter 42.)

CHAPTER 53

Get Dirty

This concept in a nutshell: Roadies can learn smooth pedaling—and a lot more—by riding a mountain bike.

Time was, road riders and mountain bikers were at opposite ends of the cycling continuum. You know the stereotypes: Mountain bikers were hairy-legged Neanderthals with plodding, square pedal strokes, spitting and grimacing up dusty climbs at 40 rpm. Roadies were elegant and imperially slim, slickly pedaling fast, perfect circles.

Now the apparent deep division between the road and the dirt has all but vanished. Elite mountain bike racers spend as much as 80 percent of their training time on road bikes in order to build their aerobic power. Tinker Juarez, the American mountain bike icon, says he's on a road bike 5 out of every 7 training days. Several top mountain bike racers, such as Australia's Cadel Evans and Spain's Miguel Martinez, have abandoned dirt to race for European pro road teams.

On the other side of the coin, riders who formerly wouldn't dream of letting their (skinny) tires touch dirt have bought mountain bikes and discovered how much trail riding can improve their ability on the road.

In September of 2001, shortly after the events at the World Trade Center, I attended the Mountain Bike World Championships in Vail, Colorado. By observing the riders and chatting with them, it was apparent what roadies can learn from their off-road brethren. Examples:

- **Steady pacing**. Mountain bike races require around 2 hours of effort at lactate threshold. Go too fast early and you blow up. Go too slowly and you'll be so far behind you'll never get into contention. At the worlds, American Alison Dunlap parceled out her energy on early laps, saving just enough to mount a last-lap charge for the gold medal. This is the same skill you need for road time trials or hammering your way to a PR in a century. Remember that Dunlap got her start on a road bike. She still competes in several road races each year.

- **Bike-handling skills**. Mountain bikers push the limits of traction and steering because they're less afraid of falling than roadies. Speeds are slower off-road, and landing on dirt doesn't hurt as much as landing on pavement. In Vail, America's Walker Ferguson got the bronze medal in the under-age-23 race even though he had to come back from an early crash. "I got a little excited, fell into some bushes 15 feet below the trail and lost about 20 places," he said. "I had to settle down and work my way back up."

- **How to love a dirty bike**. Most roadies hate to get their bikes messy, so they won't ride in the rain or on roads made muddy by farm vehicles. But you can't ride off-road without getting your bike dusty, muddy or both. Mountain bikers quickly learn that it's easy to clean a machine and make it as good as new.

It's no different for your much-loved road bike, so don't be afraid to ride it in the slop. Mechanics at the worlds hosed down and re-lubed dirty bikes, taking only 10 minutes to make each one look like it had just come off the showroom floor. Even the spacers between cassette cogs were clean!

SMOOTH STROKES

A big benefit of off-road riding is how it helps you perfect a fast and supple pedal stroke. This seems counterintuitive because we associate mountain bikers with slow-cadence grinding up nearly unridable climbs. But riding on slippery dirt surfaces requires a smooth pedaling action all the way around the circle. If mountain bikers push too hard on the downstroke, the rear wheel loses traction, which costs momentum and time. In fact, a study done at the U.S. Olympic Training Center showed that pro mountain bikers had smoother and more efficient strokes than roadies—and even pursuiters on the track. On the steep climbs at Vail, it was fascinating to watch top riders smoothly pedal up the rocky chutes.

Roadies have the advantage of riding on a relatively smooth surface. If they don't apply power evenly through the whole pedal circle, it isn't especially noticeable at the rear wheel. But on dirt surfaces, any power surge makes the rear wheel slip. It's the perfect biofeedback mechanism. An unrefined pedaler proceeds up the hill in a series of rock-spewing lurches, wasting power all the way.

Uneven power is also noticeable on the Slickrock Trail in Moab, Utah. Skilled cyclists can ride near-vertical pitches because the rock provides exceptional traction. But the steeper the climb, the more perfectly round a pedal stroke must be. The penalties for a slip are a nasty crash and substantial amounts of skin sandpapered off by the sandstone.

As a result of immediate feedback, elite mountain bikers have developed a smooth spin with almost no conscious effort. It's a skill that will serve every roadie, too.

STEPS TO PERFECTION

To refine your stroke by riding your mountain bike on trails, first you need the right equipment. Clipless pedals, supportive shoes and the right tires for surface conditions are crucial. Once you're properly outfitted, find a dirt climb about 200 yards long. It should be steep, and ideally the surface should be loose but without big rocks, water bars or logs.

First, try climbing the hill in a fairly big gear while pedaling with hard, jabbing downstrokes. Notice how your rear wheel slips? Now ride up again, but this time concentrate on making each stroke round by applying power evenly. You'll know if you're succeeding because your rear wheel will keep its grip. When you can climb the hill in a big gear at about 50 rpm without breaking traction, you've got it.

Next, use a lower gear and increase your cadence on the climb while maintaining smoothness. As your rpm goes up, it gets progressively more difficult to keep pressure on the pedals through the whole 360-degree circle. But the more you practice, the more accustomed your nervous system becomes to applying steady power. The goal is to be able to climb at a brisk and efficient cadence of around 80 rpm with nary a slip. Doing so says all of your power is being used to get up the hill.

TIP! Skilled off-road riders have learned how to use their upper-body strength to pull on the handlebar, thus adding power while still keeping pedal strokes round and smooth.

Mountain bike coach Skip Hamilton teaches his riders to climb technical terrain with considerably more upper-body movement than is often recommended. He suggests climbing in a gear that's one cog smaller (harder) than usual while lightly pulling on the bar in time with your pedal strokes and allowing your shoulders to rock a bit.

BIKE HANDLING

Riding off road hones bike-handling skills. There's nothing like sliding on loose dirt through corners to make you feel at home when your rear wheel skids on wet pavement. One of the best ways to learn is to follow better riders. In mountain biking's infancy, that's how we all did it. There weren't any instructional books or tradition. We simply rode, pushing our limits and observing riders who were smoother and faster.

Now you can find articles on how to pull every technical move imaginable. But guess what—learning from better riders is still the most effective way. Watching as your hero rides around a switchback, tackles a rocky section or bunny hops a log imprints the technique in your brain. Then all you have to do is imitate his or her moves—and practice!

Find good mountain bikers in your area to serve as your role models. Look for them in cycling clubs or on group rides. Then here are ways to learn from their example:

Play follow the leader. My descending skills improved markedly after I followed Skip Hamilton down a singletrack near Crested Butte called, appropriately enough, Deadman Gulch. Skip is a top off-road technician. He floats effortlessly over obstacles, seeming to defy gravity. In trying to keep up, I crashed immediately.

Show time: Hamilton teaches technique by example.

After dusting myself off, I figured out how to follow at about 40 feet, focusing on the trail ahead but keeping Skip in my peripheral vision. Then I simply imitated what he did. I followed his line, adopted his relaxed, cat-like stance on the bike and mimicked his speed. It was like magic. His skills became imprinted on my brain. I became a Skip clone. Try it and you'll see how well it works.

Follow good riders on climbs and technical sections, too. Imitate their gearing, cadence and line through obstacles. Often, problems stem from pedaling at the wrong cadence or not setting up correctly for the next turn and ramming the front wheel into something and stalling. Good riders get all these things right.

Ask for tips. Don't be shy. Ask for help. Nearly all good riders feel flattered when asked to share their techniques. This includes pros when they're out riding on the local trails. They remember when they started and how they learned from others, too. When I visited the Volvo-Cannondale team camp in Arizona, I made it a point follow Olympic mountain biker Tinker Juarez on the trails and ask him questions whenever we stopped for a breather. (I needed a lot more extra breathing than he did.) Tinker was gracious and highly articulate. It was obvious that he'd thought long and hard about the sport's techniques.

Watch a pro race. You don't have to ride with top pros or coaches to sponge up their skills. Go to a race and find terrain on the course that mirrors what's difficult for you. If you stall on technical climbs, spread your picnic by the meanest uphill section. Going over the bar on tough downhills? Locate the nastiest drop-offs and watch the action closely. You'll be amazed at the racers' agility and balance, but you'll also see that their skills aren't superhuman. They're within reach once you understand what they're doing with their bikes and bodies.

Go to a camp. Expert instruction is a quick way to get better. A coach will demonstrate skills, watch as you try various moves and cajole you into improvement. When you get coaching in a group of like-minded riders in a great mountain biking area, it makes the whole experience that much more effective.

Watch race videos. No pro races nearby? No vacation time to attend a camp? No problem. Simply plug a mountain bike race video into your VCR, look and learn. Rewind the tape so you can study a certain move repeatedly. Use the "pause" and "frame-by-frame" functions to examine techniques in detail. Visualize yourself riding the same trail and handling the technical sections with the same relaxed assurance. Soon, other riders will be asking you for tips.

These skills, honed on dirt, transfer directly to the road. They'll make you smoother, stronger and more powerful on hills or in big-gear situations on the flats. And they'll keep you upright in perilous situations. You'll be more confident on pavement because of the time you spend off it.

CHAPTER 54

Tapering for Top Performance

This concept in a nutshell: To peak for a big event, reduce training volume the week before but maintain (or increase) intensity.

Athletes do better in important events if they're well rested. Rest gives the body time to replace glycogen stores, and it gives the head time to get psyched for hard effort. Pioneering studies with swimmers by sports scientist Dave Costill showed that when they reduced their usual training load from a massive 10,000 yards per day to 3,200 yards per day over a 15-day period, their times improved by almost 4 percent while their arm strength rose nearly 25 percent.

So, what's wrong with us? Cyclists have traditionally ignored such findings. Road racing has a stage race tradition of hard men riding day after day with slices of raw beef in their shorts to ease oozing saddle sores and cabbage leaves under their cotton hats to protect their frying brains from midsummer heat. Our heroes come from the 3-week tours. Rest day? Okay, so let's go ride 60 miles.

But it's smarter to listen to recent studies that point the way to an effective method of tapering, one that is easy to employ and remarkably successful.

A SCHEDULE THAT WORKS

- **Continue to ride**. Don't simply lie on the couch to rest. According to Jonathan Vaughters, "If I don't ride every day, my legs feel blocked. My most important training for a stage race takes place in the two weeks before the start." The same usually holds true for recreational cyclists who ride regularly.

- **Reduce your mileage**. Although you want to continue riding, you need to cut mileage substantially to get a tapering effect. About 7 days before your important event, cut your average mileage by about two-thirds. So, if you've been averaging 200 miles per week, slice it to 65-70.

- **Continue interval-type training**. But reduce the number of intervals each day. Here's how the week before an event might look. After warming up for 20 minutes, do this procedure:

Day 7	5x3 minutes at slightly above lactate threshold
Day 6	4x3 minutes at slightly above lactate threshold
Day 5	3x3 minutes at slightly above lactate threshold
Day 4	2x3 minutes, fast
Day 3	1x3 minutes, really fast
Day 2	Light pedaling for 30-60 minutes with 2 or 3 short jumps
Day 1	Event

This tapering protocol reduces your overall workload because of the drastic mileage decrease. You have more time to recover and less strain on your leg muscles. But the intervals guarantee that you retain the muscle enzymes that help you process lactate. The fast riding also means that your neuromuscular system will be accustomed to going fast when you ask it to during the event.

This type of taper works because it combines rest with intensity. It allows recovery but encourages speed. You can fine-tune the intervals for the event you're aiming for simply by increasing or decreasing their length. If your target event is a 40K time trial, do intervals 5 minutes long at race pace and intensity. For a criterium with lots of high-speed jumps out of corners, you'd do better by starting with 10 short, hard sprints on Day 7 and reducing the number of sprints by 2 each successive day.

CAUTION! Don't make the mistake of doing too many intervals too hard during this taper. You want your legs to remember how to go fast, but you don't want to tire them in the process. So, if your target event is a century, the time trial intervals of 5 minutes described above would be plenty. Don't start with 8 or 10 intervals of 10 minutes each even though the event distance is much greater.

TRAINING TAPERS

It's smart to taper even if you don't have an important event you're pointing to. Most training plans have a 3-week "build period" of gradually increasing volume and intensity, followed by an easy week where both factors are decreased by about one-third. Then they're increased by about 10 percent in the next 3-week training block before another "rest" week. Tapering this way ensures that your body gets enough recovery to assimilate hard training efforts. It's also a great way to try different tapering protocols to see which one works for you—and in which situations.

A taper is useful, too, after you've had an uncommonly tough week on the bike, such as the high mileage of a tour. Here's a personal example to show how this works.

In January and February of 2002, I averaged 8 hours a week on the bike (including trainer time) along with another 6 hours per week of crosstraining—snowshoeing, hiking and weight lifting. Bike time included several rides of 3-4 hours when Colorado's weather permitted. I needed the long rides because I would be coaching at the PAC Tour Endurance Camp in southern Arizona the second week of March. I'd be riding a loop that covered some 620 miles (about 35 hours on the bike) in 7 days, including climbs, headwinds and brisk pacelines.

I enjoyed the camp but was tired afterwards. I experienced deep fatigue in my quads when I walked up stairs, a disturbing tendency to take naps in midafternoon, and an even more troubling predilection to fall asleep in the middle of watching NCAA tournament basketball. If I can't stay awake for great college hoops, I know I'm fried.

The chart on the next page shows how I organized my recovery. Notice how I cut back mileage drastically, at least compared to the camp week. Notice also how I didn't merely spin around but included some intense-but-short efforts. I limited most hard work to sprints to open up my legs. When I did a longer hard effort (10 minutes uphill) I limited the intense work to just one climb.

After this taper week, I wasn't as comatose, my legs had regained their life and I was ready to resume normal training. If I had stayed off the bike all week (or hammered too hard), my recovery wouldn't have been as rapid or as effective.

March 16	Last day of the tour, 86 miles from Sierra Vista to Tucson with 3,000 feet of climbing.
March 17	No ride. Drive home, 13 hours in the car.
March 18	No ride. Catch up on chores and RoadBikeRider.com.
March 19	1:20 ride at a moderate pace with a couple of short sprints.
March 20	1:45 ride with a hard 10-minute climb and a few short sprints. 1:00 walk. Light weight training.
March 21	1:20 ride with 4 hard jams of about 30 seconds each.
March 22	2:00 ride at a moderate pace

CHAPTER 55

Special Techniques of the Pros

This concept in a nutshell: Pro riders have favorite—and often unusual—workouts that give them an edge and may work for you, too.

I've been writing about this sport for 25 years. I've heard about (and tried) nearly every training technique imaginable. But when you look at training dispassionately, it really comes down to a few relatively straightforward techniques:

  – Build a good base of endurance miles
  – Include enough intensity to hone your fitness
  – Get plenty of rest

Oh, and don't forget to choose your parents wisely so you have the required genetic characteristics for success! It's simple, really, though not as simple as the classic advice, probably apocryphal, attributed to Italian *campionissimo* Fausto Coppi: "Ride your bike, ride your bike, ride your bike." In fact, in my more cynical moments, I often conclude that all training for cycling can be condensed into 2 words: "Pedal harder!"

So, it's kind of a relief to find that top pros often employ somewhat unusual approaches to training. They aren't afraid to try something out of the mainstream if they know—from experience coupled with trial-and-error—that being a bit of an iconoclast helps them be better riders.

What follows are 7 special techniques I learned in 2002 from Jonathan Vaughters at his training camp in Denver and from my 4 days of riding with the Saturn Cycling Team pros at their pre-season camp. Some of these workouts may be appropriate for you. But even if they aren't, I hope they inspire you to think outside the box. Use them as a spur to develop effective alternative training of your own.

VAUGHTERS: 10/20 INTERVALS

Europe-based roadman Jonathan Vaughters is one of the top climbers in the pro peloton, with a record-smashing ascent of Mont Ventoux in his list of wins. He's also a strong time trialist.

Vaughters maintains that "cycling isn't an endurance sport; it's a power sport." To demonstrate, riders at his camp did a 5-minute steady-pace effort at about 24 mph. Then we rode the same course but went very hard for 10 seconds and "floated" easily for 20 seconds. We repeated this pattern for the full 5 minutes. Average wattage and speed were the same for both rides. But perceived exertion was different. The fast/slow pattern was much tougher. That's how cycling—and especially racing—is, says Vaughters. You go hard to stay in the paceline or get up short hills or close gaps. Then you soft pedal in the pack for a short time before you have to hammer again.

New riders who come to the sport from, say, marathon running are amazed at the difference in intensity. Running tends to be a steady-state effort while bike racing and group training are anything but. This

Vaughters: Power pusher.

is especially true in Europe. As Vaughters observes, "American and European races both average about 40K per hour. But in Europe they go 25 kph for a while, then 65 kph, then 30 kph. In the U.S., you get a 40 kph average by going 40 kilometers per hour."

Intensity varies in recreational riding, too. You cruise on the flat, jam on a hill, coast in a tailwind and then work hard when you turn a corner into the wind. How can you accustom your body to these pace variations?

Vaughters recommends 10-20 minutes of alternating 10 seconds hard and 20 seconds easy. Start the hard efforts at only 80 percent of the effort you think you can maintain. The first 5 minutes will seem too easy, the next 2 or 3 minutes will seem hard and the final minutes will seem interminable. He suggests doing this workout once per week during the winter when you're leg weight training. He does it in the month before he starts serious racing to get ready for the abrupt nature of the peloton's accelerations.

VAUGHTERS: FAT-BURNER WORKOUT

Do you bonk on long rides even though you keep ingesting carbs? If so, you haven't trained your body to burn fat efficiently.

Vaughters won the 2001 Saturn Cycling Classic in Colorado, a 140-mile, 7-hour race with 14,000 feet of climbing at high altitude. He needed only some sports drink, an energy bar and a couple of carbo gel packets. "Some of the other riders were eating turkey sandwiches!" he laughs.

How do you train your body to ride on stored fat? Vaughters suggests doing a 3-hour ride at a steady, brisk pace so your glycogen stores are depleted. Then eat a moderate dinner that's relatively low in carbohydrate. The next morning, don't eat breakfast. Instead crawl out of bed, get on your bike, warm-up and do 45 minutes hard at about 85 percent of max heart rate. Cool down, spin home and have a big bowl of cornflakes. You'll crave carbs like never before.

This workout is unpleasant, but it will teach your body how to run more efficiently on fat reserves. To see results, train this way once per week for 4-6 weeks. Then give yourself a medal!

VAUGHTERS: LEG WEIGHTS PLUS MILES

A crucial early-season training question is how to incorporate leg workouts in the weight room with the endurance you must build. Vaughters suggests this weekly plan:

Monday	Rest day.
Tuesday	Ride 45-60 minutes, ending at the gym. Weight train for an hour, including 5-6 sets of heavy leg presses. Ride home.
Wednesday	Spin 3 hours at an easy-to-moderate pace.
Thursday	Repeat Tuesday's workout.
Friday	Repeat Wednesday's workout.
Saturday	Do leg presses in the morning and either race or do a hard training ride, preferably with a group, in the afternoon.
Sunday	Ride 4-6 hours at moderate intensity.

Recreational riders won't have time to do the mileage Vaughters does. But his pattern of lifting and riding can be duplicated. Simply reduce the time spent on the bike and in the gym.

Remember that you won't ride well during this training. "I did a local criterium in Boulder while on this routine," Vaughters laughs. "Everyone wondered why a European-based pro was riding in the middle of the pack. They didn't know that I'd done six sets of hard leg presses and then ridden until the race started."

KLASNA: HILL RUNNING

Running and cycling don't mix very well. Several studies show that running doesn't improve cycling ability, although training on a bike can improve running. There's an exception, though. Running *uphill* apparently has a positive effect on cycling ability because it's powered by the same muscles—quads and glutes—that are used in the pedal stroke.

Even so, most pro cyclists have been reticent about including much running in their programs. One exception is Trent Klasna, named North American male rider of the year for 2001. Klasna says he loves running trails and does it often during the off-season, feeling it helps his cycling.

How about during the season? Can trail running be useful then, too? Sure—once or twice a week, for anyone but serious racers, it's a great

Klasna: Zone out and get fit by running trails.

change of pace and gets you away from pavement and traffic. As Klasna observes, "It's easy to get into a zone when running but much harder on the bike because you have to watch for cars."

In terms of training time, running is faster and more efficient than cycling—great for busy athletes. But before you plunge in, heed these tips:

- **Choose good shoes.** Supportive shoes are a must for running in general, and this goes double for the rough terrain you'll encounter off-road. Because trail running has become popular, most shoe manufacturers offer models with good traction and protection. Go to a running store, tell them what you intend to do, and listen to their recommendations. Some stores have a treadmill so you can actually run in different shoes to find one that works for your degree of pronation or other gait peculiarities.

- **Start gradually.** Beginning a running program can be painful as your muscles get accustomed to the pounding, especially on downhills. The solution is to break in very gradually. Try alternating 100 yards of running with 300 yards of fast walking. Gradually alter this ratio. After about a month of working out every other day, you'll probably be able to run 5 miles with minimal or no walking.

- **Pick good trails.** Find trails in city or state parks. Sometimes, vacant land contains trails cut by motorcycles or mountain bikes. Look for dirt roads, canal bank access roads and rail trails. If you're lucky, you live near a state or national forest with a number of hiking trails that you can run. The ideal terrain is rolling—short hills of 50-200 yards with corresponding downhills. This makes it easy to safeguard your quads and knees by walking down after running up. Here in the Rockies where I live, most trails go straight up for many miles. I run the vertical pitches and walk the easier ones. Then going down, I do the reverse—walk the steep grades and run on the shallow ones.

- **Combine riding and running.** If you must travel to suitable trails, ride instead of drive. Use your beater bike, chain it to a tree, run the trail out and back, and cool down by spinning home. That's how it was done in Boulder, Colorado, by Davis Phinney, the winningest road racer in U.S. history. You'll need pedals with toe clips and straps so you can wear your running shoes. Also, plenty of fluids in bottles or a backpack hydration system.

Pay dirt: Unpaved training helps you handle it when the asphalt ends during a race or tour.

KLASNA: OFF ROAD ON A ROAD BIKE

Most of us cringe at the thought of riding our pampered road bikes on an unpaved surface. Those loops we'd love to ride but have a 200-yard dirt section? Forget it—too dusty, and the paint might get chipped.

But riding off-road on skinny tires is the best bike-handling exercise imaginable. It teaches you how to control skids and to ride lightly so you don't bang up your wheels or get a pinch flat. Riding in the dirt requires a relaxed upper body and a fluid hold on the handlebar—crucial techniques for surviving in a pack on the road. Another big benefit is the fun factor. Riding off-road is radically challenging. It greatly expands your training terrain and gets you away from traffic.

Trent Klasna, a superb bike handler, is a big fan. He actually seeks roads that begin paved and turn to dirt. Another advocate is former pro and 7-time Tour de France competitor Ron Kiefel. He still rides the dirt roads around Boulder on his Serotta road bike. Here's how to do this type of training:

- **Use an old bike and durable tires.** Klasna rides his team-issue LeMond on the dirt—but of course he isn't paying for it. Most of us non-sponsored riders will do as well on an old, expendable bike with sturdy wheels and touring tires. A cyclocross bike works great, too.

- **Use low gears**. The bike should have big rear cogs and preferably a triple crankset so you can ride up steep hills with your fast road cadence of at least 80 rpm. Road wheels with narrow tires don't have much traction on loose surfaces. A smooth spin is much more efficient than the big-gear grind that you might be able to get away with on a mountain bike with knobby tires.

- **Use easy trails or dirt roads**. This is not the right time to ride the hardest singletrack in the area. Road bikes work fine on moderate trails, but you risk trashing your equipment and getting injured if you tackle technical terrain. Honor your comfort factor. If the trail seems too difficult, it probably is.

- **Emphasize technique rather than speed**. Road bikes are extremely fast on easy singletrack. But speed isn't the purpose of this exercise. Instead, hone your bike-handling skills and have fun. Slow and easy does it.

SWEET: SPRINT PROGRESSION

It's often said that sprinters are born, not made. You either have the required number of fast-twitch fibers in your quadriceps or you don't. If you don't, you'll never truly be fast no matter how hard you work.

Australian road sprinter Jay Sweet doesn't believe that conventional wisdom. He duked it out with the fastest European sprinters during his 4-year tenure on the Big Mat team before joining Saturn. Yet coaches told him he'd never be a successful sprinter because he was too small and didn't have enough muscle mass in his glutes and quads to generate pro-level power.

Sweet didn't let that stop him. Instead, he developed a specific sprint training progression to teach himself to go fast. I'll let Jay explain it while I add comments about how you can implement it.

Sweet: 5 steps to a super sprint.

- **Sweet: "Sprint training begins in the winter. I put in a lot of miles."**

Even though sprinting is a high-intensity/short-duration activity, cycling still requires endurance. If you aren't in the lead group at the end of the race, the fastest legs in the world are useless. Fabled finisher Mario Cipollini sprinted to 6 stage victories in the 2002 Giro d'Italia because he'd built the endurance to race for more than 5 hours with strength in reserve. Sweet, too, develops his stamina with a big base of endurance miles.

- **Sweet: "Next, I do power sprints in a larger gear and strength work on hills."**

Another factor in Cipollini's success is his ability to get over moderate climbs with the contenders. Sweet, too, trains hard to develop the strength to stick with the all-round riders on climbs up to 5 kilometers long.

Power sprints of 10-15 seconds in a large gear at a cadence of 90-100 rpm develop fast-twitch fibers almost like weight training. Climbing at a lower cadence (50-60 rpm) in a large gear is another way to convert strength to power that's useable on the bike.

- **Sweet: "As the racing season nears, I do long endurance sprints of 30 seconds."**

Endurance sprints teach the body to reach high speed and then hold it longer than usual. Start with a hard jump out of the saddle. Get the gear turning, sit down, spin up to a high cadence and keep going at full effort for 30 seconds. This is tough work, so do only one set of 3-5 endurance sprints per week.

- **Sweet: "For tune-ups before races, I like fast sprints of 10 seconds on and 50 seconds easy in a smaller gear."**

Sprinting is about repeatability. It's not just the last sprint for the line that's important. Sprinters have to accelerate many times in the miles before the finish line to stick with their leadout men and retain their position in the pack.

Repeated short sprints with minimal rest intervals develop your ability to jump hard again and again. One way to do it in training is to count telephone poles. Sprint the distance between 2 or 3 poles, spin easily for 4 poles and then repeat.

- **Sweet: "Right before an important race I'll motorpace, working on sprinting around the motor and then recovering in its draft."**

Okay, here's one drill that works for a pro but probably not for recreational riders. Motorpacing in the draft of a car or small motorcycle is dangerous. It requires a skilled driver, a traffic-free road and cops who are looking the other way. A good substitute is tailwind sprints at a high cadence. Sprint for 10 seconds, ease off and let the wind maintain your momentum, then sprint again. You get the advantages of motorpacing without the danger. And in most sections of the country, windy days are easier to find than a good motorpace driver.

BESSETTE: TIME TRIAL TRAINING

Saturn's Lyne Bessette was named North American woman rider of the year in 2001. Renowned as a climber, this Canadian is also a top time trialist.

Most TT specialists now focus on keeping a high cadence. Although time trialing technique traditionally emphasized big gears and a lower cadence, the move to faster pedaling has been fostered by Lance Armstrong and his successful time trialing at 100-plus rpm. But while it pays to keep your cadence up during a competitive TT, training with higher gears and a slower cadence helps build the power necessary to turn moderate gears faster. With all the buzz about high cadence, some riders haven't done the necessary strength work to go fast.

Bessette likes to combine big-gear strength work *and* high-cadence training in one workout. As she explains, "I shift to a big gear of 53x12 or 11 and go 20 minutes hard on rolling terrain. I don't shift at all, so I'm working on strength going up and leg speed going down."

Here are 3 points to consider if you try it:

Bessette: Fast pedaling in big gears.

- **Choose the right course**. It should be gently rolling, about 5 miles long, with light traffic and no stop signs or lights. Come as close to this ideal as you can.

- **Choose the right gear**. Gearing is individual. Bessette may do fine in a 53x11-tooth but you may not. Match your gear to your strength and the terrain. Even on the uphill sections, don't let your cadence drop below about 70 rpm. And don't do this workout if you have a history of knee problems.

- **Spin on the downhills**. This is the fast-rpm part of the workout. It's tempting to work real hard going up hills in a big gear and then recover on the descents, letting your cadence and effort drop. Resist this temptation! Don't go so hard on ascents that you're blown when the road tilts down. Keep your cadence high and work on your spin. Think about good pedaling form. This is a strength workout, but it's also great for developing leg speed.

Glossary

Included are numerous terms not included in this book but which will give you a better understanding of road cycling, especially road racing.

aerobic: exercise at an intensity that allows the body's need for oxygen to be continually met. This intensity can be sustained for long periods.

aerodynamic: a design of cycling equipment or a riding position that reduces wind resistance; *aero* for short.

anaerobic: exercise above the intensity at which the body's need for oxygen can be met. This intensity can be sustained only briefly.

apex: the sharpest part of a turn where the transition from entering to exiting takes place.

attack: an aggressive, high-speed jump away from other riders.

balaclava: a thin hood that covers the head and neck with an opening for the face. It's worn under the helmet to prevent heat loss in cold or wet conditions.

bead: in tires, the edge along each side's inner circumference that fits into the rim.

blocking: legally impeding the progress of opposing riders to help teammates.

blood glucose: a sugar, glucose is the only fuel that can be used by the brain.

blow up: to suddenly be unable to continue at the required pace due to overexertion.

bonk: a state of severe exhaustion caused mainly by the depletion of glycogen in the muscles because the rider has failed to eat or drink enough. Once it occurs, rest and high-carbohydrate foods are necessary for recovery.

boot: a small piece of material used inside a tire to cover a cut in the tread or sidewall. Without it, the tube will push through and blow out.

bottom bracket: the part of the frame where the crankset is installed. Also, the axle, cups and bearings of a traditional crankset, or the axle, retainer rings and bearing cartridges of a sealed crankset.

bpm: abbreviation for *beats per minute* in reference to heart rate.

break, breakaway: a rider or group of riders that has escaped the pack.

bridge, bridge a gap: to catch a rider or group that has opened a lead.

bunch: the main cluster of riders in a race. Also called the group, pack, field or peloton.

bunny hop: a way to ride over obstacles such as potholes in which both wheels leave the ground.

cadence: the number of times during one minute that a pedal stroke is completed. Also called *pedal rpm*.

carbohydrate: a substance in food that is broken down to glucose, the body's principal energy source, through digestion and metabolism. It is stored as glycogen in the liver and muscles. Carbo can be simple (sugars) or complex (bread, pasta, grains, fruits, vegetables), which contains additional nutrients. One gram of carbohydrate supplies 4 calories.

cardiovascular: pertaining to the heart and blood vessels.

cassette: the set of gear cogs on the rear hub. Also called a *freewheel*, *cluster* or *block*.

categories: the division of racers based on ability and/or experience.

century: a 100-mile ride.

chain suck: when the chain sticks to the chainring teeth during a downshift and gets drawn up and jammed between the small ring and the frame.

chainring: a sprocket on the crankset. There may be 1, 2 or 3. Short version is *ring*.

chasers: those who are trying to catch a group or a lead rider.

chondromalacia: a serious knee injury in which there is disintegration of cartilage surfaces due to improper tracking of the kneecap. Symptoms start with deep knee pain and crunching during bending.

circuit: a course that is ridden 2 or more times to compose the race.

circuit training: a weight training technique in which you move rapidly from exercise to exercise without rest.

cleat: a metal or plastic fitting on the sole of a cycling shoe that engages the pedal.

clincher: a conventional tire with a separate inner tube.

cog: a sprocket on the rear wheel's cassette or freewheel.

contact patch: the portion of a tire in touch with the ground.

criterium: a mass-start race covering numerous laps of a course that is normally about one mile or less in length.

crosstraining: combining sports for mental refreshment and physical conditioning, especially during cycling's off-season.

cyclocross: a fall or winter event contested mostly or entirely off pavement. Courses include obstacles, steps and steep hills that force riders to dismount and run with their bikes.

downshift: to shift to a lower gear, i.e. a larger cog or smaller chainring.

drafting: riding closely behind another rider to take advantage of the windbreak (slipstream) and use about 20 percent less energy. Also called *sitting in* or *wheelsucking*.

drivetrain: the components directly involved with making the rear wheel turn, i.e. the chain, crankset and cassette. Also called the *power train*.

drops: the lower part of a down-turned handlebar typically found on a road bike. The curved portions are called the *hooks*.

echelon: a form of paceline in which the riders angle off behind each other to get draft in a crosswind.

electrolytes: substances such as sodium, potassium, and chloride that are necessary for muscle contraction and maintenance of body fluid levels.

endo: to crash by going over the bike's handlebar. Short for end over end.

ergometer: a stationary, bicycle-like device used in physiological testing or for indoor training.

fartlek: a Swedish word meaning "speed play," it is a training technique based on unstructured changes in pace and intensity. It can be used instead of timed or measured interval training.

fat: in the diet it is the most concentrated source of food energy, supplying 9 calories per gram. Stored fat provides about half the energy required for low-intensity exercise.

feed zone: a designated area on a race course where riders can be handed food and drinks.

field sprint: the dash for the finish line by the main group of riders.

fixed gear: a direct-drive setup using one chainring and one rear cog, as on a track bike. When the rear wheel turns so does the chain and crank; coasting isn't possible.

full tuck: an extremely crouched position used for maximum speed on descents.

general classification: the overall standings in a stage race. Often referred to as GC.

glutes: the gluteal muscles of the buttocks. They are key to pedaling power.

glycogen: a fuel derived as glucose (sugar) from carbohydrate and stored in the muscles and liver. It's the primary energy source for high-intensity cycling. Reserves are normally depleted after about 2-and-a-half hours of riding.

glycogen window: the period within an hour after exercise when depleted muscles are most receptive to restoring their glycogen content. By eating foods or drinking fluids rich in carbohydrate, energy stores and recovery are enhanced.

gorp: good ol' raisins and peanuts, a high-energy mix for nibbling during rides. Can also include nuts, seeds, M&Ms, granola, etc.

granny gear: the lowest gear ratio, combining the small chainring with the largest cassette cog. It's mainly used for very steep climbs.

granny ring: the smallest of the 3 chainrings on a triple crankset.

grinder: a hard, interval-like repeat marked by turning a big gear at a relatively slow cadence.

hammer: to ride strongly in big gears..

hamstrings: the muscle on the back of the thigh, not well developed by cycling.

hanging in: barely maintaining contact at the back of the pack.

headset: the parts at the top and bottom of the frame's head tube, into which the handlebar stem and fork are fitted.

hybrid: a bike that combines features of road and mountain bikes. Also called a *cross bike*.

intervals: a structured method of training that alternates brief, hard efforts with short periods of easier riding for partial recovery.

jam: a period of hard, fast riding.

jump: a quick, hard acceleration.

lactate threshold (LT): the exertion level beyond which the body can no longer produce energy aerobically, resulting in the buildup of lactic acid. This is marked by muscle fatigue, pain and shallow, rapid breathing. Formerly called *anaerobic threshold (AT)*.

lactic acid: a substance formed during anaerobic metabolism when there is incomplete breakdown of glucose. It rapidly produces muscle fatigue and pain. Also called *lactate*.

leadout: a race tactic in which a rider accelerates to his maximum speed for the benefit of a teammate in tow. The second rider then leaves the draft and sprints past at even greater speed near the finish line.

LSD: long, steady distance. An endurance training technique that requires a firm aerobic pace for at least 2 hours.

mass start: events such as road races, cross-country races and criteriums in which all contestants leave the starting line at the same time.

metric century: a 100-kilometer ride (62 miles).

minuteman: in a time trial, the rider who is one place in front of you in the starting order. So called because in most TTs riders start on 1-minute intervals.

motorpace: to ride behind a motorcycle or other vehicle that breaks the wind.

mudguards: fenders.

off the back: describes one or more riders who have failed to keep pace with the main group. Also referred to as *OTB*.

orthotics: custom-made supports worn in shoes to help neutralize biomechanical imbalances in the feet or legs.

overgear: using a gear ratio too big for the terrain or level of fitness.

overtraining: deep-seated fatigue, both physical and mental, caused by training at an intensity or volume too great for adaptation.

oxygen debt: the amount of oxygen that must be consumed to pay back the deficit incurred by anaerobic work.

paceline: a group formation in which each rider takes a turn breaking the wind at the front before pulling off, dropping to the rear position, and riding the others' draft until at the front once again.

panniers: large bike bags used by touring cyclists or commuters. Panniers attach to racks that place them low on each side of the rear wheel, and sometimes the front wheel.

peak: a relatively short period during which maximum performance is achieved.

peloton: the main group of riders in a race.

periodization: the process of dividing training into specific phases by weeks or months.

pinch flat: an internal puncture marked by 2 small holes caused by the tube being squeezed against the rim. It results from impacting an object when air pressure is too low. Also called a *snakebite*.

power: the combination of speed and strength.

PR: personal record.

presta: the narrow European-style valve found on some inner tubes. A small metal cap on its end must be unscrewed before air can enter or exit.

prime: a special award given to the leader on selected laps during a criterium, or the first rider to reach a certain landmark in a road or cross-country race. It's used to heighten the action. Pronounced "preem."

protein: in the diet it is required for tissue growth and repair. Composed of structural units called amino acids. Protein is not a significant energy source unless not enough calories and carbohydrate are consumed. One gram of protein equals 4 calories.

psi: abbreviation for pounds per square inch. The unit of measure for tire inflation.

pull, pull through: take a turn at the front of the paceline.

pull off: to move to the side after riding in the lead so that another rider can come to the front.

pusher: a rider who pedals in a big gear at a relatively slow cadence, relying on gear size for speed.

quadriceps: the large muscle in front of the thigh, the strength of which helps determine a cyclist's ability to pedal with power.

reach: the combined length of a bike's top tube and stem, which determines the rider's distance to the handlebar.

repetition: each hard effort in an interval workout. Also, one complete movement in a weight-training exercise; *rep* for short.

resistance trainer: a stationary training device into which the bike is clamped. Pedaling resistance increases with pedaling speed to simulate actual riding. Also known as an *indoor*, *wind*, *fluid*, or *mag* trainer (the last 3 names derived from the fan, liquid, or magnet that creates resistance on the rear wheel).

road race: a mass-start race on pavement that goes from point to point, covers one large loop or is held on a circuit longer than those used for criteriums.

road rash: any skin abrasion resulting from a fall. Also called *crash rash*.

rollers: an indoor training device consisting of 3 cylinders connected by belts. Both bike wheels roll on these cylinders so that balancing is much like actual riding. Also, small hills in undulating terrain.

saddle sores: skin problems in the crotch that develop from chafing caused by pedaling action. Sores can range from tender raw spots to boil-like lesions if infection occurs.

saddle time: time spent cycling.

sag wagon: a motor vehicle that follows a group of riders, carrying equipment and lending assistance in the event of difficulty. Also called the broom wagon.

Schrader: an inner tube valve identical to those found on car tires. A tiny plunger in the center of its opening must be depressed for air to enter or exit.

set: in intervals or weight training, a specific number of repetitions.

singletrack: a trail so narrow that 2 cyclists can't easily ride side by side, which makes passing difficult or impossible.

sit on a wheel: to ride in someone's draft.

slingshot: to ride up behind another rider with help from his draft, then use momentum to sprint past.

slipstream: the pocket of calmer air behind a moving rider. Also called the *draft*.

snap: the ability to accelerate quickly.

soft-pedal: to rotate the pedals without actually applying power.

speed: the ability to accelerate quickly and maintain a very fast cadence for brief periods.

speedwork: a general term for intervals and other high-velocity training, such as sprints, time trials and motorpacing.

spin: to pedal at high cadence.

spinner: a rider who pedals in a moderate gear at a relatively fast cadence, relying on pedal rpm for speed.

squirrel: a nervous or unstable rider who can't be trusted to maintain a steady line.

stage race: a multiday event consisting of various types of races. The winner is the rider with the lowest elapsed time for all races *(stages)*.

straight block: a cassette with cogs that increase in size in 1-tooth increments.

suppleness: a quality of highly conditioned leg muscles that allows a rider to pedal at high cadence with smoothness and power. Also known by the French term, *souplesse*.

take a flyer: to suddenly sprint away from a group.

team time trial (TTT): a race against the clock with 2 or more riders working together.

tempo: fast riding at a brisk cadence.

throw the bike: a racing technique in which a rider thrusts the bike ahead of his or her body at the finish line, gaining several inches in hopes of winning a close sprint.

time trial (TT): a race against the clock in which individual riders start at set intervals and cannot give or receive a draft.

tops: the part of a drop handlebar between the stem and the brake levers.

training effect: the result of exercise done with an intensity and duration sufficient to bring about positive physiological changes.

tubular: a lightweight tire that has its tube sewn inside the casing. Also called a *sew-up*. The tire is glued to the rim.

turkey: an unskilled cyclist.

turnaround: the point where the riders reverse direction on an out-and-back time trial course.

unweight: the act of momentarily lightening the bike through a combination of body movement and position. It's integral to techniques such as jumping over railroad tracks.

USA Cycling: the umbrella organization for American bicycle racing. Affiliated with the UCI.

UCI: Union Cycliste Internationale, the world governing body of bicycle racing, headquartered in Geneva, Switzerland.

upshift: to shift to a higher gear, i.e. a smaller cog or larger chainring.

USCF: U.S. Cycling Federation, the organization that governs amateur road, cyclocross, and track racing in America. A division of USA Cycling.

USPRO: U.S. Professional Racing Organization, the organization in charge of professional bicycle racing in America. A division of USA Cycling.

velodrome: an oval banked track for bicycle racing.

VO_2 max: the maximum amount of oxygen that can be consumed during all-out exertion. This is a key indicator of a person's potential in cycling and other aerobic sports. It's largely genetically determined but can be improved somewhat by training.

watt: a measurement of the power you're producing. It tells how much energy you apply to the pedals over time. A power output of 100 watts will illuminate a 100-watt light bulb. The average recreational racer can generate 200-250 watts for about 30 minutes. Lance Armstrong is reputed to pump out more than 450 watts for that amount of time.

watts meter: an instrument for measuring watts output (*wattage*) during pedaling, with the reading displayed on a cyclecomputer-like monitor. Also called a *power meter*.

wheelsucker: someone who drafts behind others but doesn't take a pull.

windchill: the effect of air moving across the skin, making the temperature seem colder than it actually is. A cyclist creates a windchill even on a calm day, a situation that must be considered when dressing for winter rides.

wind up: steady acceleration to an all-out effort.

Index